UNAUTHORIZED OFFWORLD
ACTIVATION

EXPLORING THE STARGATE FRANCHISE

UNAUTHORIZED OFFWORLD
ACTIVATION

EXPLORING THE STARGATE FRANCHISE

EDITED BY

RICH HANDLEY

JOSEPH DILWORTH, JR.

SEQUART ORGANIZATION   EDWARDSVILLE, ILLINOIS

Unauthorized Offworld Activation: Exploring the Stargate Franchise
edited by Rich Handley and Joseph Dilworth Jr.

First edition, May 2022, ISBN 978-1-9405-8927-5.

Cover by Leah Battle. Book design by Julian Darius.

Published by Sequart Organization. Edited by Rich Handley and Joseph Dilworth Jr.

For more information about other titles in this series, visit Sequart.org/books.

Contents

Chevron One Encoded: A Foreword

by Alexis Cruz

It was a rough shoot. One hundred forty-degree heat on the blistering sands. There was something in this story, though, in its energy that inspired us and kept us driven through many months of long days and long nights. We had a mission and were fully committed.

We were also in good company. I was working with legends, on the cusp of making a new one. I watched an ancient city rise up in that desert built by hand, of wood, fiberglass, pure heart and craftsmanship. I ran through its streets, coughed smoke and dust from practical effects, learned and brought a dead language back to life, and danced around a campfire eating green horned chicken that tasted like... well, *chicken*. They had told us these were themselves the same dunes that once carried the tale of another boy a long, long time ago, in a galaxy far, far away.

This boy here, though, was 19 and excited — a pen-and-paper gamer nerd from the Bronx, barely dodging bullies and bullets, who found himself a million light years from home at the turn of the century. I had just graduated from a prestigious performing arts school in New York City, the inspiration for the hit film *Fame*, which had itself been the inspiration for me as a child when I first felt the calling. "Wait, you mean to tell me that place is *real*? I can *go* there? I can learn to do this thing there... like *them*?"

Alexis Cruz's Skaara, shown here with sister Sha'uri as portrayed by Mili Avital (left). Vaitiare Bandera (right) played the character (renamed Sha're) on television, having previously auditioned for the movie role.

So I did. I took those skills with me and joined a crew of intrepid professionals of unbridled imagination. I was, of course, way out of my league, but one of the greatest lessons I learned among them was to make room for risk and growth. To make room for new ideas as they came, and to take the time to explore those ideas — to collaborate and adapt as a team. My part in *Stargate* was small at the start, but that hardly mattered. Every cog was important, and I was happy to be there for the ride, living in the moment and making the best of the materials at hand.

Now, here we are, decades later. We knew at the time that the movie was special, but we didn't dare to think that *Stargate* would come to hold a place in the hearts and minds of people all across the world. And yet, every day, it's still startling and exhilarating to see the outpouring of love for the *Stargate* franchise.

What is it that makes *Stargate* so special? So endearing and enduring? I think it's the relativity. When most people, even geeks, think of science fiction, we tend to think in futuristic terms – those things that take place far into the future. That accounts for a lot of content over many generations throughout the world, and it may be one of the largest big-tent genres there is. What makes *Stargate* stand out, though, is that it's not just extraordinary characters, it could just as well be you and me stepping through that portal. We watched family go through that gate, and as family we went with them.

There are no costumes, no suspension of disbelief in ourselves, just us contemporary humans with all of our aptitudes and follies, setting out into the vastness of the universe — today. We see ourselves in these soldiers, scientists, and explorers. These people with hopes and dreams, and kids and aging parents, and bills and hobbies. A turn here, a turn there, and any one of us could have been — can *be* — on an SG team. I think that's a big part of the magic.

Left: Alexis Cruz was one of the only *Stargate* film actors to return for *SG-1*, playing not only Skaara but also Klorel, the Goa'uld who possessed him. Right: Cruz when he's not playing an Abydonian freedom fighter turned false god.

But let's backtrack a bit together. Before ancient alien astronauts were a thing in the consciousness of the mainstream public, we hadn't quite seen this stylistic fusion of ancient mythology with high tech, and yet somehow it was instantly familiar when those first notes of David Arnold's score danced across the smooth grooves of Ra's mask, and then onward to the affable frustrations of an archeologist ostracized for seeing the future in the past. We felt that otherness and we felt the validation of ourselves as the stars opened up for him.

Can you remember that time, before the idea became almost a given, as we do today? Back then, it was nearly as esoteric and underground as having to dig through the sands itself. *Stargate* seemed to collect it all together, shape it, frame it, and present it as a homegrown starship of our very own to soar with. Its themes resonated across many intersections of human experience. And I think that's key: the *human* experience. It took these ideas dancing on our periphery, or churning beneath our consciousness, and gave us a coherent vision. "Get in, winner, no time to explain..." But then you did. *You* did explain it as you went along. Truth be told, that wasn't us, the filmmakers – it's been you over the course of decades and, most rewarding to me, across generations.

I'm consistently blown away by our audience and its engagement as I've met many of you on my vaudevillian journeys through the convention circuit. As we celebrated this pocket dimension we shared, I spoke with you, broke bread with you, heard your stories, laughed with you, dreamed with you, cried with you, shook my fist with you. I've met your children – and *their* children – just as excited as we were. *Stargate* has almost become defined by its larger collaborativeness. We, as filmmakers, were kinda flying by the seat of our pants, and that tends to happen when you're catching lightning in a bottle. We chased that for close to two decades and over three television series, building on what you were giving us along the way.

One of you built a show bible, and we used it. You told us what stories impressed on you and we dug deeper. You showed, with your love, the characters you'd like to see more of, and they came forth, personified by some of the finest artists we have had the privilege to know. This back and forth encouraged the development of an entire community that persists to this day, and I don't know if it'll ever stop. We wouldn't want it to.

My biggest challenge in that time before, as I look back, was Skaara's salute. I worked so hard on it, and I hope you can imagine the biggest smile on my face as I write this. The soldiers, the real ones, drilled me repeatedly and I asked for more. Height, degrees of tilt, proximity, pacing. I was one with that young boy Skaara, with a singular motivation of expressing an inexpressible gratitude and validation. To make it clear, in no uncertain terms, that he was there for it and would do whatever it takes to be by your side.

Now here we are, decades later, about to embark on new journeys together. New missions and new visions of an expanded modern mythos. I'm as eager as that boy back then, as I invite you to board this ship with these great new storytellers. We are all together, them, you and I, all collaborators now in a larger mythos that only requires you to step through the gate. I am honored to hold a torchlight once again to these new songs of our new peoples.

I close now with a warm smile for all of your friendship, for your confidence and creativity through all the vastness of time and space.

Old man Skaara salutes you.

—Alexis Cruz
March 2022, New York City

Snakes on a Train: An Introduction

by Rich Handley

"No, really, you *need* to watch this show. Trust me, it's better than the movie. Give it half a dozen episodes, because the first few aren't that great — but after that, it's *awesome*!"

Those words, excitedly spoken to me in early 2004, launched my fascination with the *Stargate* mythos. I'd been working at a publishing company back then, and three of my friends at that office[1] were astonished to learn I'd never seen a single episode of *Stargate SG-1*. I had been a lifelong fan of science-fiction television, and I was writing for various *Star Wars* and *Star Trek* magazines at the time, so they'd understandably assumed I would also be a regular passenger on the *Stargate* train. They were mistaken... but as I was soon to learn, the mistake had been *mine* for ignoring what would turn out to be one of my favorite franchises.

SG-1 had already aired seven seasons and would soon be launching its eighth, with Sci-Fi Channel[2] promoting the imminent debut of its first spinoff, *Stargate Atlantis*. (Its first live-action spinoff, at least. More on that in a moment.) My friends were excited about *SG-1*'s return, but they'd noticed my lack of shared

---

[1] Toni McQuilken, Denise Gustavson, and the late Paul Giachetti.
[2] Before that network had rebranded as Syfy to create a new identity for itself... which is kind of like CNN deciding it needs a totally new image and thus choosing the name SeeEnEn.

enthusiasm. I'd only ever watched the 1994 theatrical film, you see. I'd found it enjoyable for what it was: a typical Dean Devlin and Roland Emmerich science-fiction yarn, heavy with humor and spectacle, but light on substance and reliant on clichés. The movie, while certainly entertaining, had simply not inspired me to seek out further stories in that universe.

Stargate began with an Egyptian archeological dig and culminated in the introduction of Daniel Jackson and Jack O'Neil (one L), as portrayed in the theatrical film by James Spader and Kurt Russell, respectively.

Don't get me wrong, I'm not knocking the *Stargate* movie. I liked it and still do. I'd watched most of the duo's films up to that point (*Universal Soldier*, *Independence Day*, *Godzilla*, *The Patriot*, *Eight Legged Freaks*, and *The Day After Tomorrow*), and I'd found *Stargate* to be the clear standout. It's hard to go wrong with either Kurt Russell or James Spader, and this one had both, not to mention Viveca Lindfors, Erick Avari, Alexis Cruz, Richard Kind, Mili Avital, Leon Rippy, John Diehl, and the soon-to-be-famous Djimon Hounsou. It boasted effects worthy of being called special, as well as a powerful soundtrack and strong performances from its leads. Plus, Jaye Davidson's subdued, slithery slinkiness in portraying Ra was effectively weird in its approach. Yet for whatever reason, I'd not paid much attention when I'd seen commercials for *SG-1*. It was off my radar, and I was happy keeping it there, as I was too busy riding other trains to board a new one.

The quote at the start of this introduction had been uttered because one of my coworkers had suggested I marathon the first seven seasons so I could watch the season-eight opener with them. As I recall, I'd made a squinty-face and politely declined the offer of loaned DVDs, explaining that I didn't think the movie was so spectacular I needed to see more. That, apparently, was exactly what they'd expected my response to be, so they were well armed with a laundry list of reasons why I should change my mind. It was three against one. The odds were not in my favor.

With an amused sigh, I accepted the gracious offer of the first DVD boxset, along with the movie. After years of paying the franchise little mind, I at last took my first steps onto the *Stargate* train and left the station. The film offered the same lighthearted fun I'd recalled, and I had to admit the TV pilot, "Children of the Gods," was much better than I'd expected it to be. Apophis, as *SG-1*'s first major Goa'uld System Lord, was a formidable foe, and I was intrigued by the idea that there were others like him roaming and ruling the galaxy, each based on a different deity from Earth religions. Plus, the show wasn't just about angry gods and alien warriors and blatant colonialism – it was *funny*. So, I liked what I saw, even though changes made from the 1994 version were a bit jarring.

I don't mean spelling changes (Sha'uri to Sha're, Ferretti to Feretti, O'Neil to O'Neill), since I wasn't aware of those yet. I refer to things like Jack's deceased son changing from Tyler to Charlie. Or Stargate Command moving from Creek Mountain to Cheyenne Mountain. Or Abydos relocating from a distant galaxy to nearby in the Milky Way, and the Abydonians speaking English instead of ancient Egyptian. Or, most significantly, Ra having been the last of his species in the film, but on TV being one of many Goa'uld. What's more, the creatures were now snake-like, instead of the movie's ghostly entity that resembled a Roswell Grey alien – or, intriguingly, an evil Asgard.[3] Still, I enjoyed it.

I went to work the next day and begrudgingly admitted my approval, despite some awkward clunkiness and the stark differences in how Richard Dean Anderson approached Kurt Russell's character, to the extent that it was difficult to view him as the same guy. (The writers cleverly acknowledged this with an amusing in-joke about there being both a Jack O'Neil and a Jack O'Neill in the

---

[3] I made that connection later, of course, since I had no idea *Stargate*'s Asgard existed at that point.

military.) I found Anderson to be a great joy once I got used to the new Jack, though, and I was impressed at how adeptly Michael Shanks channeled James Spader's Daniel Jackson. And while Amanda Tapping's Samantha Carter and Christopher Judge's Teal'c were not given the greatest material to work with in their introductions, I had a feeling I might come to greatly enjoy them both over time (and I absolutely did). As a fan of *Star Trek: The Next Generation*, *Babylon 5*, *The X-Files*, and *Dark Shadows*, I was well aware my favorite shows have sometimes had a shaky start before taking off. *Stargate*, I suspected, would fall in that category, and I was right.

My friends were right, too. Even after just watching that two-parter, I could already tell the TV show had great potential, and so I was willing to give the franchise a chance. I kept riding that train, pulled in by the show's early narrative threads, particularly the Goa'uld possessions of film characters Charles Kawalsky (Jay Acovone, replacing John Diehl), Skaara (Alexis Cruz, reprising his movie role), and Sha're (Vaitiare Bandera, replacing Mili Avital). An appreciation for *Stargate* was snaking its way into my consciousness, and I decided *SG-1* might well be worth watching after all. And then... well, then I reached "Emancipation."

I can think of only one modern-day science-fiction TV show that has ever been as racist as this episode's portrayal of Asians, and that was in *Star Trek: The Next Generation*'s "Code of Honor," which featured the most cringeworthy stereotyping of tribal African cultures ever to grace a progressive television program. Substitute a Mongol tribe for an African tribe, and you've got "Emancipation." Plus, the degrading and sexualizing of Sam Carter was horrific, worse even than how *Star Trek*'s Tasha Yar had fared. Imagine my facepalm when I learned the two episodes, which have essentially identical plots, had been scripted by the same writer. Yes, a single individual had written the most offensive installments of two separate franchises!

I hit the brakes. "Please tell me this isn't what the rest of the show is like," I urged my friends. They assured me it would never be that bad again, and that I needed to give the series half a dozen episodes before it would hook me. They were dead-on, because that's when I experienced "Cold Lazarus," in which an alien doppelgänger, registering O'Neill's unresolved guilt and grieving regarding his young son's death, tries to comfort the real Jack by bringing him the child he longs to see. But with no concept of permanent death, the alien had failed to comprehend the depth of loss stemming from it having been Jack's own gun with which Tyler/Charlie had shot himself. The alien visits Jack's estranged wife, spends time in the boy's former bedroom, finally grasps the devastating, unending despair at losing a child, and breaks down crying.

Damn.

It was an extraordinary and heartbreaking tale, and I sat there stunned at how much it had affected me emotionally after the first six episodes had failed to do so. You see, it had only been two years since my little brother had accidentally killed himself as well. Eric was not my son, but there was a thirteen-year difference between us, so when I was finishing college, he was still just a little boy, which means he was as close to being a son as a brother can be. What Jack – and, by extension, alien-Jack – went through, I understood all too well. I suspect the episode's writer, Jeffrey F. King, must have lost someone young who'd mattered a great deal to him, too. Clearly, he understood the pain, and if *Stargate* featured writing of that caliber and sensitivity, I was in for the full train ride.

From that point forward, I embraced the franchise with great relish, enjoying the delicacies offered on the train's dining car menu. No longer was I reluctantly ingesting the lukewarm meal I'd initially been handed. Instead, I hungrily devoured every delicious morsel – and, like Oliver Twist with his empty gruel bowl, I begged for more as I completed each boxset. By the time I'd finished those seven seasons, I was ready to jump into season eight's aired chapters, and it wasn't long before I was watching each new adventure alongside my fellow *Stargate* junkies. I even tracked down the boxsets on eBay so I could start over again at the beginning. This show needed to be added to my shelves. It was *that* good, thanks to the four main leads, but also because of Don S. Davis, Teryl Rothery, Gary Jones, Corin Nemec, Beau Bridges, and so many others along the way.

But something fascinating and unexpected had happened. Right around the time I'd fully caught up, the show underwent substantial changes. Not only did Richard Dean Anderson leave, but so did the Goa'uld, for the most part! The Ori saga proved divisive due to the focus shift away from the System Lords, the introduction of a new enemy built around violent religious extremism, and the replacement of O'Neill with Ben Browder's Cameron Mitchell. Some viewers found they couldn't warm up to this new direction, but I firmly believe the Ori, along with Mitchell and Claudia Black's Vala Mal Doran, were just what the show needed. They were an enticing icing on an already delectable cake, and we all know how much O'Neill loves cake.

These new cast members and the show's latest adversaries gave *Stargate SG-1* the kick in the pants it needed at a time when the System Lords concept had admittedly run a bit stale: find a snake, battle a snake, kill a snake. Rinse, lather, repeat. Meanwhile, the late Cliff Simon's surprisingly un-Goa'uld-like Ba'al clones helped the snakeheads shed their skin and transform into something new and delightfully unpredictable. The deadly Ori threat brought the flagging *Stargate* locomotive back to full-speed, and with Ba'al aboard it was fun again to have snakes on that train (with apologies to Samuel Jackson... and to Daniel Jackson, too, I suppose).

Thanks to the extraordinary casts of *Stargate SG-1* (top) and *Stargate Atlantis* (bottom), the franchise became something much more complex than the film that had spawned it.

So, you won't hear me complain about *Stargate SG-1*'s final years because I consider them some of the show's best. Each time I rewatch the series, I admire the ambitious Ori storyline's scope and profundity even more. *SG-1* will be twenty-five years old on July 27th of this year – in fact, that was one of the motivating factors in the decision to assemble this anthology – and I personally plan to celebrate this silver anniversary by marathoning the Ori arc yet again. *All hail the Ori!*

You also won't hear me complain much about *Atlantis* or *Stargate Universe*, both of which followed the same pattern: despite a rocky start, each emerged as a worthy (albeit increasingly short-lived) successor. *Atlantis* even managed to surpass *SG-1* in several respects, thanks in no small part to the casting of Torri Higginson, Joe Flanigan, David Hewlett, Paul McGillion, Rainbow Sun Francks, Rachel Luttrell, David Nykl, Jewel Staite, and of course Jason Momoa, more recently of *Game of Thrones* and *Aquaman* fame. And while *Universe* was regrettably canceled just as it had found firm footing, Robert Carlyle, Jamil Walker Smith, Ming-Na Wen, David Blue, Louis Ferreira, Alaina Huffman, Brian J. Smith, Lou Diamond Phillips, and Elyse Levesque all put in compelling performances.

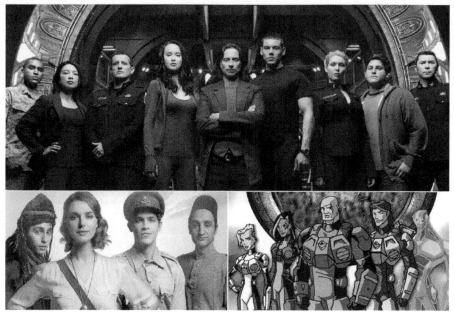

Three short-lived spinoffs, *Stargate Universe* (top), *Stargate Origins* (bottom left), and *Stargate Infinity* (bottom right), expanded the mythos to varying degrees of success.

That's why it's so frustrating neither series was afforded a satisfying ending, like *SG-1* had received with the films *The Ark of Truth* and *Continuum*. Brad Wright, Jonathan Glassner, Robert C. Cooper, Joseph Mallozzi, Paul Mullie, Carl Binder, and other producers and writers made something unique for TV, but corporate-level decisions cut them off at the knees, preventing them from concluding the compelling storylines involving *Atlantis*'s Wraith and Replicators, as well as *Universe*'s Ursini, Nakai, and Lucian Alliance, not to mention the story arcs for Elizabeth Weir and Aiden Ford. If only the intended third film, *Stargate: Extinction*, had been greenlighted, it could have wrapped up what the casts and crews had created in expanding for the small screen what Devlin and Emmerich had painted on their large canvas. If only.

The cancelations of *Atlantis* and *Universe* left plot threads unresolved involving the Wraith, the Ursini, the Nakai, the Pegasus Replicators, and the Lucian Alliance. Thankfully, *The Ark of Truth* concluded the Milky Way Replicator arc.

Now, you *might* hear me complain a little about *Stargate Origins*, the prequel webseries that revealed an untold adventure involving Catherine Langford. It was gratifying to have something new to look forward to after so long a drought, and *Origins* did have its commendable moments, particularly the introduction of two strangely unique Goa'uld (Aset and Serqet), as well as *Stargate*'s first onscreen depiction of a male homosexual relationship with Wasif and Motawk. However, it failed to fully deliver on its promise. Actors Ellie Gall, Connor Trinneer (*Atlantis*'s Michael, here playing Paul Langford), Shvan Aladdin, Salome Azizi, Michelle Jubilee Gonzalez, Daniel Rashid (as a younger version of the 1994 movie's Kasuf), Tonatiuh Elizarraraz, and the rest had little to work with script-wise. Ah, but perhaps I should leave that topic to the anthology's writers.

What you'll *definitely* hear me complain about is the much-maligned animated series *Stargate Infinity*. Why? Because that's the subject of my essay, and it's difficult to talk about *Infinity* without skewing negative, though I have endeavored to remain fair. After the other contributors had chosen assignments and none, as predicted, had requested to discuss *Stargate*'s oft-overlooked cartoon, I took one for the team and wrote the piece myself. You're welcome.

When my co-editor Joe Dilworth and I discussed the idea of proposing a *Stargate* anthology to Sequart, we knew it would fit well with the line of books the publisher had already produced, covering *Star Trek*, *Planet of the Apes*, *Star Wars*, *Blade Runner*, *Battlestar Galactica*, and DC Comics' *Hellblazer*, as well as classic movie monsters. I'd worked on all those prior books, as a contributing writer and often as a co-editor, and Joe had penned essays for several of them.[4] So *Stargate* made a lot of sense for us to tackle next. It's a member of what I like to call the "four stars of science fiction": *Star Trek*, *Star Wars*, *Stargate*, and *Battlestar Galactica*.

Stargate has earned its place alongside such giants. If you add up *SG-1*, *Infinity*, *Atlantis*, *Universe*, and *Origins*, the franchise has aired nineteen seasons across five shows, alongside three movies and a line of novels, comics, short stories, audios, and role-playing games. Even with the abrupt cancelations of *Atlantis* and *Universe*, plus the critical failures of *Infinity* and *Origins*, it's an amazing achievement of longevity, one that few franchises can boast, other than *Star Trek*, *Doctor Who*, and a few others. For newcomers looking to marathon the entire saga from beginning to end, I recommend the following viewing order:

1. *Stargate* theatrical film
2. *Stargate Origins* webseries[5]
3. *Stargate SG-1* episodes 1.1 to 8.2
4. *Stargate Atlantis* episodes 1.1 to 1.15
5. *SG-1* episodes 8.3 to 8.20
6. *Atlantis* episodes 1.16 to 2.1
7. *SG-1* episodes 9.1 to 10.2
8. *Atlantis* episodes 2.2 to 3.4

---

[4] You can read more about these books here: sequart.org/author/rich-handley/.
[5] A note about the reading order: *Origins* takes place before the theatrical film and wasn't released until after *SG-1*, *Atlantis*, and *Universe*. Still, I think watching it right *after* the movie works best for those new to the franchise, since the two are connected and one needs the film's context to enjoy *Origins*. For those commencing a rewatch, it's fine to start with *Origins* and then view the movie.

9. *SG-1* episodes 10.3 to 10.12
10. *Atlantis* episodes 3.5 to 3.19
11. *SG-1* episodes 10.13 to 10.20
12. *Stargate: The Ark of Truth* (with prelude)
13. *Atlantis* episodes 3.20 to 5.1
14. *Stargate: Continuum*
15. *Atlantis* episodes 5.2 to end
16. *Stargate Universe* season 1
17. *SGU: Kino* webisodes 1-34
18. *Universe* season 2
19. *Stargate Infinity*

Stargate is something truly special, and we're proud to bring you this anthology of insightful and thought-provoking essays, and to have such a wonderful lineup of writers. I may not agree with everything each of them says in their essays, but I'm so excited they're here to say it (and the truth is, I usually *do* agree with them). Take a well-deserved bow, Ren Cummins, Keith R.A. DeCandido, Edward Dodds, Jo Duffy, Bryanna Elkins, Kelli Fitzpatrick, Mark L. Haynes, Brandon Jerwa, Robert Jeschonek, Anastasia Klimchynskaya, Val Nolan, Frank Schildiner, and *GateWorld*'s Darren Sumner – as well as *Stargate* actor Alexis Cruz (Skaara), who provided the book's foreword. We are truly honored to have had the privilege of adding Alexis to the lineup, thanks to his friend, contributor Ren Cummins. Add the stunning cover art by Leah Battle, and there's *a lot* to love here.

I want to give a quick shoutout to author, editor, and standup comic John J. Ordover. When Joe and I initially announced this anthology under the title *Chevron Seven Locked*, John quipped, "Considering the nature of the book, I would think *Unauthorized Offworld Activation* would be a better title." John was joking, but his suggested alternative was such a vitally descriptive title, embodying both the book's unlicensed status and the show's whimsical approach to humor. My immediate response: *"Damn!* I wish we'd thought of that." Joe's: "I am beating my head against my desk right now... that is a perfect title." We loved *Chevron Seven Locked*, but we adored *Unauthorized Offworld Activation*. Sequart agreed, and here we are.

The *Stargate* train is worth riding time and again, but as fans we've come to accept disappointment. We felt it as *SG-1* left the airwaves when there was story left to tell, then with the unexpected cancelations of both its sequel shows following cliffhanger endings. We felt it when *Infinity*... well, existed. We felt it when the *Extinction* movie failed to materialize. We felt it when *Origins* proved less than fulfilling. And we felt it when Emmerich and Devlin revealed plans to make films ignoring the enormous television tapestry... and then when their intended movies were canceled, because at least there would have been new *Stargate* to enjoy.

Still, I hold out hope that *Stargate* will return, and soon, whether as a continuation of what came before or as a reboot offering something new. It's inevitable, considering Amazon's acquisition of MGM. After spending almost $8.5 billion to purchase the studio, Amazon will no doubt seek to profit from its most valued, most high-profile properties – and *Stargate* is prominent among them. It would be inexplicable for the company *not* to bring it back. Wherever the train may take us, I look forward to seeing our beloved heroes (or their successors) stepping once more through the Chappa'ai to snake their way through distant star systems and other galaxies.

Like Jack O'Neill, I wouldn't mind one last jaunt through the old orifice.

Taking the Space Out of Deep Space

by Ren Cummins

Space. The final frontier. These... oh wait. No, you haven't opened the wrong book, and I haven't explored the wrong franchise. We're talking about *Stargate*, yes, and assuming for a moment that this isn't the first time you've heard of it, let's go ahead and proceed with that expectation. Glowing pale rounded portals, wormholes connecting across the vastness of space, right? Right. Lovely science-fiction adventure tales taking place out there in the great dark beyond, or more locally sourced high-tech, bleeding-edge funkiness set upon the ash-coated ruins of the Now. But let's get real. I cut my teeth on a galaxy far, far away. I was born just before the first Moon landing. I am all about this great big, tremendous cosmos. So, let's talk about the majestic unknown. But first, let's talk about what lies at the heart of all these space stories: adventure.

Any good adventure needs risk. Threats. There absolutely must be the chance of perilous death or bodily harm or psychological mayhem, if your point is to be thrilled by the story being presented. Certainly, there are multitudinous elements to science-fiction storytelling, and not all of them fit into one of Joseph Campbell's journeys. However, setting aside everything not directly associated with traveling, let us focus for the moment on that which remains. To wit: distance.

As we push the "engage" button, let's look at the *long, long time ago* part of our journey. Let us set the WABAC machine to the tales of the wild, wild West –

of gold hunters, of trappers, of those who tamed the western regions of what would become the left half of the United States of America. Anyone who's spent a decent quantity of time out there will know of what I speak when I refer to the majesty and divinity that only nature can present: Yosemite, the awe-inspiring redwoods, the cragged and otherworldly beaches of Monterey and Carmel or Crater Lake, the painted bands in stone of what is now Arches National Park. The Black Hills. The Grand Canyon.

Every place in the world was untouched until someone walked up and touched it. Every place was lost until it was found. Everywhere was off the map until a cartographer wandered by. Most of the world sat unseen in the fog of "here there be dragons" and then, one day, we swept aside that shimmering mist and slapped a name on the many things we found hidden therein. But in those moments just before those unknowns were known, some hapless explorer stood, rode, or sailed on the brink of death when that fog parted, and the darkness cleared.

What was there? What would they find? Was death awaiting their trembling hands? Sometimes, yes. But usually, no. Any horizon passed over revealed another horizon yet to be conquered. The next hill, the next mountain, the next river or ravine, the next sea. Next, next, next. Each new step toward That Which Is Not Known took us one step further from That Which Is. Of course, now we look at these things and have forgotten what the world was like when we hadn't shaken hands with it.

Today, most of these former mysteries have their own gift shop. We can check them out on our phones, witnessing them virtually and visiting them on our computer screens without even getting out of our beds. We can hop onto the websites and order the T-shirt. Many kinds of exploration have rather lost their teeth in terms of the risk inherent and the dangers untold that lead to these marvelous places. But it was not, in fact, so long ago that to attempt to make these journeys would lead loved ones to offer a tearful goodbye, secure in the knowledge that they might never see their intrepid adventurers again.

There is a highway that forms a line from west to east across the American landscape – Interstate 80, connecting California to New Jersey. An interesting observation is that this highway passes through a major city approximately every four or eight hours at the outside. Between those points, where larger cities are absent, smaller towns or rest areas take up the gaps, ensuring that at least every two hours drivers may stop, care for their needs, and proceed on.

Traversing great distances without provisions can be risky, so the stargate network, much like U.S. Interstate 80, features frequent stops for wary travelers—where, inevitably, the situation soon turns perilous for the SG-1 team.

Why is this? Why so mathematically consistent? The answer is simple: the average American car needs to refill its gas tank at least every two to four hours of full freeway-speed driving. So do the drivers and passengers – two to four hours ensures that food, drink, and... other facilities can be accessed at standard intervals. Every eight hours? Hotels. Restaurants. Malls. Shopping centers. Entertainment. The need for these facilities emerged at the onset of interstate driving – build it and they shall come.

A century earlier, the gaps were consistent, but tailored to the needs of train passengers (as well as the needs of the trains themselves), horse and carriage, or even simply horseback riders. Track the average daily distances attained via these various forms of transportation from coast to coast, and the end of a day's journey will find the traveler at a new establishment of goods and services, eager to make a penny by providing to the new arrivals. Many of these roadside communities still stand today: my very own home of Seattle was the launching point to the Alaskan gold rushers and grew into a fair city literally on the foundations of the mining prep community of the 1800s.

Those early explorers knew well the risks of going into the wilderness without proper provisions and were willing to pay the added fees placed on these items. What was the alternative, really? Travel these days is not without its perils, but thanks to the availability of wireless phone service, ease of transportation, a comprehensive shopping network, and interstate commerce protections, the wild whatever yonder isn't quite as wild and wooly as it once was – at least, not in many parts of the world.

There do, of course, remain many places on Earth where the miles matter, but just for curiosity's sake, imagine if you had no vehicle, no cell phone, no access to your credit or debit cards, and the like. How far would you feel safe to travel? Five miles? Twenty? One hundred? And how long would it take you to cover that distance, even if you stuck to established roads? Unpaved roads? No roads at all? Through swamps? Deserts? Jungles? Across a white-roiling river? Around a lake? Across an ocean? Nearly all classic science-fiction films were based on this premise. "You're a long way from home" became a common phrase in these books and films, keying into a common fear (or excitement, for the adventurous among us) that increases our adrenaline when it becomes clear that getting back to where we belong is going to be much harder than we thought.

The COVID-19 pandemic has asked us to remain safely ensconced in place to lessen the chances of our catching or sharing the coronavirus. This means that many of us have either been mostly at home or, in some challenging cases, away from our homes for the better part of the past two years. This has caused us to yearn for some get-out-of-home free time or, alternatively, it has filled us with dread at the notion of setting out toward the horizon. I find that I tend to pack a bit more into my messenger bag than I used to. "You never know" has become something of a motto, but it was not always so – an upgrade to "be prepared," perhaps. Prolonged crises have an effect on us.

The point is that the weight of risk adds a heightened perspective. In fiction, this can be achieved through a variety of methods, but in deep-space science fiction, the risk is right there in the name. Being far, far away from everything the characters know and love offers a subtext of drama and intensity. Being taken so far from their comfort zone is a fundamental part of creating a setting of fear, and the greater the distance, the greater the implied risk.

In space, a thousand things can go wrong, and with help being on the far side of the world, the other end of the solar system, the opposite horizon of the galaxy – that, in and of itself, becomes a substantial obstacle placed in the path of our heroes' safety. *The Martian* took place just one planet away; *Apollo 13* was only a few days' flight between Earth and the Moon. Help was so close, galactically speaking, yet still so very far away though the vacuum of space.

Then science-fiction writers had to go and conjure up ways to cross that vastness — concepts like warp speed and hyperspace, folding space, artificial (or natural) wormholes, Einstein-Rosen bridges, or whatever else you want to call them, as well as teleporters — all intended to bring the different points in space closer together. J.J. Abrams was once asked how long it takes to travel between planets, and his answer amounted to "as long as the narrative needs it to be." But does that even work? How dramatic can deep space actually be, once it's no longer so deep?

This, then, is the conundrum that *Stargate* makes me ponder. You dial an ancient otherworld ring to its programmed coordinates, stroll into the glowing whirlpool of light and wonder, and step out onto a planet on the other side of the universe in the time it takes Thanos to snap his fingers. All things being equal, the distance alone should make us nervous for our protagonists.

In the original movie, there was a problem that was discovered almost immediately: the team needed seven symbols to dial the stargate and return home. Without those specific symbols, they would not be able to activate the ring and open the wormhole to get back. That was, in fact, the entire snag in their initial plan: they couldn't just keep dialing up random combinations in the hopes of finding the right one. By the way, in case you were wondering, there are apparently some 1,987,690,320 possible unique combinations in total on the Milky Way stargates, but since that wasn't my math, feel free to check it.

On Abydos, however, they had the first six symbols figured out, which does raise the question of why they didn't just enter the first six and then try each of the other characters to determine the seventh. Would that count as a wormhole plot hole? But I digress. *Stargate Atlantis* and *Stargate Universe* would later add an eighth and ninth chevron, respectively, but that's an entirely different math equation, which I shall leave for others to pursue.

While there is a form of obstacle in the original film — the loss of the full cartouche containing the address to return home — this eventually stops being a point of concern on the television shows. In the film, returning home is the primary objective for Daniel Jackson and most of the military support with whom he has traveled, and finding that full dialing code represents what they most urgently require to achieve their ultimate goal. Certainly, they did not originally intend to start a revolution, Jackson was not looking for a love interest, and Jack O'Neil was not looking for closure over the death of his son. The plot is spelled out clearly: they needed to open the gate and go home, and that's how we see distance used as a plot device.

The stargates and the wormholes they open allow instantaneous interstellar travel without the need for space vessels, but the writers were careful not to diminish the risks and lessen the dramatic impact.

From the aggressive frustrations conveyed by the team of soldiers against Jackson to the somewhat subdued concerns voiced between Charles Kawalsky and Colonel O'Neil, we come to feel the fundamental threat of their inability to return to Earth as an oppressive weight on everything they did. Even though the more dramatic narrative leads them to inspire an uprising against Ra, the true victory conditions – and even much of the ensuing action – bring them inevitably back to the stargate. Of course, the final view we have before the end credits is the triumphant swirl of stars and hyperspace once more through the gate itself. Not a view of Earth or cheering crowds, but just the now-familiar vortex inside the gate.

That is the primal draw of the stargate in terms of its movie narrative, but then we come to *SG-1*, *Atlantis*, *Universe*, and even the cartoon, *Stargate Infinity*. Let's be honest, if every single episode was about being trapped or isolated millions of light years away from home, then it would have become tedious. I mean, there are only so many ways to underscore "We're not in Kansas anymore!" before the recurring drama gets a bit one-note.

Thankfully – mercifully – the writers managed to use enough episodes at the start of each new series to establish the inevitable risk of deep-space travel without having to lean too heavily into the same danger, and without having the stargate be the primary source of the characters' anxiety. For many episodes, there were plenty of other threats against our protagonists, and the way they came and went was barely a blip on their radar. But if you stray too far from the original conceit, then the drama fades, the fear withdraws. So, for every few episodes with alien plagues, personal incidents with the main cast, or general threats against Earth or the rest of the universe, a crisis of the week would center around the crew being trapped eons away from home.

In early episodes, *Stargate Atlantis* stranded our heroes in a distant galaxy with no way back to Earth.

Atlantis and *Universe* both began with that very premise, in fact. Even though each diverged into other events or threats, they rarely strayed too far from the reminders that, in the event of something endangering their ability to go home, the characters would find themselves stranded. *Universe* took the themes of distance and exploration to a deeper level, of course, by adopting the same *Lost in Space* through-line and keeping our heroes farther from home than any other crews had previously been. In fact, the entire premise of the show was based on an alien ship far, far, far from Earth, with the hope of one day returning home. Ultimately, though, *Universe* was cancelled before this could be accomplished.

There are various ways to instill the subtext of dread, risk, and a resulting exuberant victory when crafting deep-space science-fiction stories, and clearly the simple (?) act of pointing out "You're a long way from home, kid!" isn't the only way. It is, however, an ever-present facet of science fiction to establish that the story is a long way from the reader geographically, technologically, or even conceptually. Space – dark matter, mysterious phenomena, and all the bits whose nature we can merely guess at, as well as the things we do know – is vast, fascinating, and usually dangerous. But being far from home, even if it's just up in our near stratosphere through the exosphere, can make it very dangerous to remain or return. Shoot, you can break your neck just falling wrong off your roof (or so my mother always warned me), so going up into the near edge of space is clearly worse by many magnitudes.

Stargate Universe saw those aboard the spaceship *Destiny* moving ever farther from home.

As a fun little exercise, the next time you're watching one of the movies or episodes, or reading any of the *Stargate*-verse stories, ask yourself what the threats are. In what ways are the characters at risk? Is there, at that moment, a direct danger or impediment preventing the characters from going home? Is it obvious that all they have known or loved is in danger of never again being seen? Or, has the show up to that point already well established the risk, but not yet taken that risk for granted?

That, perhaps, is the worst risk the material has ever faced: taking space for granted. The moment traveling to the other side of the universe doesn't feel like a risk, they've failed in one of the most basic tenets to science fiction, and at that point they might as well not leave Earth at all. *Stargate*'s writers did a fair job of striking a delicate balance between deep space and personal conflict. Mostly. Enough of the episodes do the heavy lifting for the deep-space elements necessary for the overall theme, but there are a few that seem to coast on the good graces established by the rest. Here are a few examples:

SG-1, season two, episode #21, "1969": Now, I enjoy a time-travel romp as much as the next guy, but this episode simply replaces the "space" distance with "time" distance, so it technically fulfills the general deep-space challenge, even if only by swapping it out. Also, I personally have some issues with the way time travel is used so flippantly in many science-fiction shows. While it technically manages to maintain the "far from home" element here, I wish they wouldn't fall back on such an overused trope. But at least it isn't...

SG-1, season seven, episode #3, "Fragile Balance": Great, so now we have *Big* meets *Stargate*. Or *13 Going on 30*. Or *The Kid*. Or maybe *17 Again*. I remember similar episodes of *Justice League* and *Muppet Babies* and... well, you get the picture. Sure, they had to throw in the added caveat that O'Neill[1] was dying, but still. It's a bit much, even for the seventh season of a science-fiction show. In what season do most shows jump the shark when they add a baby? Probably the seventh.

Atlantis, season three, episode #15, "The Game": To be fair, nearly all dramatic shows have one or two episodes per season that are more lighthearted and do not cater to the serialized "big bads," but this one pursued the silly notion that an entire civilization could be at the brink of war simply due to the actions of our crew, who had thought they were playing a strategy game. Though it is a premise unlikely to be found in a non-fantasy or non-science-fiction genre show, it leans so far into the comedic considerations implied by the conceit that it all but throws away the series' theme. While a dramatic show needs its moments of lightness if it is to avoid being too dark to be enjoyable, it completely removes the sense that there is really any danger or risk at all. Gratefully, the episodes that follow draw viewers right back into *Stargate*'s usual tone and flavor, making this one more of a fluke than a genuine narrative catastrophe.

To be fair to the franchise, these are the exceptions. For the most part, *Stargate* – especially *Universe* – leans heavily into the "space is dangerously far from home" conceit. Although most of space, for whatever reason, ends up looking like the wilds of Vancouver, BC, the writers generally treat space travel with the respect and risk such jaunts involve. Perhaps there's something to be said for the notion that repetition encourages familiarity, which in turn removes fear and trepidation.

Maybe you don't need to remind everyone each week, "Hey, we could possibly die when we step through the glowing ripples of space-time, but – screw it, let's go!" So, I'm willing to give them the benefit of the doubt that after multiple shows, seasons, episodes, graphic novels, books, movies, and so forth,

---

[1] When *Stargate* transitioned from movie to TV, Jack's surname acquired a second L.

maybe hopping through the twirling chevrons might not be such a terrifying concept, in and of itself. Then again, once you turn something so extraordinary into a trivial process, it dramatically removes all inherent science-fiction drama. It's something to consider, I suppose.

Stargate, in all its various iterations, managed to bridge that terrible gap of exploration and the risks inherently found in space (repeat after me: "Space is wonderful but dangerous") by addressing the most complicated narrative device – distance – but not leaning so heavily on it that it became weakened or superfluous. For all their adventures and dramatic conflicts, their greatest results came when they struck that tenuous balance between the ever-present challenge of deep space with the challenging adventures of seeking out and finding the unknown and unimaginable, within the far reaches of the cosmos.

Vivid Determination: The Power of Women in *Stargate*

by Bryanna Elkins

> Science is not a boy's game. It's not a girl's game. It's *everyone's* game. It's about where we are and where we're going.
> — Nichelle Nichols

When I was a young girl, some of the most cherished memories I can recall involved spending the evening on the couch with my mother, watching endless episodes of *Stargate SG-1*. It became a ritual for us to watch and rewatch the show, time and time again. There were many reasons for this, ranging from the brilliant storytelling to the fantastical settings, to the vast mythos and the worlds beyond. But there was one thing I held dear above all else, one thing that drew me back to the show, something that kept me watching: the women who inspired me from their place on the screen.

Now, you may be thinking it's a bit over the top to state that it was specifically the women of *Stargate* who brought me back again and again. In the impressive world of science fiction, there are plenty of female-identifying characters, from *Star Wars* to *Star Trek* to *Battlestar Galactica*. But at the time, as the young woman I was, characters who were defined by their actions and not their beauty or sex appeal were few and far between. I would even say that now, not much has changed. In fiction, there has been a great deal of progress with diversity and representation, and it is through science fiction that a large part of this progress has been made. But this was not always the case, not even twenty years ago.

Stargate, however, was one of the first shows that put women with strong wills and stronger minds in the spotlight. Not only that, it was a show that let them take the spotlight, that let them shine. One of my biggest inspirations came in the form of Doctor Janet Fraiser, portrayed by Teryl Rothery. In fact, I would consider her my largest fictional inspiration. She was intelligent, well-spoken, and strong in every definition of the word. It was a representation that was realistic, that valued who women are, that valued their ability and skill.

I can count on one hand the shows I have watched on which women were scientists and valuable contributors. In *Stargate*, I had a place where I felt I had a future. Watching Fraiser and Samantha Carter (Amanda Tapping) alongside my mother was what ultimately led me to decide not only that I would join the military, but that I would also become a physician. Although I found myself unable to join the military as I grew older and faced chronic illness, the inspiration sparked in me by Fraiser's character has pushed me to continue my pursuit of a career in medicine. You may think my dream sounds eminently reasonable nowadays, and it may well be for some. However, when I was young, becoming a military doctor felt like an unscalable mountain.

I was not alone in my thinking. My dream was born at a time when I recall many women being told they simply could not join the military, and even I personally had been told that women were not as capable or as useful as men in any role. Many women, arguably *most* women, had been told the same. It was not simply something we were told, but also *shown* everywhere around us. It was a stereotype, nothing more, but it was a dangerous one. Media perpetuated it, often sexualizing female characters or putting them in the role of soft-spoken damsels in distress. Their independence, strength, and intelligence were stifled, and so of course their agency would be impossible to find even under a microscope.

More consistently problematic is that even in films or shows labeled as progressive, there is a seeming tug of war between women and their team. Alternatively, their portrayal as a "hero," though there are exceptions to the rule, often leads to their being diminished to the role of sidekick. Very rarely do female characters receive the chance to headline as a true, equal team member, and they are sometimes even reduced to foils or character-development tokens for male team members to emphasize the latter's importance. This is frequently done to the woman's detriment. Women may be present, yes, and their presence may qualify as representation – but the quality of their representation is lackluster. There are very few instances of a female hero truly being portrayed correctly, and many of them fall into the trap of "providing emotion while watching the action."[1]

Even more concerning is the male domination of the teams we see, with women who are present rarely engaging in any substantial contribution among themselves. Many people know to judge this by the Bechdel test, named after cartoonist Alison Bechdel,[2] which is used as a method of determining the importance of women's roles in media. Essentially, it requires at least two named female-identifying characters discussing something other than men. As recently as 2009, well into the postfeminist era, it was estimated that up to half of all films nominated for an Oscar would have been tabled had they been required to pass this test.[3]

By my own count, as well as the analysis conducted by others,[4] at least half of the episodes or films throughout every iteration of *Stargate* thoroughly pass the Bechdel test. Some pass multiple times within the same story. The exception is the theatrical film – but we all know we have diverged from *that*. It serves as inspiration, but *Stargate* has gone beyond. That is to say, *Stargate* has blown this all out of the water. Not only does the franchise consistently pass the analysis of critics who rightfully demand role models for women from young to old in fiction, it does so in a matter-of-fact way that nobody, even for a moment, seems to question. There is no *why* for the women present – they simply *are*. They are a

---

[1] Kac-Vergne, Marianne. "Sidelining Women in Contemporary Science-Fiction Film." *Miranda*, no. 12 | 2016, 2 Mar. 2016, doi.org/10.4000/miranda.8642.

[2] The test originated as a joke in a 1985 comic strip from Bechdel titled "Dykes to Watch Out For," then was picked up and used as an earnest tool of feminist analysis because media representation is often so abysmal it cannot pass this absurdly basic bar. Bechdel attributes her inspiration for that joke to her friend Liz Wallace and to the works of Virginia Woolf. Source: Garber, Megan. "Call it the 'Bechdel-Wallace Test.'" *The Atlantic*, 25 Aug. 2015, theatlantic.com/entertainment/archive/2015/08/call-it-the-bechdel-wallace-test/402259/.

[3] Harris, Mark. "I Am Woman. Hear Me... Please!" *Entertainment Weekly*, 6 Aug. 2010, ew.com/article/2010/08/06/i-am-woman-hear-me-please/.

[4] Pass-The-Bechdel. *Stargate SG-1 Full Series Review*. Tumblr, 6 July 2020, pass-the-bechdel.tumblr.com/post/622035937867808769/stargate-sg1-full-series-review/amp.

vital part of the team, and they have a role to play. They are independent, they're empowered, and they have agency.

It is important to note what agency is, and some qualities that strong female-identifying characters have, so that we can dissect how *Stargate* places women in positions where they display agency. Agency is commonly defined as a person having rights and being aware of these rights, paired with their ability and belief that they can exercise these rights. Both of these conditions must be present. While one's agency can be used to help others or collaborate with diplomatic approaches, it can also be displayed through traditionally "negative" methods. The main point is that the person in question has the ability to identify their goals and choose their method of achieving them. In the case of science fiction, I would posit that alignment on a moral scale does not matter for characters displaying agency, and in fact villainesses can be extremely good indicators of how healthily a franchise portrays women – often, villainesses are unchained from societal expectations, are aware of this fact, and can work toward their ultimate desires.[5]

I remember my friends feeling the very same way that I did about *Stargate*. I would tell them the stories and show them the episodes, and they too would fall in love with the franchise's incredible women. I found that as I grew older, I was ever more impressed. As the later seasons of *SG-1* and its sequel shows, *Stargate Atlantis* and *Stargate Universe*, came and went, I witnessed other women grow to love the show as well, and I even saw the perspectives of men change when exposed to the characters within.

Sam Carter is probably the most well-known woman of the *Stargate* franchise. Amanda Tapping provides a remarkable portrayal of Carter, one that resonates with nearly all who watch the show. She is portrayed as intelligent from the moment she first appears, refusing to bend to the pressures of a male majority and, instead, taking every opportunity to effortlessly prove herself. She is not only a part of the Stargate Command team, but also a *vital* part of that team. She is extremely specialized in her knowledge, surpassing many – if not all – of those within the *Stargate* program.

From the moment Carter enters the room in the very first episode of *SG-1*, she has no problem keeping up with those around her. Her quips to Colonel Jack

[5] Davies, Bronwyn. "THE CONCEPT OF AGENCY: A Feminist Poststructuralist Analysis." Social Analysis: *The International Journal of Social and Cultural Practice*, no. 30, Berghahn Books, 1991, pp. 42–53, www.jstor.org/stable/23164525.

O'Neill and others consistently prove her wit and her awareness – and, more than that, her determination. She is immediately portrayed as fearless, having spent time actively in war, and is very dedicated. Sam is herself respectful, but ultimately intolerant of disrespect received. She refuses to allow the men present to minimize her or her accomplishments.[6]

This is only compounded time and time again as both *SG-1* and *Atlantis* progress. What starts as a pointed introduction evolves into Carter being an indispensable part of the teams on both shows. She is not given extra attention due to her *gender*, but rather due to her expertise, strength, and capability. It is because she is trusted and respected. Furthermore, it is because she is brave and willing to stand up for herself, even so far as putting the System Lord Ba'al in his place with a well-aimed punch and an effective retort when he refuses to help her and condescendingly questions her intelligence.[7] There is no question of whether or not she is able, at least not that would not be presented to any man in her position, but she continues her ascent past her initial role of captain to colonel for *Atlantis*.

It is both refreshing and empowering to have a woman in a field that has a measly thirteen percent of total academic authors, such as physics.[8] This empowerment is also supported by her U.S. Air Force background, which is composed of only twenty-one percent women.[9] She displays her ability and is treated no differently than anyone else. It is precisely the inspiration we need. Then we have Doctor Fraiser, who is portrayed in a similar light. In a male-dominated field, she is as determined and as no-nonsense as Carter. Aided by a

---

[6] *SG-1*'s "Children of the Gods." This is, quite frankly, one of my favorite scenes in any franchise: the way Sam so matter-of-factly addresses them all, outdoing every single one of their expectations with a single sentence, and the portrayal by Tapping is flawless. She gives Sam a visibly powerful personality, one further defended by the script. The undercurrent of slightly campy humor makes it even better. It is one of the best introductions of a character that I think exists!

[7] *SG-1*'s "The Quest, Part 2."

[8] Yes, it's true, only 13% of authors in the academia of physics are women – as evidenced by this study: Holman, Luke, et al. "The Gender Gap in Science: How Long until Women Are Equally Represented?" *PLOS Biology*, vol. 16, no. 4, 2018, doi.org/10.1371/journal.pbio.2004956.

[9] And yes, only 21.3% of the USAF are women as well: "Demographics of the United States Air Force." *United States Air Force*, 2022, afpc.af.mil/About/Air-Force-Demographics/.

consistently incredible presentation by the talented Teryl Rothery, Fraiser's role is just as important as any other.

This is especially true given that women only make up anywhere from twenty-seven to thirty-one percent of healthcare leadership worldwide – with absolutely no number available regarding the percentage of women as physicians in military leadership roles.[10] Fraiser is courageous, selfless, and capable, able to easily balance her personal life with her duty, as evidenced by her adoption of Cassandra.[11] More than once, she proves to be an integral part of saving the SG-1 team and even Stargate Command as a whole. She does so alongside Carter in *SG-1*'s "Legacy," as well as in multiple other instances. Her courage is also frequently displayed. She is not only active on base, but in the field, just as Carter is, and her fearless devotion is what leads to her tragic death.[12]

A similarity shared by both is that they are free from the dependency that plagues many female characters. Part of the point of the aforementioned Bechdel test is that often, women are possessed by a need for validation by male characters – especially love interests – and they exist to prop the men up further by discussing them in a way that validates their masculinity. Both Carter and Fraiser offer a solid characterization of women who are independent. They may have romantic interests, but such does not define their character. Even when placed in situations in which men are in extremely dominant or overbearing roles, such as in *SG-1*'s "Emancipation," the women are far from conforming to these demands of an even more ancient society and their gender roles.

Claudia Black's Vala Mal Doran arrives on the scene as the polar opposite of many of the women who'd appeared on *SG-1* before her. From her first appearance in "Prometheus Unbound," she is fiery and intelligent, crafty and confident. Over time, we learn more about her, including her darker past as a thief and, more generally, as a criminal – which only proves to display Vala as

---

[10] This study only covers non-military roles, for it is quite difficult to find any statistical analysis of women in the military: Yang, Jenny. "Female Representation Global Health Workforce Ranked by Influence 2018." *Statista*, 8 Sept. 2021, statista.com/statistics/1102621/females-global-health-workforce-by-role/. Another study provides some insight for those interested, but it focusses on family-practice physicians so it is not as relevant as one would like: Massaquoi, Mariama A et al. "Perceptions of Gender and Race Equality in Leadership and Advancement Among Military Family Physicians." *Military Medicine* vol. 186, Suppl 1 (2021): 762-766, doi:10.1093/milmed/usaa387.
[11] *SG-1*'s "Singularity" and "Rite of Passage."
[12] *SG-1*'s "Heroes, Part 1" and "Part 2."

someone who is in possession of her destiny and her growth. Hers is the story of a woman who overcomes the more terrible potentialities of life, instead growing strong and certain enough of herself and her abilities to continue to learn and improve – not for any man, but for herself.

Despite their differences, Vala Mal Doran (Claudia Black) and Samantha Carter (Amanda Tapping) made a formidable team and unlikely friends.

Vala is more than that, however. Frequently, such as in the case of *SG-1*'s "Beachhead," when she sacrifices herself to stop the construction of the Ori supergate, Vala displays heroism that surpasses many of even the original long-term characters. Her bravery is unrivalled in nearly every situation into which she is placed. And in an expression that is often overlooked, Vala is in command of her desires outside of career. She displays sexuality in a way that is not degrading to her character, and in fact her comments show that she is not afraid to speak her mind regarding the topic – something rare among women in media.

Alongside Colonel Carter reprising on *Stargate Atlantis,* Teyla Emmagan is introduced to us in "Rising," portrayed by the brilliant Rachel Luttrell. She is thoroughly confident and graceful, despite being the equal of men around her. Even when pregnant, she does not allow anyone to view her as weak. When mocked by a villager in *Atlantis*'s "The Kindred," she fights back against them. She shows that motherhood is not a weakness, the same as Fraiser does in her own way, and in fact openly displays that she is just as tough as anyone who is *not* carrying a child.

Rachel Luttrell portrayed Teyla Emmagan, the noble warrior-queen of the Athosians.

Atlantis's "Missing" provides a similar display of her personality. Not only is Teyla able to overcome internal conflict regarding her own feelings of guilt when faced with a perhaps greater duty (something that gives her a relatable and humane depth due to its nature), but she shows a full range in the episode. She is caring yet ruthless, and powerful yet calm. This is who she is, a woman aware of her decisions, of the consequences they might have, but who believes in them and knows how to both handle and defend herself.

The noteworthy heroines of *Stargate* extend into *Universe*. That show's team reaches even further into the legacy started by *SG-1*, offering a multitude of roles that display women as talented and courageous. Camille Wray is a character who deserves mention here, as she is another woman who thrives under pressure. With consistently noteworthy performances by the talented Ming-Na Wen, Wray becomes extremely memorable. She is displayed as devoted to her work and her morals. The character is also extremely important in other ways, as she is representative of ethnic diversity as well as of the LGBTQ+ community. Moreover, it's done in a way that is not inappropriately utilized through oversexualization, a tactic that is often a method of tokenization and reduction for queer women.[13]

Neither of these facets are to the detriment of Wray's character – as they indeed should not be. Beyond this, she is a consistent voice of her own beliefs, and they seem unshakeable. Even her most extreme actions are supported by a belief that it is the right thing to do, as in *Universe*'s "Divided," in which Wray initiates a coup alongside Nicholas Rush in favor of the civilians aboard the *Destiny,* believing the existing military leadership endangers them all. Camille exhibits awareness of her right to a voice but is even more acutely aware of her moral code and her ability to abide by it, despite the existence of the men in power.

Ming-Na Wen's Camille Wray proved to be one of *Stargate Universe*'s more intriguing characters as the show, and Wray's complex arc within it, progressed.

---

[13] The latter is quite important, as despite the queer community making up approximately 7.1 percent of the American population, Nielsen reports published as recently as last year indicate that only 7.6 percent of recurring characters overall in television are queer-identifying, which is purportedly even less for women, or for women of color. This should be 7 percent per show, but it is nowhere near that number. Sources: (1) Jones, Jeffrey M. "LGBT Identification in U.S. Ticks up to 7.1%." Gallup, 18 Feb. 2022, news.gallup.com/poll/389792/lgbt-identification-ticks-up.aspx. (2) "Being Seen on Screen: Diverse Representation and Inclusion on TV." Nielsen, 12 Feb. 2020, nielsen.com/us/en/insights/report/2020/being-seen-on-screen-diverse-representation-and-inclusion-on-tv/.

The miniseries *Stargate Origins* also provides a remarkably strong female lead in its portrayal of Catherine Langford (Ellie Gall). Drawing on the role of the older Langford, who had appeared both in the *Stargate* theatrical film (portrayed by Viveca Lindfors) as well as on *Stargate SG*-1 (played by Elizabeth Hoffman, Glynis Davies, and Nancy McClure), the younger Catherine of *Origins* is exactly what one would hope she would be. Although she initially appears potentially unremarkable, this perspective is quickly shattered.

The many faces of Catherine Langford: (top, left to right) Kelly Vint, Ellie Gall, and Nancy McClure as younger iterations; and (bottom, left to right) Glynis Davies, Viveca Lindfors, and Elizabeth Hoffman during the character's later years.

Langford, like many female characters in *Stargate*, is a woman of intelligence and ambition, and one who is pursuing a career in archaeology. She displays an impressive amount of agency during the first episode alone, standing by her decisions and consistently exercising her independence. Yet she does not do this at the cost of her family, which is something important to her. Langford is fiercely defensive of her father Paul and his work, but it is balanced – she is just as defensive of herself and her own rights.

The most notable element of Langford's character is her toughness, which has been consistent throughout the various actresses' interpretations of the role. Despite being quite classically feminine in her attire and style, she is not someone with whom to trifle. She dispatches a captor entirely alone in *Origins*, for example, enabling her to find and rescue her father. She is confident, courageous, and determined – more so than any of the men around her, in fact. When it comes to rescuing her dad from the other side of the stargate, she is the only one of the trio who is unafraid and willing to take the plunge. She takes charge and maintains charge the entire time, directing the men with orders and creating plans to aid them in survival.

Catherine's independence enables her to command the situation, as well as make her own decisions, and her quick thinking and boldness allows her and her cohorts to survive the constant dangers they face. Catherine burns brightly at every turn, and on more than one occasion she is shown quite literally staring into the face of danger and refusing to back down. Whether against god or man, Catherine knows her worth and fights fearlessly for what she believes.

Even the villainesses deserve recognition. They are fearsome, cunning, and not at all to be trifled with. Suanne Braun's Hathor, despite her own failures in her initial appearance in the *SG-1*, episode "Hathor," rises to the rank of System Lord and amasses a notable powerbase. While she is portrayed initially as a woman who uses her sexuality to achieve her goals (and while her methods are not something that should be glorified) – which, while often critiqued, does not make her appear weak – her failure is simply in that she seemingly underestimates the women of Stargate Command. In consecutive encounters, she is portrayed as both quite clever and ingenuous, able to bend any slight advantage into benefit. Her entire position is based on her possession of agency. She crafts her own decisions and makes them with conviction, utilizing her control over both external and internal.

Morena Baccarin's Adria follows in the same path. She is utterly ruthless. Terrifying, even. She follows much the same path as Hathor, possessing vital self-efficacy despite her indoctrination by the Ori. She makes decisions that benefit her, displaying caring for her mother as much as her own knowledge and beliefs allow, but similarly uses her extreme intelligence and capacity to frequently gain the upper hand. In fact, the arc Adria follows is a well-crafted display of how, despite her indoctrination, she became something more and claimed power once she was separated from the Ori. It becomes clear, in *The Ark of Truth*, that she learns her own power over the period of time in which we see her. With the Ori dead, she develops a dangerous awareness and powerful agency, far beyond what many desire her to have.

There are multiple other female characters whose contributions could be dissected, all of whom are incredible and significant in their portrayals. There is no woman who should be overlooked – and no woman who *can* be overlooked. If I have not mentioned them here, it is not for lack of wanting, but due simply to the fact that it would take up all the pages of this book with descriptions of them all and praise for their talented portrayals.

However, even more important than simple gender diversity and the breaking of the glass ceiling through characters is that it comes in the form of representation of women with racial diversity, which I touched on above. While some of the races portrayed may be fictional, the effects of representation are, regardless, very clear. *Stargate* has never been without racial diversity in its portrayals, but many science-fiction franchises find themselves devoid of such. And as is the case with women's representation, many more have ethnic diversity that is little more than token. Approximately only twenty-seven percent of television shows have a recurring cast member who qualifies as racially diverse.[14]

It may be difficult to present strong cases of diversity in science-fiction settings, given the requirement for extraterrestrial species and the complexity of scenarios, but it is far from impossible. In fact, as outlined above, it is *crucial* for media – especially media that presents a fantastical view of reality – to embrace diversity through as many avenues as possible. Gene Rodenberry, in casting Nichelle Nichols as Nyota Uhura on the original *Star Trek*, helped to break multiple glass ceilings since Uhura, a black woman, was featured prominently as a bridge officer at a time when the Civil Rights Movement was still taking place. Martin Luther King Jr. famously thanked Nichols, in fact, for her portrayal of Uhura.[15]

I would state that fiction, especially a franchise such as *Stargate*, which centers around the United States and contains reference to political realities and even subtextual displays of its socio-economic strata, should find it a necessity to represent all forms of diversity. While *Stargate* initially seems to fall into the same pitfall as many franchises, the show's iterations do demonstrate an

---

[14] See the same source in 13.
[15] "Nichelle Nichols Remembers Dr. King." *StarTrek.com*, 7 Mar. 2019, startrek.com/news/nichelle-nichols-remembers-dr-king.

important feature: growth. In fact, I am reminded of a quote from Vala herself, in which she seemingly breaks the fourth wall to provide a tongue-in-cheek critique about the fact that Earth "[...] seems to have a rather interesting, if somewhat limited, gene pool."[16]

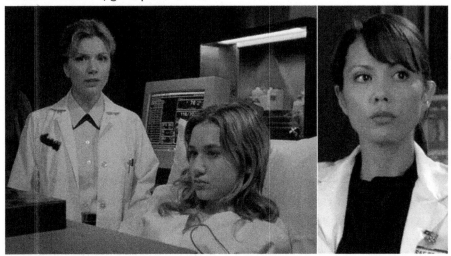

Teryl Rothery and Colleen Rennison (left) were endearing as mother-daughter team Janet and Cassandra Frasier. Lexa Doig (right) became the late Doctor Frasier's replacement, Carolyn Lam.

Stargate quite obviously embraces diversity in its casting choices, but even more importantly, it creates narratives in which women of all ethnicities are empowered and noteworthy. Characters such as Adria, Camille Wray, Teyla Emmagan, and Doctor Carolyn Lam (Lexa Doig) — even though some are on entirely different sides of the moral spectrum — provide poignant portrayals of women with both determination and strong will. Though someone like Adria may not be the ideal role model, she does display an undeniable power and an extremely memorable contribution. Doctor Lam displays the same capability as Doctor Fraiser, taking on her role as chief medical officer and shining brightly in such episodes as "Origin" and "Babylon." And, as discussed previously, Wray is impressive in all facets, while Emmagan is a powerhouse who proves time and time again that there is a reason she was the Queen of the Athosians.

---

[16] *SG-1*'s "Avalon, Part 1."

In the world of media, in which gender and ethnic representation rarely or insufficiently intersect, as referenced by multiple authors,[17] and/or do so in a diminutizing or de-emphasizing light, *Stargate* portrays women who surpass the often-seen boundaries of class, gender, and ethnicity. It allows women of any background to take on any role – and, more importantly, it gives them the space in which to do it well.

Science fiction is meant to be transgressive. It is meant to surpass where we are now. It is often informed by political undercurrents. It is thoroughly inspired by the seemingly endless limits of humanity, and it thrives on the stories of those who go beyond. There is no place for complacency here – and while we should never stop evolving, *Stargate* went beyond and provided women like me with visions of ourselves among the stars. From Janet Fraiser to Samantha Carter, from Vala Mal Doran to Teyla Emmagan and Camille Wray, *Stargate* proved to me – and to others – that if *they* could do it, so too could I.

A big thank-you to Will Kendall, Alli Kozarec, Michelle Elkins, and Emberley Broadhead for their help in editing, especially on such a tight schedule. An even bigger thank-you to Beth Walloch for providing me with the chance to Q&A with so many Stargate fans regarding this topic. You guys are amazing!

---

[17] While there are numerous authors who promote intersectionality, I invite those reading to delve into the works and words of Samuel R. Delany (especially in *Starboard Wine*), as well as Octavia E. Butler, to further explore the perspective I gained through them, especially the importance of intersectionality in speculative and science fiction.

Inhabiting This Human Form: The Metaphysical Personhood of Ra

by Kelli Fitzpatrick

In the opening credits sequence of the 1994 *Stargate* film,[1] Ra's headdress is the focus, with the camera panning over its intricate textures in close-up detail. It isn't completely obvious initially that it *is* in fact a headdress, as it appears more like stone architecture or ornate sculpture. But as the credits conclude, the camera zooms out and we see a metal face staring back at us, accompanied by ominous-sounding music.

That symbol of a mask, something that conceals the face, is an apt motif to kick off the story, given that the character of Ra is a possessed being (an alien lifeform inhabiting a human body). While later iterations of the *Stargate* franchise deal heavily with the concept of bodily possession, particularly with the Goa'uld,[2] the original film places possession front and center in its villain but

---

[1] Russell, Kurt, James Spader, and Jaye Davidson, actors. *Stargate*. Directed by Roland Emmerich, MGM, 1994.

[2] Those who have watched *Stargate SG-1* know that Ra is revealed to be a Goa'uld. In order to reach a sufficient depth of analysis, this essay will focus only on the theatrical film, but I encourage you to bring any knowledge you have from other

spends little screen time considering the metaphysical implications of this state of being.

In many cases of science-fiction possession, the philosophical assumption is that what makes a person the *same* person through time is having the same mind or consciousness, that the thing that makes you *you* is separate from your body, an immaterial entity who can be transplanted into a different body. At first glance, *Stargate* seems to fall into this camp of recognizing the psyche of a person *as* that person, treating Ra in human form as the same being as Ra in alien form, but closer analysis reveals some evidence to the contrary: the cinematography of the film suggests the body may play an important role in defining metaphysical personhood (for Ra, at least). I argue this discrepancy is not an oversight by the filmmakers but rather a clever leveraging of the tools of film to emphasize a key message of the story.

The film boasts the utterly wicked and utterly fascinating character of Ra as its primary antagonist, played by actor Jaye Davidson. (Kieron Lee portrays the masked Ra in the movie, while others would play him post-film: Jay Williams in *SG-1*'s "Moebius" and *Stargate: Continuum*, and Vico Ortiz in *Stargate Origins*.) The ancient Egyptian symbol of the "eye of Ra" appears several times in the film (on Catherine Langford's necklace, on the placard in the mining settlement) before Ra[3] himself arrives and is revealed, through much foreboding fanfare, to be an alien possessing a human body.

We get most of Ra's backstory via cave inscriptions that Doctor Daniel Jackson translates, which explain that Ra's original body, shown as having grey skin, an elongated face, and sharp teeth, was dying and his species going extinct.[4] Ra thus went on a quest to find "a way to extend his own life," and came upon prehistoric Earth. "He realized," the inscription reads, "within a human body, he had a chance for a new life." So, without asking permission, Ra abducted a human

---

iterations of *Stargate* (or from philosophy, for that matter) to bear on your interpretation of Ra's personhood as you read.

[3] This is likely obvious from context, but since this essay deals with metaphysics, it is worth clarifying that references to "Ra" in this essay, unless otherwise specified, refer to the fictional character in the *Stargate* film, not to any person or figure in the real world, fictional or otherwise. When I make claims about Ra's metaphysical personhood, I am making claims about how the metaphysics of the character might operate within the fictional world, given what is shown and discussed on screen.

[4] Intriguingly, the alien looks rather like a sinister version of *SG-1*'s Asgard – a species who are, in fact, revealed to be going extinct. Could Ra be a Goa'uld-possessed Asgard, in turn possessing a human?

youth and "possessed his body, like some kind of parasite looking for a host." Then, "inhabiting this human form," he set himself up as a god-ruler and enslaved humans to mine the mineral that maintains his technology.

Jaye Davidson's unmasked Ra was a fascinating foil for Daniel Jackson (James Spader) and Jack O'Neil (Kurt Russell), shown here with the nuclear weapon that brought down the false god.

Ra's inhabitation of a human host is a classic case of science-fiction body swapping, and as such, presents some very interesting philosophical questions. Specifically, body swapping presents a useful problem case for an issue philosophers call "metaphysical personhood," which refers to what makes a person the *same* person across time. Is the Ra that Daniel Jackson and Colonel

Jack O'Neil[5] meet on the moon in the Kaliam Galaxy[6] the same person as the Ra who traveled from distant stars, whose species was going extinct? Is the Ra they meet the same person as the human boy who walked toward the light one fine prehistoric evening? Or is the answer perhaps both – or neither? Furthermore, what are the appropriate criteria we should use to answer this question? Does having the same psyche make one the same person? What about having the same body?

Before we even get to Ra's entrance in the film, the issue of metaphysical personhood makes a subtle cameo toward the beginning in the operation of the stargate itself. The gate seems to function like a wormhole, a portal connecting distant places in the universe. To travel through it, a person undergoes "molecular deconstruction" and is then reconstructed on the other side. Since, for the duration of the journey, the traveler has no cohesive body yet is treated as the same continuant person upon arrival, it seems like the film is establishing the view that a person is something more than molecules, more than matter. The first-person point of view of the roller-coaster trip through the gate suggests that the traveler remains conscious for the journey, despite their molecules being separated. The person, therefore, must be their mind, the thing that is awake.

There are many different permutations of this philosophical position that states a person is some aspect of their mentality. For example, John Locke argues that you are the same person if you have the same consciousness.[7] Joseph Butler argues that you are the same person if you have the same soul.[8] Each of these positions is complex and nuanced, and they can't truly be lumped together effectively, but for the purposes of this essay, I'm going to use the general phrase "the psyche" to denote whatever the relevant mental aspects are. We can call the corresponding philosophical theory "the psyche theory."

If the film espouses the psyche theory, then what happens to the psyche of the human boy when Ra takes possession of his body, and what does that mean

---

[5] O'Neil's surname has one L in the movie's credits, whereas the name of the TV version played by Richard Dean Anderson has two Ls.

[6] Later retconned, on *Stargate SG-1*, as Abydos, a planet located within the Milky Way.

[7] Locke, John. "Of Identity and Diversity." *An Essay Concerning Humane Understanding, Volume I*, 1690, gutenberg.org/files/10615/10615-h/10615-h.htm#link2HCH0030.

[8] Butler, Joseph. "Of Personal Identity." *The Analogy of Religion, Natural and Revealed*, 1736, pp. 301-308, anglicanhistory.org/butler/analogy/dissertation1.html.

for the resulting person who calls himself Ra? Option one is that the boy's psyche is obliterated instantly the moment Ra possesses him, essentially killing him, and that the being in the pyramid ship is fully Ra, the same Ra who left the alien body. This seems to be the assumption most of the characters make (or, at least, their behavior indicates as much). However, we do get one sign that an aspect of the human boy's psyche may have survived in Ra: his spirit of boldness.

Top: Ra, portrayed in masked form by Kieron Lee, surrounded himself with young children. Were their deaths morally justified? Bottom: Jay Williams (left) took on the role for *SG-1*'s "Moebius" and *Stargate Continuum*, while Vico Ortiz (right) portrayed him in *Stargate Origins*.

There is plenty of evidence that Ra exults in his human form, decorating it, parading it around, but the historical account in the cave states that Ra chose this particular human not for appearance but because "curious and without fear, he walked toward the light." Ra could have abducted any human for any reason, but he chose a host based on *personality* traits, on *intellectual* properties. Why would personality traits matter if only the body survived possession – if the host's psyche died? It seems to me that one does not screen for a desired property one intends to immediately delete. It is possible that Ra simply took the first host available, the one who walked toward him, but I think he's both too powerful and too vain for that. I'm convinced he got exactly what he wanted.

That brings us to option two: Some (or all) of the boy's original psyche remains inside Ra, repressed – in other words, Ra exists as fully himself in a new body, but there is a separate person buried beneath. There is no evidence of this in the film, however. No one speaks of the boy as if his consciousness still exists. There is no indication of a divided will or split personality, and Ra never wavers or second-guesses his choices. If the boy's discreet psyche is still in there somewhere, it is not discernible from what we see on screen.

Option three is that some (or all) of the boy's psyche was fused with Ra's, creating a new being who is not the same metaphysical person as either Ra or the boy pre-possession. This option has some merit. It explains why Ra wanted a bold host, so he could absorb those desirable personality traits into his own. It also fits with the parasite analogy Jackson gives – most parasites feed off their hosts, sometimes influencing their behavior but rarely taking over their minds completely.[9] However, this option does not fit well with Ra's vanity and obsessive quest to preserve himself. Fusion means the original beings no longer exist as distinct from each other.[10] This does not seem like Ra's goal.

Finally, option four is that the traits Ra desires in the host are physically encoded in the brain matter of that body, allowing Ra to take advantage of them even after he eliminates the host's psyche. From a real-world scientific perspective, this sort of integration would likely be difficult to achieve because brain physiology adapts to the person using it and the habits of the body it is controlling. In the case of Ra, the habits of the human body change drastically

---

[9] See this article for the notable exception of "zombie parasites": Bates, Mary. "Meet 5 'Zombie' Parasites That Mind-Control Their Hosts." *National Geographic*, 24 Oct. 2018, nationalgeographic.co.uk/animals/2018/10/meet-5-zombie-parasites-mind-control-their-hosts.

[10] Some philosophers believe that fusion means the original beings no longer exist at all, while others, like David Lewis, hold a perdurantist view that both beings still exist post-fusion but share temporal parts. Ra is not the sharing type, so neither of these arrangements seem like they would appeal to him. For more on perdurantism and identity, see this source: Lewis, David. "Survival and Identity." In *Philosophical Papers: Volume I*. New York: Oxford University Press, 1983, 55-72.

upon possession. As author Dean Barnett writes for *The Guardian,* in a body-swapping scenario:[11]

> The mind now occupies a brain It hasn't developed alongside/from, so the brain has a lot of features that will be unfamiliar. For example, memories are physically stored in the brain. Even if the newly transferred mind brings its own memories with it, now there are two sets of memories in one head (one physical, one purely mental)? That's going to be disorientating, to say the least.

While this difficulty might pose an obstacle to humans swapping bodies with each other using our current scientific understanding, Ra's technology is presented as incredibly advanced and could likely overcome this hurdle. Therefore, I see this option as viable.

If some vestige of the boy's psyche does remain, could Ra be un-fused, giving the youth back his body?[12] What would happen if Ra were mortally wounded, even killed, and placed in the sarcophagus chamber? Jackson says he was dead before he was placed in the sarcophagus, and Sha'uri is as well when she goes in. They are both revived as themselves. Whose psyche would wake up in a killed and revived Ra? Still Ra, or the boy he possessed? Ra's regular tune-up sessions in the chamber don't seem to affect him as a possessed being, but what if he were dead for a while? Is there a post-death window of opportunity during which Ra's psyche would be gone from his possessed human form, but the body could still be revived? We'll never know since Ra is vaporized before any sort of rescue operation can be attempted, or even considered. Interestingly, no one in the film seems concerned for the fate of the boy whose body was stolen.

Perhaps the reason they are not concerned is that they assume the boy is long dead and gone (option one above), but if he is *not* gone, it could be argued that he would have had good reason to fear being possessed, had he known what was coming. In his well-known essay "The Self and the Future,"[13] English moral philosopher Bernard Williams argues that the prospect of having one's body

---

[11] Burnett, Dean. "Body Swapping: The Science Behind the Switch." *The Guardian,* April 2014, theguardian.com/science/brain-flapping/2014/apr/02/body-swapping-the-science-behind-the-switch.

[12] As *SG-1* would reveal regarding Apophis, Ba'al, Qetesh, and other Goa'uld, the removal or death of the symbiote does, in fact, free the human host from possession – at least, for that show's serpent-like Goa'uld. Whether or not it's true of the non-serpentine Ra alien is anyone's guess.

[13] Williams, Bernard. "The Self and the Future." *The Philosophical Review,* vol. 79, no. 2, Apr. 1970, pp. 161-80.

tortured inspires dread (as is rational), and that being told your memories and desires will be overwritten by someone else's will only make the impending experience seem *more* horrifying, not less. William's point is that when viewed from the first-person perspective (ours), body swapping seems more like mind derangement, because we care about what happens to our bodies. The human boy may very well be in this sort of Williams-esque predicament while possessed by Ra. His body is arguably being tortured, by being used without his consent for tyrannical purposes, and his psyche has been apparently overwritten by someone else's.

What if the psyche is *not* the seat of metaphysical personhood? An alternate view is that you are your body; we can call this the "body theory." In this view, which is championed by philosophers like Judith Thomson,[14] the body *is* the person. Same body, same person. Different body, different person. As Thomson states, this is perhaps the "simplest view of what people are." It is fairly straightforward, until one gets into problem cases like possession.

From a body theory perspective, the metaphysical person of Ra died when his alien body perished, despite the fact that his psyche was transferred. A body theorist would say the person riding around in the pyramid ship is the same human boy who used to live on Earth – he just experienced a drastic personality shift and a sudden onset of immortality that coincided with the arrival of a spaceship on his planet. Same body, same person, remember? At first glance, the film does not support this view. We are made to believe that the being in the pyramid ship, the entity subjugating the human workers, is Ra the alien, and not a youth from prehistoric Earth. All the dialogue in the film points very clearly to the psyche making the person, not the body.

But the film's cinematography shows a very different perspective – and, interestingly, it has more to do with Ra's body than the boy's. At several points throughout the film, a glowing shadow of Ra's alien visage shines through his human face. Sometimes only his eyes glow, but in a few scenes, other facial features can be seen shining through in blue-white light. This phenomenon is most clearly noticeable in the climax sequence when Ra realizes his ship is about to explode. His face turns completely to the alien countenance, emoting in surprise (or is it fear?). As the bomb goes off, we see Ra's alien body gruesomely stripped of flesh by the nuclear blast.

---

[14] Thomson, Judith Jarvis. "People and Their Bodies." *Reading Parfit*, edited by Jonathan Dancy, Oxford, Blackwell Publishing, 1997, pp. 202-29.

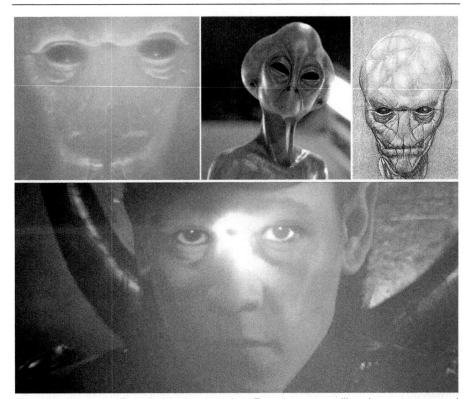

The alien known as Ra, who'd possessed an Egyptian teen millennia ago, appeared to view himself not as his human host, but as his original alien body – which more resembled one of *SG-1*'s Asgard than the show's serpentine Goa'uld. (Sketch: production designer Patrick Tatopoulos's concept drawing of Ra's original form.)

What should we make of this cinematic choice? What is being implied by showing Ra's alien form through his human skin? Let's unpack what might be going on here physically before we consider the metaphysics. Ra's alien flesh has been physically gone for millennia. It is clearly stated that ten thousand years ago, Ra's alien body was dying – "decaying and weak" is the phrase Jackson translates. It is unlikely that any of Ra's actual alien tissue was incorporated into his human form (via grafting or bioengineering or an unknown alien process) since Ra tells Jackson he can sustain human bodies indefinitely due to their relative simplicity, but he obviously could not maintain his own alien body. Ergo, his alien form cannot be part of the body he is, in fact, maintaining. Whatever we're seeing, it's not his old, physical form.

That means that physically, the image of his alien body must be a construct of Ra's technological (or biotechnical) skill. He was somehow able to preserve or recreate a photonic echo of his old likeness in his new shape. It only shines through at specific times: when he is acting angry, vindictive, or threatened.

Moments when he is losing himself in the twisted pleasure of torturing someone or is vulnerable and afraid. Moments when he is arguably most *himself,* in an unfiltered way.

And that brings us to the most interesting metaphysical insight in this analysis: despite having possessed a human youth, Ra views himself *as his alien body*. He subscribes to the body theory of metaphysical personhood but views himself as a body that *no longer exists*. That is intensely interesting, since the one thing the body theory normally requires is the presence of the same body. This interpretation works whether the flashes of his alien face are intentional or unintentional. If they are unintentional, it simply means that Ra's attachment to his alien form is so strong that not even transplanting his psyche could disconnect him from it. If, on the other hand, this capability is by design, then the association is even stronger, as it means Ra chose to engineer a way for him to retain this part of himself. Regardless of what the writing on the wall says about him taking a new host, regardless of how the entire cast of characters speak to him, Ra is, in his own assessment, an alien body that must be preserved at all costs.

Further evidence for this interpretation manifests in the additional bizarre things going on with Ra's physical form. His headdress, the one we saw in the opening credits and that he wears when he first meets Jackson and O'Neil, *morphs into his human face* when it retracts. The headdresses of the guards Anubis and Horus[15] collapse *around* their faces, possibly retracting into a device near their necks, but Ra's appears to dissolve directly into his skin. Ra's voice is also heavily distorted, matching neither the tone nor the pitch one would expect from a human youth. Ra has done more than inhabit a host; he has dragged some of his original physicality into this new arrangement. Or perhaps, from his perspective, the original physicality is all that matters.

We are left, then, with a disconnect: most of the film's dialogue points toward metaphysical personhood being grounded in one's psyche, while the visuals of Ra as a possessed being point toward personhood being grounded in one's body. I would argue this discrepancy between what the film *says* and what the film *shows* is not a mistake but a literary device that underscores the story's message: that things are not always what they seem – and, in particular, that authoritarian solutions are never simple and always backfire. Both sides eventually taste this truth, as both attempt authoritarian moves. O'Neil, as a

---

[15] In the movie, Ra's guards are humans named Anubis and Horus, who are separate from the same-named Goa'uld introduced on *SG-1*.

proxy for the U.S. military, secretly brings a nuclear weapon through the stargate, with the incredibly presumptuous intent of destroying any perceived "danger." When Ra is dying, he steals a human body and enslaves a species to mine the mineral he needs to maintain his dominion. Just blow up the threat. Just take whatever you want. The parallel of assumed entitlement is clear.

But it turns out it's not that simple for either side. The warhead's presence only causes chaos for O'Neil and his team, introducing the potential for unnecessary violence, and as a result, the weapon is hijacked and is nearly used against the people of Earth. Ra's solutions also backfire: the humans he subjugates rebel – repeatedly – and he still perishes, even in his new body, even with all his technological prowess. Barging in and taking control of something that is not yours (a body, a civilization, a stargate, a planet) is not a choice the story rewards, nor should it be.

Instead, bad decisions earn even harder choices later on, and our heroes' choice to nuke Ra's ship is a morally grey one. At the film's climax, Ra has been injured and is retreating from the planet in his pyramid vessel. He poses no immediate threat to the people on the surface who have liberated themselves, and since the workers now know the truth, that Ra is not a god, it is unlikely they will be easily subdued again. They seem to have won. Jackson says to O'Neil, "He's leaving. Turn it off."

True to theme, it's not that simple, for the bomb cannot be disarmed. O'Neil brought a nuke into the mix, and now it is live and has to *go* somewhere. They (understandably) don't want to die, so they choose to destroy Ra instead by beaming the bomb onboard his ship. I find this choice an unexpected and slightly dark final note to O'Neil's character arc, which had been bending *away* from self-destructive violence thanks to the not-so-subtle proddings of Jackson and the time Jack spends with Kasuf's tribe, particularly Skaara (Alexis Cruz). True, O'Neil does not commit suicide or strand himself on the planet alone, as was his original plan, but he still sets off the bomb, an unequivocal metaphor for self-destructive tendency. The villain may be ousted, but it's not a clean success.

Even more unexpected is that Jackson's arc bends *toward* violence. Up until the climax moment, Jackson behaves as if he is appalled by the presence of the warhead and disgusted by the thought of the team using it. His first reaction is: "What the hell were you thinking? What did you come here for?" He speaks these lines *after* learning Ra is a despot, and while being held hostage. At that point, he doesn't like Ra, but doesn't want him dead. And yet, at the end of the film, Jackson has the thought to nuke Ra at the same moment O'Neil does. I can't help but wonder, if the clock had not been running on the nuke, would Jackson and O'Neil still have chosen to beam it aboard Ra's ship while he was retreating, killing not only the villain but also the human host's body, along with all the children and guards still aboard? Would the duo have felt that decision was morally justified? If not, why does the addition of a ticking clock – *their* ticking clock, no less – make it justified?[16]

Ra's first line in the film turns out to be chillingly prophetic: "You have come here to destroy me." They *do* destroy him, with the bomb they brought, and they do it in the same manner by which Ra was planning to eradicate Earth: by using his own technology against him. Unfortunately, they also kill all the kids in Ra's retinue in the process, seemingly without remorse. While their universe will certainly not hurt for having one less tyrant, the fact that human-created violence machines always, *always* result in the death of innocents is a point as unmissable as the giant blue nuclear blast that sweeps the sky.

The language in the film suggests that body swapping is clean and easy if you have enough power and knowledge. The flesh says otherwise: it's more complicated. Messy. By carefully comparing the film's verbal narrative with its onscreen imagery, we see that Ra's metaphysical personhood is portrayed as fraught and unstable, a failed case of forced fusion. The possession didn't quite take. Ra doesn't quite fit in the human form. This discrepancy serves as an effective thematic parallel for Ra's failed subjugation of humanity, and for the moral failures of Earth leaders who hide warheads in first-contact teams.

---

[16] This dilemma might be viewed as a science-fiction version of the famous Trolley Problem. For more on that thought exercise, see this source: Davis, Lauren Cassani. "Would You Pull the Trolley Switch? Does it Matter?" *The Atlantic*, 9 Oct. 2015, theatlantic.com/technology/archive/2015/10/trolley-problem-history-psychology-morality-driverless-cars/409732/.

The Furlings: From Paradise Lost to Lost Opportunity

by Jo Duffy

> The Furlings? Aw, not *those* guys! I just can't imagine cute, little, furry things making big, powerful weapons.
>> — Colonel Jack O'Neill, living in perpetual hope that someday, one of our advanced alien allies will give us some big, honkin' space guns

> The reason why you would want to build more ships is that, like other men, you like big machines with big engines that fire big missiles... because you have a deep-seated need to compensate for your own shortcomings.
>> — Vala Mal Doran of SG-1, definitely *not* talking to Jack O'Neill

I never planned, when I set out to write about the mysterious Furlings, to compose a feminist diatribe, condemning the underlying misogyny and male supremacy of the fictional *Stargate* universe. Nothing could've been further from my intentions, so I am not going to do that.

I love *Stargate*.

I have loved *Stargate* pretty unreservedly from my first exposure to it. In fact, one could make a compelling argument that I was predisposed, if not pre-destined, to love *Stargate*. Because to me, *Stargate* has always been all about the story's original central character, Doctor Daniel Jackson, about his physical and spiritual journey and his legacy.

Doctor Jackson is kind, altruistic, and perceptive – and yet, as a side-effect of how unbelievably smart he is, he frequently comes off as a high-functioning idiot, so in touch with dozens of languages and complicated pictographs and cryptograms and complex, humanistic, and cosmically important concepts and principles that he is often completely out of touch with the physical reality of the world and those around him. This is to the extent that one sometimes wonders how he ever fumbles his way through mundane matters like survival, not annoying those who have authority over him and his well-being, making money... or even just managing to dress himself.

How could I not love Daniel Jackson, when in fact I had met in passing and fleetingly admired (as someone likely to grow up to be a bit of a heartthrob) the actor who'd originated the role, James Spader, a good twenty years before *Stargate* had hit movie theaters? How did I manage that? It was something that could have happened to anyone... anyone who happened to attend Wellesley College... and who'd had a room across the hall from that of Annie Spader... and had met Annie's too-cute-for-anyone's-good younger brother when he'd visited her on campus, long before he became a professional actor.

James Spader did a phenomenal job portraying Daniel in the theatrical film. And lifelong favorite Kurt Russell marvelously embodied Daniel's tormentor, protector, and future buddy, the tough, capable, and desperately grief-stricken, recently bereaved career soldier, Jack O'Neil (one L). Having liked both pairs of these characters and actors so much, I was pleasantly surprised by how much I continued to enjoy and appreciate Jackson and O'Neill (two L's) when they went from saving humankind from evil, parasitic aliens (later called the Goa'uld) on the movie screen to doing the same and more during their weekly adventures on the TV screen, while being played by Michael Shanks and Richard Dean Anderson.

When *Stargate* moved to the small screen, it was natural that it added new core characters. These included General George Hammond, who – as portrayed by the late Don S. Davis – consistently achieved a fine balance between being an exasperated, hard-as-nails toughie and a supportive and insightful friend; formidable alien warrior and former-foe-turned-invaluable-ally and nation-builder Teal'c, masterfully and appealingly played by hunky Christopher Judge; and the beautiful and brilliant Air Force Captain with a doctorate in theoretical astrophysics, Samantha Carter.

I should have adored Sam on sight and wanted to be her new best friend… but when *Stargate SG-1* debuted a quarter century ago, I was instead eye-rollingly skeptical and suspicious of a character who seemed designed specifically to serve as eye candy for the male fans… and to undercut and diminish the importance to the team and overall excellence of Doctor Jackson. After all… *he* was the person who, sixty-plus years after the discovery of the immense stone ring called the stargate beneath the sands of Egypt, had figured out how to get the freaking thing working, and how to use it to open wormholes that enabled members of Stargate Command (SGC) to simply walk into the event horizon of a subspace portal on Earth and instantly exit through an identical stone-and-subspace portal – of which there are many thousands – located worlds and even galaxies away.

But when Sam Carter was introduced, not only was she a proper, gun-toting, chain-of-command soldier and a first-rate scientist… we were also told that properly she was/should have been the one to open the gate… except that she had been so busy and in demand, doing such a vast variety of other vital and wonderful things elsewhere, that she hadn't quite gotten around to it yet. For good measure, we were told that the only reason Daniel's solution even worked in the first place was that he had accidentally hit upon virtually the sole instance in which a gate could be opened without Samantha's wonderful intervention. And then, lest we still missed the point, the series' creators broke Daniel's glasses, roughed him up, and had their interns key his car.

Okay, not really… but figuratively? For sure! All these years later, it still looks to me as though certain key creators on the series, though demonstrably quite talented, either didn't like, didn't get, or simply could not figure out how to use so nerdy a character in an action-adventure series. Could they use a formidable, alien warrior? Yes. A couple of crack soldiers? Absolutely! A hard-sciences expert on rockets and computers and tech… *and* she's hot?! Bring it. But a linguist-cryptographer-puzzle-solving archeologist whose head is in the clouds and who wants to befriend everyone and avoid conflict? Wellllllllll… insert the sound of crickets here.

In case we have missed the point, in the early episode "The Torment of Tantalus," we meet Ernest Littlefield, the long-lost love of Catherine Langford, Daniel's original-movie mentor, who is lost because *he* actually opened the stargate first, before Daniel was even born;[1] went through it; and then was unable to open a wormhole through the stargate on the other side so he could return to Earth. At least it was Daniel who discovered Ernest's story and found a way to locate him and bring him back, at long last, to Earth and to Catherine. (One of the things I consistently enjoy about *Stargate* is that, without ever descending into sappiness, it is quite unabashedly and unapologetically romantic.) Of course, Ernest's return trip could only be accomplished by means of Sam's massive and way-cool science stuff. Luckily, by this point, Sam – aided by some lovely writing and a quirky and engaging performance by Amanda Tapping – had completely won me over and definitely qualified for the coveted role of Fictitious Bestie.

With Ernest, the members of SG-1 (the premier team of soldier/explorers who travel via stargate) also learned of the Four Great Races, a galaxy-spanning alliance of vastly wise, advanced, and benevolent aliens who look after lesser beings from more primitive planets, like us; try to protect us all from science too dangerous to be trusted to us until we are a little less quarrelsome and quick on the trigger; and, whenever possible, shield us all from the depredations and machinations of would-be conquerors like the parasitic and totalitarian Goa'uld. The ongoing tale of the Four Races – as we learned of them, met and interacted with them, and their stories tantalizingly unfolded – was one of the narrative through-lines of *Stargate* mythology, from which countless wonderful stories grew and were developed. The Four Races are:

The Ancients (originally called the Alterans): brilliant scientists and benevolent humanists, the creators of the vast network of stargates and of the gates themselves. The Ancients were once human, but they'd developed philosophically and spiritually to such an extent that they left their physical bodies behind and ascended to a plane where they now exist as pure energy. They are (mostly) committed to not meddling in the lives of lesser beings such as ourselves... except for a particularly malevolent cadre of former Alterans called the Ori, beings so deliciously vile, evil, and power-hungry that they constituted *SG-1*'s chief antagonists for the two final seasons of the series and one of the two concluding movies. The Ori quite literally sicken me – meaning that, as villains, they are compelling, chilling, and highly watchable. I love to hate them.

---

[1] At least until *Stargate Origins* flipped the script by showing that, no, Catherine and her father Paul Langford had already done so but had forgotten!

The Asgard: a completely fantastic hybrid of the type of skinny, bulbous-headed, long-fingered aliens that we science-fiction and flying-saucer nerds like to call Roswell Greys, with the key figures of Norse mythology, highly scientifically advanced, and — kindly but condescendingly — determined to befriend and protect us, in the guise of big, armor-wearing, Scandinavian-looking humans. Why? Because they rightly suspect most of us would be downright freaked out at meeting little, grey men in massive spaceships who go by names like Thor, Freyr, Heimdall, and Loki.

The Asgard are wonderful and a boatload of fun... but they are not nearly as smart as they ought to be and think they are, having led themselves down an evolutionary blind alley to the point at which they can only reproduce by cloning (*Boooo!*), and the taste of their completely inorganic-looking food, which they still seem to enjoy, makes Sam exclaim in horror. The Asgard also gave their own greatest enemies, the mechanical, exponentially increasing-in-numbers Replicators, a second whack at destroying them when an Asgard scientist, following the Replicators' initial defeat, thought it would be okay to bring a couple of seemingly inert Replicator components aboard his ship... to study. Dope.

The Nox: By contrast, the Nox differ from the Asgard in just about every way possible... except that they, too, are intelligent, wise, and entirely benevolent. They live in the woodland of their world and look irresistibly like a cross between the botanical fairies of Victorian painter Cicely Mary Barker and the Faeries (from the book of the same name) by Alan Lee and Brian Froud... and like Froud's character designs for the movie *Labyrinth*. The Nox seem sweet, peaceful, and innocent... which Jack O'Neill takes at face value, ignoring a few significant clues, such as their ability to successfully treat and repair any physical injury, however grave, up to and including death. He decides to protect them from harm in the kindest and most condescending way imaginable — which the Nox appreciate, though they hardly need the help.

What no one from SG-1 manages to put together is that the Nox don't need protecting. They are gentle, they are peaceful, they live in harmony with their world and with nature... and they are safely able to do so because their science is so advanced as to look to us like actual magic. The Nox have kindly decided that we mere humans are too immature and too warlike to hang with them yet... and so, they rarely appear.

Three of the Four Great Races were (left to right) the Alterans, the Asgard, and the Nox. But who were the fourth member of this alliance, the mysterious Furlings?

Then there are the Furlings. About whom, for the longest time, we knew literally nothing but their name. We did not know of anything catastrophic that had actually happened to them... but *SG-1* went on and on, year after year after year, without the team ever meeting them or learning much of anything about the Furlings beyond their name and the fact that they had the usual characteristics of wisdom, intelligence, scientific advancement, and general benevolence that qualified them to be one of the Four Great Races.

Though we may never have encountered the Furlings (opinions differ on this point), in the season-six episode "Paradise Lost," we did meet up with some of their tech – including a rather whimsical teleportation portal key that looked less like a device and more like a big, pretty, solely decorative toy bug. Jack O'Neill and Harry Maybourne – a formerly joyless, trite, win-at-any-cost, tin-plated military-cliché-turned charming, maddeningly scapegrace frenemy, zestfully played by Tom McBeath – got to enjoy a heaping helping of the Furlings' hospitality.

Except the Furlings were not actually in residence. What they had done was set things up so that asylum-seekers hankering after peace, safety, and a preindustrial, agrarian life would be transported – like willful wives on *The Honeymooners* – to the moon, a balmy and beautiful paradise (soon to be lost), where weapons (or what the Furlings recognized as weapons) were not only banned but were prevented from being brought there, thanks to a filter built into the bug controller and the matter transmitter it activated. (You know, the more I think about that bug gizmo, the more probable I begin to find it that the Furlings were every bit as cute and goofy as their name led me to fear!)

In any event, things did not work out for Maybourne (who was sincerely determined to retire to the kind of unspoiled, natural loveliness the episode's title seemed to imply), thanks to the machinations of an unnamed Goa'uld who – for simple spite, I guess, given that there didn't seem to have been any obvious profit or tactical advantage in destroying what appears to have been a simple vacation spot and sanctuary – brought the entire place to rack, ruin, and death for all inhabitants. This Goa'uld had circumvented the anti-tech filter by bringing in a seemingly harmless plant, remarkably like arugula, but naturally so laced with paranoia-inducing toxins and hallucinogens that the residents of the erstwhile paradise went mad and killed themselves and each other. Since this scheme very nearly put a period to the lives and careers of both O'Neill and Maybourne, I am at least happy to be able to report that the Goa'uld who had hatched this dastardly and idiotic plot had himself fallen victim to it, along with all the other residents, long before the humans arrived.

And that about sums up what we can expect from the Four Races.

On a positive note, our pals the Asgard have said on several occasions that we humans of Earth (or we Tau'ri, if you prefer to use our interplanetary name) are on track to become the Fifth Race of that alliance... though I do worry a bit that, in the last few years, we may have had some setbacks on that journey, as a consequence of some notably retrograde, unevolved, and regressive behavior on the part of a number of our fellows.

In preparing for this essay, I immersed myself anew in *Stargate*, rewatching the theatrical film, all ten seasons in order of *Stargate SG-1*, and all five seasons of the spinoff series *Stargate Atlantis*, also in order. I then capped things off with fresh viewings of the last two TV movies, *Stargate: The Ark of Truth* and *Stargate: Continuum*, each of which I've seen recently and often, because I love them both, and they remain in pretty constant rotation on cable TV.

What I did not expect was what the nearly thirty years since *Stargate* was first launched, and the ten-plus years since those last two films and *Atlantis*'s infuriating, mid-story cutoff, have done to how I perceive the material. It has made me realize how far the world has come within a few short decades, despite the efforts of those same souls I mentioned above, who are determined to prevent us from becoming the Fifth Race by trying with all their might to drag us and our notions of fairness and justice backward.

As the previous paragraph pretty clearly telegraphs, I have been a feminist since my teens and am also an ardent liberal. My personal ideal, to which I aspire and hope to achieve, is to respect all others to the best extent that I can, treating them as I would like them to treat me and trying to treat them as they might wish. No wonder Daniel Jackson – with so many fun and exciting heroes to choose from in these adventures – inevitably became my pet character. Yet, some of what I found in the narrative this go-around turned out to be utterly unexpected and often unpalatable.

Far from instantly resenting Sam, I cringed in sympathy with what she routinely had to endure, even when the men around her did not mean to be bullying or misogynistic. On her first appearance, not only did she have to point out that having her "reproductive organs on the inside rather than the outside" – a line I still find clever despite the determined mockery with which the writers were treating it by the end of the series – did not disqualify her from being able to do her job... but she also had to reassure male soldiers of lower rank that, though she called herself Sam, she had still "played with dolls" – clear code for her having been a proper little girl. In other words, for not being gay! As if there would have been anything wrong with that. As if it were anyone else's business.

Long ago as that era now seems, it was, after all, early, but firmly, within the period when the official position of the U.S. military on issues of sexual orientation was already "Don't ask; don't tell." Nowadays, this seems crazily regressive and backward... but coming just a short while after the horrible era when being gay could and did get a soldier, scientific genius, or fabulous writer thrown into prison, *Stargate* was, for its time, extraordinarily progressive.

I do not believe for an instant that the creators of *SG-1* are or ever were anti-LGBTQ+ bigots. I think they were protecting themselves and their chances of keeping their wonderful series on the air by reassuring potentially easily spooked local programming affiliates and nervous viewers that there was "nothing to see here." The boys, young and old, who enjoyed the series could safely fantasize about Sam and watch her be romantically pursued by a huge number of the human and alien males she met – including a Mongol-style warlord (Cary-Hiroyuki Tagawa) who made her wear pretty dresses and scorned her for her inability to spin fiber and weave cloth – hah! Finally! Something I can do that Sam the Perfect has not yet had time to master!

Even when, late in its run, *SG-1* had begun to move forward with the times, we still had to endure pushback on these issues within the stories from a number of characters... including the usually-too-noble-to-be-true Teal'c and his fellow Jaffa warriors, who initially objected to "their" women taking up arms and joining the fight instead of staying home, cooking, cleaning, rearing little Jaffa, and making whoopee with big, bad Jaffa fighting men. Progress was gradually made, though. *Atlantis* had a female commander for most of its run, and the show's core team boasted *two* ferocious alien warriors, one of whom was played by the now-notoriously hunk-alicious *Aquaman* star, Jason Momoa, and the other of whom was a woman, Teyla Emmagan, played by Rachel Luttrell. Even more tellingly, Vala Mal Doran, played by Claudia Black as an entertainingly oversexed and very funny former Goa'uld host and confidence trickster, joined the *SG-1* team *without anything having happened to Sam*, finally breaking the seemingly inviolable "bunch of guys and just one chick" rule that had dominated the composition of action-adventure teams for decades.

We are living in a different world now, where (at least in fiction) women can be bosses without being bitches who need to be broken, where LGBTQ+ men and women appear in stories as a matter of no great import, where minorities can be leaders without attracting rude and infantile comment, and where whom one loves is a matter of choice, independent of appearances or narrow and traditional rules. That got me thinking about an aspect of *Stargate* that had never, to the best of my recollection, previously occurred to me, despite my having studied psychology during my years at Wellesley and having learned all about sexual imagery and the symbology of power – a topic that infallibly strikes pretty much every adolescent undergrad as irresistibly hilarious.

Spaceships? Rockets? Guns? As Vala was pointing out, about the time this essay got rolling, the usual trappings of science-fiction adventure stories are pretty much all phallic symbols, emblems of male supremacy and potency. Yet when *Stargate* launched, though there were firearms aplenty, and though Daniel Jackson, the dweeb (O'Neill's word, not mine) on whose expertise and lightning insights his teammates' lives and safety often depended, was nonetheless being mocked, reviled, and physically bullied by the Real Men of the U.S. military... without either Daniel or O'Neill ever thinking to object... there were virtually *no* spaceships. The means of transport, the flying carpets that took us to wondrous, strange, and perilous new locations, was an orifice – a doorway, a ring through which one stepped, then emerged – rather like one was entering Narnia... or being born.

I find it hard to believe how asleep at the switch my inner psych student and giggling adolescent must have been to have failed to immediately perceive that the stargate was an unabashedly female symbol... not even when the creators who were eating their hearts out at working on *StarGATE* rather than *Star TREK* or *Star WARS* found ways of introducing into their stories a steady stream of big spaceships, complete with big, honkin' space guns and *beaming* teleportation technology, for crying out loud! By the time Jack O'Neill and General Hammond had retired and been supplanted by SG-1-fanboy and fighter pilot Cam Mitchell (Ben Browder) and General Hank Landry (Beau Bridges), the SGC was using ships more than the stargates... and some of those ships – as well as a great number of missiles and projectiles – were being launched or fired *through the stargates!* Holy Moley!

I suppose, with all of this powerfully masculine symbology – complete with accompanying violation imagery – flying all over the screen, it should hardly come as a surprise that we have seen very little of the Nox, and almost nothing of my beloved-but-still-utterly-mysterious Furlings. The Nox tend gardens, wear flowers, heal others, guide children, and protect animals. In other words, they embody feminine values and energy. I can live with not having seen as much of the Nox as we have of the Asgard and the Ancients, because at least we know how powerful the Nox are, and they have been wonderfully realized and presented.

But where does that leave the Furlings?

The notion of the mysterious Furlings has always fascinated and maddened me in a rather delightful way. When I first heard their name, I thought the Furlings could be anything! That the "fur" in their name might be a coincidence or a red herring, and was not meant to be literally descriptive, though it did tend to suggest that it might have something to do with soft, little animal creatures. For that reason alone, I rather wished that the Furlings would turn out to be somewhat like the Ancients and the Asgard: sophisticated, superior, snooty... and utterly technologically advanced.

But, if they *had* turned out to be that type of alien, we would undoubtedly have seen them charge impressively into the heart of the storyline and play a huge and dramatic role in the unabashed sausage-fest that is *Stargate SG-1*. Given how quickly the more traditionally feminine Nox were brushed off the narrative canvas and hidden away, how likely is it that cute, little, furry aliens would ever play a role at all?

And when we *did* see them (if see them we did – they were presented to us as characters in the guise of fiction-within-fiction... but by a storyteller who was himself from outer space and, therefore, arguably may have been in a position to know) the Furlings were of a cuteness to be marveled at! So that would seem to settle that... except...

When we talk about the Furlings, we really ought first to discuss their antecedents... and no, I am not talking about any other fluffy creatures within the

Stargate continuity from whom the Fourth Great Race might be descended. Nor do I refer to the identically named, but completely dissimilar furry, anthropomorphic children in the 1993 animated film, *Once Upon a Forest*. Despite having two stellar musical stars in its voice cast in Michael Crawford and Ben Vereen – *plus* a host of devoted fans – and despite their having been created a year before the release of the original *Stargate* movie, those Furlings have nothing whatsoever to do with ours.

No, I am talking about the artistic roots of the Furlings' probable creation, roots which lie in my own creative past. I would vehemently argue – though without documented evidence, and obviously without my having actually been in the room – the likelihood that our Furlings were inspired by *Star Wars*. By the Ewoks. By the noble, charming, furry, little teddy bears that have been part of the *Star Wars* continuity since the 1983 release of the third installment of the original film trilogy.

The Furlings seem to have been inspired by *Star Wars'* Ewoks and their forebears (excuse the pun), the Wookiees. At center is an Ewok-themed issue of Marvel Comics' classic *Star Wars* title, penned by this essay's author.

Oh, what a tangled path we tread when we talk about influences and inspiration, and even the most seemingly obvious connections, and artistic symmetry. The Ewoks are cute. The Ewoks are beloved. I had a marvelous time, in fact, collaborating with several terrific artists and co-creating the Ewoks' adventures for Marvel Entertainment's *Star Wars* comic.[2] But they owe their own existence to a combination of limited filming budgets and the relatively primitive special effects technology of forty-odd years ago. The immediate ancestors of the Ewoks are *Star Wars'* own Wookiees. And the original ancestor of them all is the original Wookiee hero himself, Chewbacca – who, in turn, owes his existence to

---

[2] See the above Ewok-centric cover to Marvel's *Star Wars* #94, for instance.

a long-ago fired-up-writer idea from creator George Lucas. He had created a fantastic space-cowboy antihero in the character of Han Solo. And he had the Cool Idea of Han having a dog. And like all good dogs, in life and in art, Han's dog would be his Best Friend. And then Mr. Lucas had the Coolest Idea of All: what if the *dog* could fly the spaceship?

From that idea came Chewie and the entire Wookiee species. And when it turned out – even at a time that the *Star Wars* movies constituted a virtual license for the studio to print money – that filming part of the third movie on the Wookiee planet would be both impracticably expensive *and* beyond the special effects capabilities of the time, a compromise was reached, in the form of a scaled-down version of the idea. The Wookiees got to appear in the some-say-legendary, some-say-infamous *Star Wars Holiday Special*... while a literally scaled-down and more manageable version of the Wookiees, with the syllables of their name reversed, were created for *Return of the Jedi* and two spinoff telefilms: the Ewoks.

Since I was busy editing and trying to get to press Marvel's comic book adaptation of *Return of the Jedi* (by the incomparable team of Archie Goodwin and Al Williamson), I was unable to attend the private advance screening of the film Lucasfilm had arranged for Marvel. But the next day, I heard a wonderful story about it from my friend and colleague, Peter David, who in addition to writing for Marvel was then part of the company's direct sales department. It has stuck with me all these years, though I wasn't there to overhear for myself the conversation Peter recounted... so this is strictly my own, possibly imperfect recollection of an anecdote I heard almost forty years ago. My memory of what Peter said then is that the first time an Ewok appeared onscreen, a collective sigh went up from the audience... and Marvel's then-head of finance, Barry Caplan, leaned over and said to the head of sales, Ed Shukin, "Ewok... $9.95."

Peter told me that Barry continued making these jokes throughout the film, as cute, new variations of the characters appeared. "Ewok with spear... $11.95. Ewok with baby? $14.95." Peter recently confirmed to me that he did overhear and experience this all those years ago, and that he did indeed tell me of it at the time. He also made a point I had not really focused on, much as I have always loved that memory. Every item Barry spotted as a potentially lucrative toy license subsequently did appear in stores, at pretty much the prices he had predicted. Wow! We should all have, or know someone who has, that kind of acumen.

The Furlings were almost certainly inspired by the Ewoks (and the Wookiees). I contend that when they finally did appear in the 200th episode of *Stargate SG-1*

– appropriately titled "200" – they were exponentially even cuter and more appealing than either of my beloved, long-time *Star Wars* favorites, and that they should, therefore, have possessed that same kind of marketing and merchandising appeal.

The episode "200" depicts the Furlings as adorable giant Teddy bears, but it's unclear whether this was their true form or merely the imagination of amnesiac alien turned TV writer Martin Lloyd.

The Wookiees were originally based on and inspired by dogs. And yes, I adore dogs and find them irresistibly appealing. Lassie, Big Red, Daddles, Lad: A Dog, and their ilk were the fantasy friends of my childhood, and I still love them all... though I am a dog aunt rather than a dog owner, having found cats even more congenial. The Ewoks, meanwhile, were based on sweet, little teddy bears – teddy bears who sincerely and incongruously believed themselves to be ferocious, meat- (and even space-cowboy-) eating bad-asses... which made them even cuter!

But the Furlings blow right by even the Ewoks for cuteness, by virtue of three important factors. The first is that they come in a variety of fur/pelt colors. Any real-world animal lover can tell you that part of the appeal of our non-human brethren on this – or any other – planet is enjoying and marveling at the cool and beautiful colors they can come in. Moreover, the Furlings are the fruit of the far greater and more versatile special effects developed by the time they appeared onscreen in 2006. They move well and look real. They can twitch their freaking ears, for crying out loud. Most importantly of all... they are based upon koalas.

When you bring a koala to a cuteness fight, it is game over for the other competitors. In a cuteness battle, being a koala trumps everything. Being a long-awaited, vari-colored, ear-twitching species of space koalas who briefly get to hold hands with and be gazed at in warm and soulful reverence by Doctor Daniel Jackson? I repeat, Game Over. All the other adorable, anthropomorphic space animals will just have to pack it up and go home.

Very late in the writing of this essay, someone involved in the project briefly took into his head the fear that I had failed to grasp the analytic nature of this volume and was engaged in writing Furlings fanfic. (!!!) There was never any danger of that, not least because I am fully aware that we here are writing ABOUT *Stargate*, not writing *Stargate* itself. And I am sorry for the mix-up, not least because it alarmed my poor friend, who was afraid our esteemed publisher was going to be forced to reject my submission (and really peeve me).

The entire thing was a non-event, born of exactly the kind of Silly Misunderstanding that was central to and fueled the narrative of who-knows-how-many? classic sitcom episodes, and – like any proper Silly Misunderstanding – was cleared up quickly and completely by a clear exchange of simple questions and answers. So, in retrospect, I find the whole kerfuffle entirely hilarious. But it landed on me when I was deeply focused on this essay, in the throes of my analysis; and I was sufficiently exasperated THEN to spend a few minutes fantasizing about actually writing and turning in a Furlings adventure, just to be a jerk...

Which was how I learned something that absolutely amazed me. Much as I love the idea of the Furlings, and the Furlings themselves, and much as I love *Stargate*... I had no idea how to bring those adorable, sweet, fluffy little peaceniks onto the center of the canvas without absolutely throwing our whole absorbing, maddening, adrenaline- (and testosterone-) fueled narrative – from Earth to Atlantis, and through every alternate dimension we have yet visited – completely off-kilter. If the Furlings are one of the Four Great Races, they are too powerful and wise to be dismissed or easily defeated.

And *that* is when I found myself truly understanding and endorsing the previously-bitterly-resented story choices made by the series' creators... and on their behalf by onscreen, lovable, alien-immigrant-turned-television-writer/producer Martin Lloyd (the late Willie Garson, in one of the most enjoyable roles in a résumé crammed full of them) during "200," in an episode of *Wormhole X-Treme!*, the *SG-1*-inspired TV-show-within-a-TV-show. For seconds after we finally got to see SG-1 meet and interact with the Furlings... the Furlings' planet was blown to smithereens.

The writing team have indicated no actual Furling appeared on *SG-1*, likely rendering Daniel Jackson's charming encounter with this furry fellow a fun but farcical flight of fancy.

Ten years. For ten years, they'd teased and tantalized us and kept us waiting to meet the little guys... and within a matter of seconds, when we had barely had time to take in their massive cuteness, sigh, and say, "Awwwwww..." the Furlings were toast. Burnt toast. Dry, burnt toast. It was unforgivable... an outrage. And, to my own astonishment, I now know that if I were writing a Furlings adventure, it would be very difficult to resist the temptation to do exactly the same thing. (Though, of course, if I ever actually *had* the job, I could probably reconsider the above and find a loophole.)

I get it. I really do. The Furlings are adorable, powerful, mysterious, and benevolent... and they also can be defeated by a Goa'uld wielding an *evil salad*!!! So, I love them, but even so – despite the missed merchandising opportunities, which I still seriously think someone ought to revisit – they kind of have to either tantalizingly never show up at all... or be written out shortly after they do.

The Furlings are just plain silly.

Star Gods: Do They Live Up to Their Hype?

by Frank Schildiner

Oh Ra,
You God of Life, you Lord of Love,
All men live when you shine.
— Prayer to the God Ra, tomb of Shep-en-Mut (25th Dynasty)

Could it be that God was an extra-terrestrial? What do we mean when we say that Heaven is in the clouds? From Jesus Christ to Elvis Presley, every culture tells us of high-flying bird men who zoom around the world creating magnificent works of art and choosing willing followers to share in the eternal glory from beyond the stars. Can all these related phenomena merely be dismissed as coincidence?
— Erich von Daniken, *Chariot of the Gods*, 1968

I created your civilization. Now I will destroy it.
— Ra, *Stargate*, 1994

Gods, Goa'uld, System Lords, Snakeheads... whatever you call them, they were the main antagonists of the *Stargate* franchise throughout the first eight seasons of *Stargate SG-1*. Conceptually brilliant, the idea of evil aliens imitating human pagan deities (or vice versa) was not a new one, but it had never been so lavishly and enjoyably written prior to the creation of this universe. From the first time Ra strutted into view dressed in his golden Egyptian funerary mask in the 1994 theatrical film, the Goa'uld entranced viewers.[1] As a lifelong student of mythology, as well as a writer whose first published works involved ancient astronauts, I place myself among those ranks. One question always occurred to me every time one of these villains popped up on the screen, though: how close were they to their mythological counterpoints?

The Goa'uld System Lords included (top, left to right) Ra (Jaye Davidson), Apophis (Peter Williams), and Hathor (Suanne Braun), along with (bottom, left to right) Heru'ur (Douglas H. Arthurs), Nirrti (Jacqueline Samuda), and Sokar (David Palffy).

Let's establish a few rules before continuing: This essay will not cover every single Goa'uld who appeared on *SG-1*. The episode "Summit"[2] introduced viewers to a gaggle of "gods" who shared screen time, for example. Examining each one based on only a few lines of dialogue would take an entire book. Instead, let's stick to those who had some impact on the overall mythos. For example, Hathor will be discussed, whereas Morrigan, Olokun, Tanith, Zipacna, and Svarog will not receive analysis. (In truth, Tanith was on the edge, but his

---

[1] Their species would not receive that name until *SG-1*'s pilot, "Children of the Gods."

[2] Season 5, episode 15, original airdate: 22 Mar 2002.

impact turned out to be less than expected.) The comparisons of the Goa'uld will be based on their behavior as compared and contrasted with that of their mythological counterparts.

This will not be a history of each System Lord. The rating scale will be one to five smiling Daniel Jackson faces, with a "5" rating being the most on-point mythologically, and there will be no use of half-points (since a half face would be a little too creepy). That being said, let's begin with the legendary Supreme System Lord himself, Ra. Viewers met this Goa'uld in the original *Stargate* film, played by model turned actor Jaye Davidson. Ra was a jealous and terrifying being who ruled his human slaves fiercely, and fans later learned that he led the other Goa'uld with a tyrannical, iron fist.

The Egyptian god Ra was considered the King of the Gods, one of the creators of the universe, and the bringer of light, life, and warmth. Each day, Ra steered the solar boat, known as the *Mandjet* or the *Boat of Millions of Years*, across the sky and illuminated the world – and every night, he drove the *Mandjet* through the underworld, where he encountered the snake monsters, Apophis and Mehen, who sought to swallow the Sun. The god Set rode the boat each night, as he was the only being mighty enough to fight off the demons of the dark.

Not quite the embodiment of the Supreme System Lord, eh? Mythology's Ra did not engage in battles, as his duty was simply to steer the *Mandjet* each day and keep the Earth alive. His "King of the Gods" title was derived from the importance of his duties, rather than from fierceness in battle. In truth, the Goa'uld Ra possessed many characteristics of mythological Ra's three daughters, referred to as the Eye of Ra.

These goddesses were called Bastet, Sekhmet, and Hathor, and their duties were as follows: Bastet protected the ruler; Sekhmet was the terrible warrior spirit of the Sun god; and Hathor represented vengeance, as well as the gentle joys of life, such as music, dance, and drink. The Goa'uld Ra seemed to hold a piece of each of them, with almost none of the benevolence his mythological counterpart represented. Other than the title of Ruler of the Gods, the similarities were sparing at best.

Rating: 1 smiling Daniel Jackson head

The next Goa'uld introduced on *Stargate*, and the first archenemy of the SG-1 team, was the System Lord Apophis. According to the *Stargate* mythos, Apophis was the brother of Supreme System Lord Ra and was the fiercest of their people. His symbol was the snake, and his guards wore serpent-adorned helms in battle.

Mythologically, Apophis was the serpent demon who embodied chaos. His creation spawned from Ra's umbilical cord, making him a semi-demi-twin of the Sun god. Apophis was Ra's most terrible enemy, a fierce, cunning, evil being who hid each night, awaiting a chance to destroy the King of the Gods. He had no worshipers but was a part of many prayers symbolizing his defeat each night at the hands of the other deities.

The Goa'uld version of this being displayed numerous similarities to his original namesake. A mighty warrior with a cunning mind, he planned battles strategically and often joined his Jaffa guards in fighting enemies. Violence and dangerousness were the only known traits of the demon in this tale. The Egyptian myths possessed few additional characteristics beyond cleverness and ferocity, serving as a symbol more than a being.

The Apophis whom Teal'c served, and whom the SG-1 team battled, possessed greater development. He could be quite theatrical, as well as cruel, like many of his species. The killings of men, women, and children were easily undertaken actions in his quest for greater power. On a positive note, Apophis loved his mate, Amaunet, and his son, Klorel. He even went so far as to kidnap Sha're in the hope of keeping his wife alive. Since the Goa'uld version possessed far greater depth than his mythological counterpart, the comparison is quite good, but not perfect.

Rating: 3 smiling Daniel Jackson heads

The SG-1 team's next encounter was a quite memorable one: the Goa'uld Queen, who adopted the identity of Hathor. In Egyptian mythology, Hathor was a goddess with dualistic identity. She was the vengeful side of Ra, one of his three protectors/daughters/consorts, and she also represented many of the gentler aspects of life, such as love, sex, dance, music, and femininity. A beloved goddess, Hathor was viewed as one of the creators of life, both with other gods and by herself. Many of her festivals involved drinking alcohol in excess, as well as dancing. Her best-known holiday, the Festival of Drunkeness, was a celebration of eating, drinking, and joy – all of which are lost after death.

Hathor was a fertility goddess who received the prayer of women for successful pregnancies and safe births. In her myths, she acted as the mother of several gods by serving as consorts to Ra, Horus, Atum, Amun, and Khonsu. The connections between the mythological Hathor and her *Stargate* analogue are quite obvious. The *SG-1* iteration used seduction as her main force in seeking power. She seduced the males at Stargate Command, used Daniel Jackson as her consort for the purpose of breeding Goa'uld larvae, and later stole and seduced Jaffa belonging to other System Lords.

Stargate's Hathor was dangerous and vengeful when crossed, though that was of course a common characteristic among the Goa'uld. She was beautiful but displayed no benevolent features, and she was a villain likely intended for only a short stay on the show. Still, the similarities between the mythical and *Stargate* versions were remarkable.

Rating: 4 smiling Daniel Jackson heads

Another Goa'uld on the series was based in ancient Egyptian mythology as well. Heru'ur (aka Horus) was a feared System Lord whose fighting skills and genius were considered among the most powerful among their deadly species. Beloved as a fellow warrior by his Jaffa, Heru'ur served as the main rival to Apophis for the position of Supreme System Lord until his destruction by his enemy's cloaked warships.

In mythology, Heru'ur was among the ancient and most beloved gods of the Egyptians. His earliest importance was as the embodiment of the Egyptian Pharaoh in life. This was a cosmic power, an ethereal concept that placed the ruler of Egypt as a being greater than any who walked the Earth at that time. Later, Heru'ur absorbed the power of Ra and other gods, becoming the deity of the sky and the Sun, as well as the protector of Earth. His battles with Set, who embodied the desert, chaos, bloody warfare, and might, were symbolic representations of the joining of Upper Egypt of the south with Lower Egypt of the south. It was also the war between the life of the fertile lands as the barrenness of the sandy deserts that surrounded those lands.

Heru'ur was considered the greatest warrior of the gods of Egypt, the only being wily and powerful enough to survive warfare with the terrible Set. He was beloved by the Egyptians and considered the symbol of Pharaoh's right to rule the people of the Earth. One title held by Egypt's rulers was "Golden Hawk," which is another representation of Heru'ur.

Conversely, there is one area in which the Heru'ur of myth was quite unlike that of the *Stargate* universe: cruelty. The mythical being was a protector and a warrior, symbolizing the positive features of royalty and the honorable warrior.

SG-1's Heru'ur had little compunction about torturing his enemies in the hope of increasing his power and control. Despite that, the similarity was remarkable.

Rating: 4 smiling Daniel Jackson heads

Nirrti was another early enemy of the SG-1 team, a frightening Goa'uld who sought power and slaves as subjects for her horrific scientific studies. Her appearances were always terrifying, since Nirrti had little interest in warfare, but more in power and the twisted actions derived from her machinations. In every situation involving the System Lord Nirrti, viewers were treated to true evil and often terrible events caused by this being.

The mythical Nirrti, a Hindu goddess, was the embodiment of darkness, sorrow, and destruction. She was also a mother goddess whose children's names were translated to mean Death, Fear, and Terror. Vedic prayers to her involved requests that she not involve herself in the lives of her supplicants. She was a terrifying goddess in each of her forms, and her tales called her the mother of the god embodying Hell.

The writers of *Stargate SG-1* were very inspired when they based a Goa'uld upon this ancient goddess. Even her fellow System Lords were not spared her evil throughout the series. When she finally died, it was the result of her own terrible, twisted ways coming to light. The character had an impressive connection to her mythological roots – one of the closest, in fact.

Rating: 5 smiling Daniel Jackson heads

Sokar was a game-changing Goa'uld when he first appeared. Considered one of the most violent and terrifying of his people, he had suffered exile from Ra, until returning in 1999. Sokar's first acts were the destruction of Apophis's forces, as well as attacking Heru'ur. According to Daniel Jackson and others, he was viewed as the embodiment of evil, even becoming known as the biblical fallen angel, Satan. Based on his chalky skin, yellow eyes, and black vein-covered skin, Sokar embraced this evil persona completely.

The mythical Sokar was an Egyptian god based in Memphis, and this deity represented the coffin portion of the complex funerary rituals. He was a benevolent entity whose duties included assisting in the resurrection and rebirth of the dead. An important god for the Egyptians, he was celebrated by the people, along with Osiris, for his importance regarding their reverence of life after death. Thus, other than his name, there were no connections between the two versions of Sokar. The character's name might have been based on his

Egyptian counterpart, but his actions and behavior were closer to that of the Devil of Judeo-Christian mythology.

Rating: 0 smiling Daniel Jackson heads

Rounding out the System Lords were (top, left to right) Setesh (Robert Duncan), Cronus (Ron Halder), and Yu-huang Shang Ti (Vince Crestejo), as well as (bottom, left to right) Osiris (Anna-Louise Plowman), Anubis (David Palffy), and Ba'al (Cliff Simon).

Setesh (aka Set) was the previously mentioned god of chaos, deserts, might, and murder. He first appeared as a Goa'uld who'd existed throughout human history, founding cults of a bloody nature. In ancient Egypt, he took the name Typhon and later founded a cult in England whose members each committed suicide at his command. By the time the SG-1 team discovered him, he was the leader of a New Age religion in Seattle. Though he only appeared once, his presence had a later impact that proved to be of some importance to the series' overall arc.

Setesh was a major force to the Egyptians, a terrible god whose power was revered and respected by the people since the days of city-states. Though feared for his rage and bloodlust, he was the protector of the *Mandjet* as Ra steered it through the underworld. Evil, yet important, Setesh was a being of duality who even rose to become the patron of several of history's most important Pharaohs.

Seti I, father of Ramesses the Great, reestablished the power of Egypt, reconquering lost territories and hailing Set as one of the forces he worshipped.

There were several similarities between the mythical Setesh and his *Stargate* analogue. Both versions were embodied as the evil Greek monster called Typhon and were devoted to bloody warfare. This Goa'uld's guards dressed in masks based on classic images of Setesh from the art of ancient days. Death and unhappiness surrounded both the mythical Setesh and the version from television, but this is where the similarities ceased.

In truth, Setesh's true counterpart seems to have been derived from a completely different fictional universe. In the Hyborian world of author Robert E. Howard, the main evils included followers of the snake god Set. The cultists who followed that bloody god were occasional obstacles to the legendary Conan of Cimmeria. In the 1982 film based upon Howard's work, the primary villain was the high priest of Set, Thulsa Doom. Played by the incredible James Earl Jones, Doom controlled the cult of Set in the same way that *Stargate*'s Setesh did through his years spent living as an exile on Earth.

For all the lack of connection between these two characters, the presence of Setesh did provide viewers with a rare understanding of Jaffa-style comedy, when Teal'c told his teammates a joke about Goa'uld followers in these immortal words:[3]

> A Serpent guard, a Horus guard and a Setesh guard meet on a neutral planet. It is a tense moment. The Serpent guard's eyes glow. The Horus guard's beak glistens. The Setesh guard's... nose drips.

Rating: 1 smiling Daniel Jackson head

Cronus was among the better-known mythological beings to appear on *Stargate*. In mythology, he was the king of the Titans and the father of the Greek King of the Gods, Zeus. Stories about Greek mythology are part of our culture, and the name Cronus is one that has appeared in countless texts and fictional tales. In the *Stargate* mythos, Cronus was one of the most powerful System Lords who served beneath Ra. Viewers discovered, in backstory, that he'd murdered Teal'c's father, causing the latter to swear allegiance to Apophis, Cronus's greatest enemy. A cruel, deadly being, he posed a major threat to SG-1 and other teams until his death at Teal'c's hand.

---

[3] You aren't laughing. You must not be a Jaffa.

In ancient myths, Cronus was infamous for his actions toward his children and the uglier offspring of his mother Gaia. Having learned that one of his progeny would overthrow him, Cronus swallowed the first Olympians, with Zeus being saved by his mother from sharing their fate. He also imprisoned the terrifying hundred-armed beings called the Hecatoncheires, as well as the one-eyed Cyclopes, despite promising their shared mother otherwise.

The cruelty and evil of both versions of Cronus might appear similar, though it does not seem there was anything particularly distinct about the *Stargate* version. He was a cruel, vile, tyrant like the Greek Titan, but that description could fit nearly any of the System Lords. The writers used the name properly but did not provide viewers with any actions on Cronus's part that would distinguish him from most of the other System Lords introduced so far. Still, it was a decent effort.

Rating: 2 smiling Daniel Jackson heads

Yu-huang Shang Ti (aka Yu) was one of the most fascinating Goa'uld ever introduced on the TV series. A powerful System Lord, he was calmer and less cruel than any of his contemporaries. Yu was a powerful and ancient member of the species, and his actions were often those of an absolute ruler rather than of an evil, crazed megalomaniac. An occasional ally of the humans, he opposed Apophis, Cronus, Anubis, and Ba'al, and he proved to be a match for them all until his age weakened his capabilities.

Yu's ancient counterpart derived from two sources in mythology. The first was Yu the Great, the possibly real Emperor of China and the founder of the Xia Dynasty. Yu was said to have designed a series of canals and other controls that saved the Chinese people from flooding. This was a major achievement and a means of spreading civilization to the Neolithic tribes of the region.

One title of the *Stargate* version matched that of Yu the Great: the Jade Emperor, who was one of the supreme deities of the Taoist religion. He was said to have defeated the King of Demons and other evil entities, though not through pure might. The Jade Emperor's true power derived from unlimited benevolence and knowledge. To this day, many places throughout Asia still pay homage to the Jade Emperor.

The mythological and *Stargate* versions of Yu were in complete harmony. Both were powerful beings who ruled their domains. Neither used warfare as a means of establishing themselves, preferring diplomacy and careful planning before resorting to violence. Neither held reputations as tyrants, and they were more highly regarded than most of their contemporaries. Yu, in both forms, was a fascinating character.

Rating: 5 smiling Daniel Jackson heads

Osiris was one of the most important gods in Ancient Egypt. Therefore, it is no surprise said deity appeared on *Stargate SG-1*. According to the show, Osiris and his queen, Isis, rebelled against Ra but were betrayed by Setesh. Osiris and Isis were removed from their hosts and placed in canopic jars, then remained in stasis for thousands of years. Isis's jar broke and the symbiote died, but Osiris's survived until Dr. Sarah Gardner removed the seals. Osiris, in Gardner's body, later became an underlord beneath the returned Anubis before being captured by Daniel Jackson.

In mythology, Osiris was said to be the first Pharaoh of Egypt, as well as the god of fertility, the underworld, and resurrection. He, too, was betrayed by his brother Setesh, though in the mythical tales, Osiris was torn to pieces. Beginning in the earliest kingdoms of Ancient Egypt, the Pharoah took a name based on Osiris's as a means of symbolizing their connection to this important being.

Sadly, other than the treachery of Setesh, there were no similarities between the mythological Osiris and his *Stargate* counterpart. The former was a god who was important to the daily life of the average Egyptian. Osiris in Egypt was benevolent and the ruler of the underworld, a place where all beings eventually ended up. In *Stargate*, Osiris was a typically malignant Goa'uld, complete with a love of violence and rather poor behavior toward "lesser" beings. This one was a miss.

Rating: 1 smiling Daniel Jackson head

Ah, Anubis, one of the most mysterious of the Big Bads in the history of the *Stargate* franchise. Anubis's very name shook and stunned multiple System Lords. An entire book could be written about his history, but that is not the purpose of this article. He was the only being capable of uniting the majority of the Goa'uld beneath Ra as active resistance to his taking control of the universe. He had power greater than that of any other members of his species, creating weapons of such terrible impact that he singlehandedly risked all life in the cosmos. Manipulative, treacherous, controlling, and insane, Anubis was as close to a god of evil as the *Stargate* mythos ever presented.

In Ancient Egypt, Anubis was the protector of the underworld, as well as the judge of the dead and the god of mummification. When Egyptians died, the priests of Anubis undertook the duties of preparing their body for burial and praying for the dead. Once the spirits of the dead arrived in the underworld, this god weighed their hearts against a feather. Those with sinful deeds outweighing their good were immediately consumed by Ammit, a demon that was equal parts lion, crocodile, and hippopotamus. Good people went to the afterlife, guided by Anubis.

One of the best-known gods of Ancient Egypt, Anubis was the guardian of tombs and graveyards. His image was among the most frequent in appearances in paintings, statues, and hieroglyphics. A beloved deity, he was among the most prevalent symbols of Egyptian mythology and ancient art. Obviously, other than the name, there were no similarities at all between the myth and the modern villain. Anubis was never viewed in a negative light in the old world, whereas *Stargate*'s Anubis was a malevolent Lovecraftian monster for much of his run, the mystery of which was an important aspect in his story and overall design. (Still, that period was great fun for viewers.)

Rating: 0 smiling Daniel Jackson heads

Though a few lesser Goa'uld appeared while Anubis warred on everyone, their impact was ultimately quite minimal. For example, Imhotep pretended he was a Jaffa as a means of recruiting the rebels to his cause. He lasted one episode and had zero connection to the real Imhotep – who designed Earth's earliest pyramids and was one of the greatest ancient doctors. Nor did he have any derivation from Universal's same-named Mummy, played by Boris Karloff, Lon Chaney Jr., Arnold Vosloo, and others. Still, the presence of such Goa'uld was felt on the show, even though these characters were used for their names rather than for their mythological tales.

On the other hand, Ba'al, the last of the System Lords, played a far greater role in the *Stargate* universe. A powerful System Lord who served with Sokar and voted for Anubis's return to their council, he later replaced Yu as leader of the resistance. Assisting in the destruction of Anubis, he seized much of that System Lord's weapons and armies, then rose to become the most powerful of their species. For a time, Ba'al's power was unchecked, until the Replicators and the humans brought about his end.

In addition to the dozen or so primary Goa'uld featured in the theatrical film and on *Stargate SG-1*, the franchise introduced an array of other nefarious Goa'uld, varying widely in mannerism and personality.

Ba'al, like Yu, was a dangerous Goa'uld, but one who kept his darker impulses in check. Outwardly amused and sardonic, he was as ruthless as Ra or Apophis, as deadly as Sokar, and as self-interested as every Goa'uld. Yet like Yu, Ba'al also proved capable of working with humans in the face of greater threats, though with the caveat that he could use these maneuvers as a means of advancing his personal power.

The difficulty in studying the mythology of Ba'al is the disjoined nature of the concept. Ba'al literally means "lord" in many Near Eastern languages, and it was a title given to many gods of storms, fertility, war, and the like. The Baalim, as they are sometimes called, were a means of identifying a greater being in some ancient religions. On the other hand, there was one character in ancient myths to which the name Ba'al would be considered closely connected. This was Ba'al Zəbûb (aka Beelzebub), the demonic Lord of the Flies. He was the Prince of Demons in some writings, the destroyer of kings and a being most associated with the sins of pride, gluttony, and idolatry. Beelzebub was said to be the second most powerful follower of Satan, and he was cited as the seducer of evil in the witch trials of Aix-en-Provence and Salem.

Considering the connection between Sokar (the Satan of *Stargate*) and Ba'al (the conjunction between Ba'al and Beelzebub), the closeness in ties was far greater in this situation. *Stargate*'s Ba'al behaved more like a seductive demonic character than the often-ranting megalomaniacal members of his people. By ignoring the ancient aspects of the identity, the writers homed in on one version of Ba'al and fit the character nicely into the mythos.

Rating: 3 smiling Daniel Jackson heads

First two rows: Goa'uld also included an Unas host (middle), as well as Ares and Mars as depicted in the comics (second row, right). Bottom row: Residing in the host bodies of all Goa'uld was a parasitic symbiote, or *prim'tah*, that controlled their actions.

There you have it: *Stargate*'s major Goa'uld and their mythological counterparts. One could write a small book just citing those who appeared briefly in the spinoff comics and novels (such as Ares and Mars), or who merely had a short moment or three on television.[4] Those discussed above, however, made the most impact on the franchise, and I was sorry to see many of them leave the show.

---

[4] stargate.fandom.com/wiki/List_of_Goa%27uld

Ancient Astronauts and Project Stargate: The Mythology Behind the Franchise

by Edward Dodds

Ask your average critic of television, film, or literature what makes for high-brow fiction, and they might parrot the normative – and dreadfully boring – proposition that only austere human dramas, devoid of escapism or any fanciful elements, may lay claim to the exalted title of literary sophistication. There's no doubt that the best works of this genre are compelling constructions of gripping realism. But I would put forth another proposition, that the deepest, most sophisticated and most critically underrated form of fiction is that form which underpins the very genesis and very purpose of storytelling, culturally, psychologically, and, thanks to new insights in the field of evolutionary psychology, even biologically: the myth.

The myth, and all its fantastic elements and improbable events. The fairy tale, and all its wondrous, faraway lands and dazzling creatures. The fantasy legendarium or the sensational smorgasbord – some might say "theme park" – of the superhero genre, and its elves, heroes, and storm gods. The science-fiction story and its gates to distant realms and evil alien overlords, from that seminal mythic tale of flying machines, treks to distant planets, and encounters with their strange inhabitants given to us by the ancient Roman writer Lucian of Samosata, to that tapestry woven from the strands of modern myth, folklore, ambient culture, and the reinterpretation of the antiquarian by Roland Emmerich, Dean Devlin, Brad Wright, Jonathan Glassner, Joseph Mallozzi, and talented others.

I invite you on a journey through the wormhole into the uncharted depths of the human mind, the strange and archetypal space of our collective unconscious, past the veil of metaphor into the world of mythology and dimly remembered history. I invite you through the stargate. The rich world of evolutionary psychology, and its intersection with the advent of storytelling and mythmaking, is our first destination.

Literature, poetry, stories, and songs – often considered the provenance of the humanities – when viewed through the lens of modern science, take on new life as useful and adaptive forms of instruction. Spun by human brains (designed and optimized by the blueprints of our genes, thus reflecting in all their output, in some way, deeper evolutionary truths), they are passed on to others, either as tales of ostensibly literal truth, as was common in the myths of ancient storytelling or the "discovered journal" genre of the 19th century, or in a sufficiently immersive form for its underlying messaging, usually moral, to be nonetheless unconsciously accepted as true. This is more common – albeit with viral exceptions, such as the "found footage" of *The Blair Witch Project* – in modern storytelling.

The term "didactic literature" – stories that teach a particular message or argument – is often used with some disdain. However, insomuch as every story has a moral, and as every story teaches the recipient some vital combination of messages that typically orients one toward imitating (or shunning) the behaviors of its characters, and as every story is crafted by human brains for human brains, whose every inclination toward enjoyment (and discrimination regarding what is enjoyable) has been carefully optimized by millions of years of natural selection, then it could be said that the very purpose of storytelling is fundamentally didactic and survival-oriented. This remains true even though the warm glow that good stories generate in our brain may mask their true and sober usefulness.

Perhaps we simply reserve the term "didactic literature," and its associated air of vague contempt, for stories that hit the nail on the head a little too painfully, operating at the level of crude and contemporary sociocultural argument, rather than slipping their subtly utilitarian, survival-conducive teachings into the human mind through the pathways of our own instinctive, evolutionarily honed impulses to enjoy certain narrative elements over others. Nonetheless, if storytelling did not serve some vital, likely didactic purpose, as play does in kittens and in our own children, then evolution would not have permitted its existence, much less crafted brains that enjoy storytelling to the degree ours do.

Furthermore, the suspicious convergence of narrative traits across human storytelling, well-outlined in the famed monomyth of Joseph Campbell and any analysis of comparative folklore, would suggest that the specific archetypes, tropes, and clichés of our stories have been squeezed out of a bottleneck of genetic and memetic selection pressures. Reinforcement of these archetypes clearly promotes human flourishing on a deeper level than any merely culturally mediated incentive structure.

We find merely sitting still and consuming the archetypal content of stories, reading words etched on paper or listening to an orator around a campfire so that we might almost hallucinate their reality, or watching a moving screen, so incredibly entertaining that billion-dollar industries, a considerable proportion of the resources and talent of our entire species, have been created around giving the most immersive possible life to things that are not literally true and serve no superficially obvious purpose or function. This has been the case since before the invention of industry or even the wheel, for prehistoric men were drawing cave art not because they lived in caves (for indeed, they largely did not), but because, as recent discoveries have revealed, they specifically utilized caves as primitive theaters, using cunning, crisscrossed lines and multiple, overlaid images to create illusory, flipbook-like motion pictures in the shifting light and shadowplay of their flickering flame torches.

Children beg to be read storybooks, yet rarely beg to go to school or read their homework assignments. Teenagers part with what little money – abstracted tokens of exchange – they possess to watch a movie on a stereotypical first date, but they are rarely so powerfully and naturally inclined to enjoy a good old lecture on microeconomics. From this, we can only surmise that evolution, in shaping reward circuits of serotonin and dopamine to incentivize the pursuit of useful activities, has incentivized the consumption and production of stories, and their distinctly, remarkably convergent narrative and mythological tropes, for reasons greater than the overtly apparent. Evolutionary biologist Bret Weinstein would say such stories reflect evolutionary "metatruths." Archaeologist Daniel Jackson would say, "This could be incredibly important, Jack."

In light of this premise, any *mere* yarn attains a new, awe-inspiring, even humility-provoking weight, and stories that utilize the fanciful and fantastic, the tropes and archetypes of myth, are exposed not as primitive exercises of escapism to amuse children (or the adults of an ostensibly infantilized culture, a common criticism spuriously leveled at the comic books, theme park rides, and "silly" science fiction and fantasy of contemporary popular fiction), but as the most complex and most sophisticated form of storytelling. The astonishing popularity of such works and their implausible characters, from the Thor of the Marvel Cinematic Universe to another Thor of distinctly slimmer frame and lesser hair, is revealed not as a sign of crude or decadent literature that appeals to a lower common denominator of entertainment consumption, or even a uniquely ascendant geek culture, but a sign that these stories are, in a sense, the truest, their tropes the most effective memes of cultural replication and moral, didactic, and evolutionary value.

The same psychological forces, rooted in our very biology, that gave rise to the Thor of Norse myth also gave rise to the mythmaking of today. One cannot help but notice the strange and wondrous similarities between the fandoms of popular works of fantasy and science fiction, in their vastness, their fervent following, and the meaning and social cohesion they provide the lives of their fans, and the religions generated by the uncannily similar stories of ancient myth. As with the religions of yesteryear, the inspiration of moral behaviors and modes of being is often ascribed to childhood and reinforced adult exposure to such stories, with fans, casual and dedicated alike, frequently claiming that works such as *Star Wars* and Harry Potter taught them their very morality.

This gives rise to cultural forces that explicitly imitate their example in arenas widely ranging from the individual, private consultation of "What would Luke Skywalker or Daniel Jackson do?" when facing uncertainty, to wholesale political activism galvanizing the many through metaphor and example. Even if the advancement of science has obliged modern audiences to accept their foundational stories as fictional, these contemporary myths are nonetheless complex, deeply rooted, and extremely compelling combinations, variations upon the same recipe, of ancestral narrative elements that may not be literally true so much as *literarily* true. This is true insomuch as they provide a useful – or, indeed, most useful – blueprint around which to orient the moral and social lives of both the individual and the populace at large.

Science fiction emerges as a particularly weighty form of modern mythmaking with which to contend. In abstracting and projecting the moral and social issues of our world to the analogical issues of faraway worlds, it extracts the latent content from our aspirational values and projects them in ways more palatable to our minds, sidestepping the cognitive biases generated by preconceived beliefs, sociopolitical affiliation, and other forces so as to slip the *patterns* of moral behavior into the receiving unconscious, even where the exact details might have tripped us up. If one can accept the diversity of values, lifestyles, and physical appearance of alien refugees seeking shelter beneath Cheyenne Mountain, for example, one can more easily accept the equivalent when facing such in real life.

If one searches across the entire domain of science fiction, there are few examples more saturated in myth, more connected to the religions, folklore, and stories of antiquity yet simultaneously more forward-thinking and aspirational in its values, more didactic – and I use the term with the fullest praise it should connote – in both scientific education and moral messaging, than the franchise known as *Stargate*. At last, on our journey, so armed by the knowledge with which to analyze its detail, we come to the worlds of Roland Emmerich and Dean Devlin, and of Brad Wright, Jonathan Glassner, and Joseph Mallozzi.

To truly comprehend the mythology of *Stargate*, one must first understand the history and folklore of the modern myth of unidentified flying objects (UFOs). In 1947, pilot Kenneth Arnold reported seeing a formation of extraordinary aerial craft. This initially generated skepticism, but a wave of similar sightings that year swiftly engaged the popular and media interest, particularly when the very commercial airline pilot who had somewhat infamously dismissed the Arnold sighting as lights reflecting off a cockpit window, then saw the anomalous craft himself a few days later. That pilot described the shape that would become ubiquitous in popular culture for decades to come: like two saucers joined together, one on top of the other.

The "flying saucer" was born.

The phenomenon swiftly ensnared public attention to a degree oft underestimated by those born after that era, and it was all the newspapers could talk about. World leaders, from the United Kingdom's Winston Churchill to successive U.S. Presidents, took the issue quite seriously in private, consulting scientists and advisors regarding what "flying saucers" could possibly be. Generals, other military officials, and intelligence operatives wrote a variety of official, now declassified documents that opined the phenomenon was entirely real, possessed remarkable commonalities in physical behavior and appearance, demonstrated aerial behaviors impossible for any craft of this Earth, and required serious scientific investigation.

Some even believed mass extraterrestrial landings were imminent and began to quietly sound the alarm, for while the populace then largely believed "flying saucers" – rebranded as "UFOs" by the American government in order to distance serious investigation from the media craze, and again rebranded as unidentified aerial phenomena (UAPs) in more recent years for similar reasons – were experimental military craft, those within the upper echelons of military and government knew well that they possessed no such physics-defying flying discs.

Cases far more compelling and unusual than the original Arnold sighting swiftly piled up. Later in 1947, Air Force officials announced in a press release that a crashed flying saucer had been recovered from a ranch in Roswell, New Mexico, only to correct the record with the revelation that the alleged saucer had been a weather balloon, before correcting the record *again* decades later, claiming it had been a top-secret intelligence-gathering balloon as part of Project Mogul – despite the fact that said project didn't exist until years later. An officer posed for a photograph next to aluminum foil and other clearly conventional debris as proof, though said officer later claimed he had been instructed to pose with fake debris to cover up the truth that something extraordinary *had* actually crashed, with other Air Force and military personnel claiming they had been enlisted in a sudden, high-priority, and secret mission to airlift bodies in small coffins, ostensibly retrieved from a crashed craft, to a military facility in Texas.

Trained military aviators, NASA astronauts, commercial pilots, scientists with doctorates performing meteorological observations, and eventually even future President Jimmy Carter all reported seeing the anomalous craft, often at close range and for tens of minutes at a time, often alongside dozens of witnesses of comparable profession and expertise. Sometimes, there would be radar data to corroborate visual observation, as with the 1952 Washington incident, in which fighter jets were scrambled to intercept clusters of unknown bogeys converging on the U.S. capital.

Videos and photographs came forth, with analysts concluding several were authentic and truly showed physical objects at the distance described by accompanying witness testimony, traveling at great speeds. Some cases would only emerge years later, when details came to light or witnesses came forward, as with various incidents of ostensible UFO intrusion into nuclear launch facilities, with declassified documents and testimony from multiple military personnel attesting to large, disc-shaped, and impossibly fast UFOs hovering over, tampering with, and even discharging beams of light – taken by the observers to be analysis probes rather than weaponry – at missile silos across a shocking number of highly sensitive sites.

The reality or non-reality of the UFO phenomenon, as well as any potential explanations in the case of the former, from a bizarre and insufficiently documented natural atmospheric plasma phenomenon to something even more spectacular, is not the scope of this essay. But what can be said with certainty is that the powerful cultural splash of the UFO phenomenon created the mores of ambient culture, of government conspiracy and possession of extraterrestrial technology, of furtive visitation and secret government projects, that underpin the worldbuilding and mythology of the *Stargate* franchise. Inspiration for the character of Doctor Daniel Jackson, in fact, can be seen in the so-called "invisible college."

Answering public outcry and demands for transparency, the U.S. Air Force put together the successive Projects Sign, Grudge and Blue Book to investigate the UFO phenomenon, hiring scientists to compile, catalog, analyze, and preferably "debunk" reports, paying particular attention to credible, classified military reports from bases and ships throughout the world that featured corroborating sensor data. Project Blue Book was shut down after many years of operation due to a dismissive, externally sought conclusion known as the Condon Report. However, the lead scientists who had worked for Blue Book the longest – astronomers Doctor J. Allen Hynek, who had started as a skeptic infamously dismissing certain sightings as marsh gas, and Doctor Jacques Vallée, who had seen a stereotypical flying saucer with a transparent dome in his native France – concluded the UFO phenomenon to be real and extraordinary.

Hynek and Vallée wrote several books on the subject between them, eventually presenting to the United Nations their belief that the UFO phenomenon "be[spoke] the action of some form of intelligence." Various astronomers, meteorologists, and physicists who had read the Condon Report, not merely the allegedly foregone conclusion by the eponymous Doctor Condon (who had seemingly not even read the report bearing his name), concluded that the phenomenon presented a genuine scientific mystery, as did other scientists who had written their respective sections of the report. This formed what Vallée termed an "invisible college" of scientists who met regularly and investigated the phenomenon (including materials with unusual isotopes allegedly left by UFOs as molten slag) in their own time, keeping a low profile to avoid public ridicule or career backlash.

Top: An authenticated government photograph, taken by an aerial survey plane of the National Institute of Geography of Costa Rica in 1971, shows an unidentified flying object estimated to be 220 feet across. Bottom: Doctors Allen Hynek and Jacques Vallée brief officials on the UFO phenomenon at a U.N. meeting.

We see this in *Stargate*. In the theatrical film and on *Stargate SG-1*, Daniel Jackson is banished to the fringes of academia due to his having espoused theories about alien involvement in human history that are immediately and reflexively dismissed as pseudoscience. He, too, is hired by the Air Force to lend his academic credentials and expertise to a mystery hypothesized to be extraterrestrial in nature, and he gains access to privileged data that his peers in academia lack, allowing him to reach and reaffirm a radically different conclusion than his orthodox colleagues while studying ostensible extraterrestrial technology composed of unusual material.

Some have suggested the strange hovering objects visible in medieval and Renaissance paintings, often firing destructive bolts of light at the surface, may depict ancient extraterrestrial visitations.

The "ancient alien" premise of the *Stargate* mythos, that extraterrestrials visiting Earth gave rise to the gods of Bronze Age (and later) mythology, traces back to similar territory. While H. P. Lovecraft had already popularized the idea within science-fiction and weird-fantasy circles through *The Call of Cthulhu* and *At the Mountains of Madness*, the premise was considered by scientists more seriously during the height of UFO mania. One year after Vallée published *Anatomy of a Phenomenon*, oft considered the first serious scientific inquiry into UFOs, famed astrophysicist Carl Sagan, along with Soviet astronomer Iosif Shklovsky, penned a chapter on the possibility of ancient narratives and anomalous historical reports representing descriptions of encounters with visiting extraterrestrials, in Sagan's 1966 book *Intelligent Life in the Universe*.

Vallée agreed. He had not missed the similarities between the modern UFO phenomenon ensnaring the interest of the Western powers and Eastern bloc alike since 1947, and the ghost rockets (which resembled a commonly reported UFO shape variously described as a flying cigar, a butane tank, a pill capsule, or a Tic Tac) over Sweden in 1946, the glowing "foo fighters" reported during World War II, the "airship" sightings of the 19th and early 20th centuries, and a medley of earlier reports of flying "discs" and "cylinders" of great speed and instantaneous, erratic motion, rising from oceans and flying beneath clouds. These were documented yet forgotten alongside other visually and behaviorally distinct categories of aerial phenomena, now explained as meteorites (dismissed as superstition until the 19th century) and ball lightning in old astronomical and meteorological journals.

Left: The goddess Bastet slays the evil Apep; this depiction inspired the emblem of *Stargate's* Apophis, adorning the foreheads of his loyal Jaffa. Right: Pharaoh Akhenaten worships the Aten. Erich von Däniken and other advocates of the "ancient astronaut" hypothesis interpret the Aten to be a flying saucer, rather than the solar disc aspect of Ra it actually depicts.

In his 1969 work *Passport to Magonia*, Vallée made his case that UFOs had been seen throughout history, possibly even antiquity, based on seemingly sober yet incredible descriptions of flying "circular shields" and amazing, abruptly maneuvering celestial lights from ancient Roman, Chinese, and medieval European sources. Vallée suggested that they may have represented actual intelligence – extraterrestrial, interdimensional, or otherwise otherworldly in origin – interacting with humanity on a prolonged basis. But it was *Chariots of the Gods?*, a 1968 book by hotel manager Erich von Däniken, that established the core features of the stereotypical "ancient alien" hypothesis now familiar to viewers of *Stargate* and History Channel's infamous *Ancient Aliens*, such as alien involvement in constructing the pyramids.

Dismissed by Sagan himself as "sloppy" butchery of an otherwise plausible concept, von Däniken's work nonetheless achieved acclaim and popularity as an unexpected international best-seller, propelling a crude and overtly pseudoscientific form of the "ancient alien" hypothesis, filled with what archaeologists deemed to be fabrications, misinterpretations, and dishonesty, to a measure of public attention. While it is clearly this strawman form that inspired the Goa'uld, Asgard, and Ancients of *Stargate*, embracing the more populist interpretations of von Däniken provided the franchise with a far greater richness of ancient myth to draw upon than merely old meteorological reports and cold modern UFO encounters. This crafted a world of greater narrative complexity and more intimate psychological significance, while preserving the veneer of plausibility required for any good story to circumvent or suspend audience disbelief. Thus, the surrounding folklore of the UFO phenomenon both directly and indirectly inspired the worldbuilding and mythology of *Stargate* lore.

On the one hand, the Asgard represent a gestalt of modern ufology and adjacent paranormal tropes. Their physical appearance resembles that of the diminutive, childlike "UFO operators," with their big black eyes and grey skin, allegedly seen in a handful of "close encounter" reports – or sleep paralysis experiences.[1] Their ships produce blindingly bright beams of light capable of abruptly taking humans up into their craft, a common feature of the "alien abduction" reports that first leaped into popular culture through the experiences of Barney and Betty Hill, as well as *Communion* author Whitley Strieber. Indeed, *SG-1* episode "Fragile Balance" reveals an unethical Asgard geneticist called Loki who kidnaps humans to perform medical experimentation, clearly a reference not only to the abduction literature, but to the trickster behaviors ascribed to UFO operators in some "close encounter" reports.

On the other hand, the Asgard represent a modern reinvention of Norse mythology, demonstrated not only through names such as Loki, Thor, Heimdall, and the species' name itself, but through the Norse-descended peoples of Cimmeria, and the explicit usage and repackaging of Norse myths in a technological context, such as Thor's hammer, Thor's chariot, and Thor's own

---

[1] Popularized by *The X-Files*, along with many other horror and science-fiction series

holographic disguise as a bearded storm deity. Vallée himself speculated phenomenological ties between the "little people" of Celtic fairy faith and alleged UFO occupants, and it could be argued that *Stargate* drew upon pre-existing links in meshing old European mythology with modern "visitors." The malevolent Goa'uld represent a similar amalgamation of pseudoscience and myth.

The Asgard known as Hermiod, at left, demonstrates a fictional phenotype identical to the stereotypical "gray alien" of UFO folklore, such as the one at right, from *The X-Files*.

Interestingly, the Ra of the original *Stargate* film was more directly tied into UFO lore than the Goa'uld of *Stargate SG-1*, with his "true form" not being a small, snakelike parasite, but rather a stereotypical Grey alien of the "tall" subtype.[2] In transferring such links to the Asgard, the mythology of *Stargate* lost none of its potency. The Goa'uld became far more frightening and psychologically compelling thereby, conjuring the deeply rooted fear of snakes stemming from neurological programming left over from the arboreal environment of our primate ancestors, and its frequent invocation in religion and myth, from the serpent of Genesis to the Satanic dragon of Revelation to the malevolent drakes of Medieval mythology. Worming into the brain to assert control over their hapless victims, the Goa'uld represent the paralysis of utter terror from the very first appearance of Amaunet, the primordial goddess of Egypt, in the pouch of a Jaffa priestess in "Children of the Gods."

---

[2] See "Inhabiting This Human Form: The Metaphysical Personhood of Ra," by Kelli Fitzpatrick, elsewhere in this volume.

Such frightful connotations continue unabated with Apophis, the Egyptian serpent god of chaos and the night. The mythological deity's battles with Ra inform the *Stargate* worldbuilding of feuding Goa'uld warlords, with *SG-1's* Apophis revealed to have been a rival of the *Stargate* film's Ra. The prehistoric, predynastic Egyptian culture of Naqada I – clearly the namesake of the Goa'uld's favoured mineral *naquadah* – features depictions of a serpent fighting a solar deity, suggesting Apophis predated the first pharaohs of Egypt. In light of *Stargate's* interpretation of Apophis as a malefic alien, such terrible antiquity takes on almost Lovecraftian overtones, with the final, tragic emergence of the suppressed mind of Apophis's host body, in "Serpent's Song," masterfully presenting cosmic horror entwined with psychological horror.

The concept of utilizing Egyptian chaos deities as alien arch-villains is not original to *Stargate*, with Sutekh of *Doctor Who*'s "Pyramids of Mars" representing the execution of a similar concept that may have inspired *Stargate* mythmaking. *Star Trek* also explored the notion of ancient Earth gods having been space travelers, including Apollo, Zeus, Hera, and other Olympians (*The Original Series*' "Who Mourns for Adonais?"); Mesoamerican god Kukulkan, Aztec deity Quetzalcoatl, and the Chinese dragon (*The Animated Series*' "How Sharper Than a Serpent's Tooth"); and even Christianity's Lucifer (*The Animated Series*' "The Magicks of Megas-Tu"). Still, *Stargate* pushed the concept's envelope from such isolated tales as "Pyramids of Mars" and Lovecraft's "Nyarlathotep" to the entire foundational precept of its mythology, thereby rooting its world entirely in the primordial stories of ancient myth.

Further villains achieve their compelling presence through the reinterpretation and combination of other myths and beliefs. Sokar, an underworld god of the Memphite necropolis, incorporates and utilizes the sociocultural and psychological power of contemporary religious concepts,[3] with the original Egyptian deity's activities in *The Journey of Ra* myth, punishing the souls of the wicked by casting them into an eternally burning lake of fire, allowing for seamless stitching with the Satan of Judeo-Christian tradition, and opening the doors of Hell before the protagonists in the Netu arc. The fanatical Ori, drawing from the obsession with the purity of fire found in Zoroastrianism, the

---

[3] See "Star Gods: Do They Live Up to Their Hype?", by Frank Schildiner, elsewhere in this volume.

Medieval Inquisition, the Crusades, and the practice of burning heretics at the stake, as well as the excesses of religious intolerance in contemporary culture, ascended as a daemoniacal and allegorical fusion of some of the worst aspects of the past and present.[4]

Although myth was utilized in less overt ways in *Stargate Atlantis* and *Stargate Universe*, the similarities between the life-sucking Wraith of *Atlantis* and the blood-sucking vampires of European folklore are difficult to miss. What's more, the central premise of *Universe* is revealed to be a quest for answers to a question generated by the marriage of modern science and ancient religion: whether the universe may, in fact, originate from some form of intelligent design, from a supernatural god to a materialist simulator. Moreover, the nature, existence, and activities of the Stargate Program itself are grounded in UFO folklore, conspiracy theories and actual, sometimes incredible government projects.

Numerous peculiar statements from various individuals throughout the years, ranging from high-ranking intelligence and military personnel to former CIA Director and President George H. W. Bush, have lent "true believers" all the ammunition required to believe in a government cover-up. Indeed, Hynek alleged that his military superiors often behaved in a furtive manner contrary to open scientific investigation, deceptively handling data and insisting he explain away cases that seemed inexplicable. In the Blue Book files, Vallée recovered a classified document, clearly mixed up in the paperwork, that seemingly revealed the existence of a separate, completely unknown military project, composed of a committee of anonymous scientists who took the phenomenon far more seriously and had access to thousands of higher-quality reports that, per the recommendations, were *deliberately* not shared with Blue Book. They even recommended the military deliberately stage UFO sightings, presumably to determine which sightings represented something unknown to science, and which could be ascribed to clandestine foreign activity.

Vallée traced the names and acronyms within the document to private aerospace companies and government contractors. The idea that the reality of the UFO phenomenon was being concealed by shadowy elements of the U.S. government, protected from freedom-of-information requests through special-

---

[4] See "Faith and False Gods: Religion in *Stargate SG-1*," by Darren Sumner, also in this anthology.

access programs, the usage of private industry, and the unique privileges of NORAD, picked up momentum throughout the decades. This was reinforced by various supposed whistle-blowers, deathbed confessions, and even public statements from former Senate Majority Leader Harry Reid and senior Department of Defense officials outlining their well-informed beliefs that Lockheed Martin possessed retrieved UFO materials, along with their failed, rebuffed attempts to gain access to secrets they were told were classified via the Pentagon.

The lay of the land in the *Stargate* franchise, with a highly secret and segregated Air Force program collaborating with, competing with, or fending off intrusions from nosy senators, NORAD, NASA, and the shadowy, former-government-turned-private NID, often involving opaque military and government factions in which the left hand is unaware of the activities of the right, clearly draws from such conspiracy theories. Attempts by Stargate Command personnel to quash leaks or cover up extraordinary events, such as Sam Carter trotting out a hologram of an Asgard on live television in order to discredit an aerospace industrialist and former journalist who had discovered the truth of alien life in *SG-1*'s "Covenant," clearly parallel alleged similar cover-ups, such as the aforementioned Roswell incident, or the mysterious tandem-act of the public Project Blue Book and the secret, parallel Project Stork uncovered by Vallée.

The name of the Stargate Program, in fact, invokes an actual secret U.S. military unit established by the Defense Intelligence Agency and a scientific research contractor: Project Stargate, terminated in 1995 due to a lack of useful results. The similarities between the real program and the franchise's eponymous fictional program are quite remarkable, even if intentional inspiration is unclear. While Project Stargate primarily focused on parapsychological experiments involving "remote viewing" and psychic phenomena (failing to demonstrate any actionable evidence of telepathy), its experiments included attempts at "astral projection" to other planets, including a mental trek to Mars featuring giant alien pyramids. Moreover, among the Stargate documents released by the CIA following lawsuits and freedom-of-information requests can be found multiple UFO reports. Perhaps the "giant aliens" of *SG-1*'s "Crystal Skull" would have liked to have known about giant Martian pyramids!

In light of such remarkably well-connected detail, the mythology of the *Stargate* franchise emerges as one of the deepest and most sophisticated examples of worldbuilding in science fiction. In presenting government secrecy, dysfunction, and conspiracy in such a plausible and nuanced manner, *Stargate* draws the audience into a remarkably immersive parallel world, almost close enough to touch. In drawing upon myths of the modern world that have reinterpreted myths of the ancient world, *Stargate* speaks to the curiosity within all of us, while simultaneously spinning allegorical tales of moral and social subtlety, as well as instilling in the audience a deeply abiding fascination with science, the frontier of our technological advancement, the limits of our understanding, and our eternal quest for meaning and truth.

It is the convergence between the narrative world and reality, the perceptible plausibility of its premise contrasting with the fantastic elements of its content, that makes the mythology of *Stargate* so compelling. Its call to adventure will surely be heard for many years to come.

Faith and False Gods: Religion in *Stargate SG-1*

by Darren Sumner

In one of the final moments of *Stargate: The Ark of Truth*, Vala Mal Doran and her former companion Tomin sit on the edge of a bed in a small and spartan guest room inside Stargate Command. Thanks in part to Tomin changing sides, the armies of the powerful, ascended Ori have been defeated, not through conquest but by revelation of the true nature of the Ori – who are not gods but only beings who were once very much like humans, who'd evolved to a higher plane and now gained power from the worship of mortals.

Tomin has made a long journey in his faith. He'd lived his whole life under the teachings of Origin, reading its book and hearing its stories. Healed from a disability by the power of the Ori Prior, Tomin took up the call to join an armed crusade to the Milky Way Galaxy. As a commander, he put the will of his gods into action, forcing the subjugation of numerous worlds. But Tomin felt a nagging sense of the immorality of it all – that this crusade did not line up with his own understanding of his faith. After the Priors began interpreting the stories of Origin out of context and for their own crude ends, Tomin came to doubt the entire enterprise ("Line in the Sand").

Although Tomin turned his back on the Priors and their armies, he did not give up his faith but took this road in pursuit of its real truth. As his story closes,

Tomin tells Vala: "When I was being tortured by the Prior, the teachings of Origin gave me the strength I needed. There's still so many things about it that mean a great deal to me."

This scene is paradigmatic of the way in which *Stargate*'s writers, on *Stargate SG-1* in particular, approached the topic of religion. The Goa'uld posed as gods from various ancient Earth cultures, using religion as an instrument of power and manipulation. Through the character of Teal'c, opposition to the Goa'uld and generations of oppression provided a central pillar of the show's storytelling. Then came the Ori, ascended beings so powerful that they not only posed as divine beings but, for all intents and purposes, from the vantage point of the mortal plane they appeared in fact to be all-powerful gods.

This theme has always resonated with me, not only as a person of faith but also as a student of religion and theology. I was a seminarian when *SG-1* concluded its run and found it noteworthy that the show's writers avoided adapting as characters on the show any major religious figures who are widely venerated today: Thor and Apophis and Nirrti, yes, but not Yahweh, Muhammed, or Gautama Buddha. And clearly the writers had no answer for those fans who would occasionally ask, "Was Jesus a Tok'ra?"

But from time to time, I have also encountered others who took *Stargate*'s treatment of religion to be outright hostile. After all, *SG-1* made it its mission to go around killing "gods." Because they preached no gospel of their own, doesn't this mean that the show and its writers derided religion as foolish superstition at best, and programmatic oppression at worst? Do the Goa'uld stand in here for all religious belief? The conclusion of the Ori storyline in 2008's *The Ark of Truth* provided an opportunity to explore this very question.

Upon the film's release, I spoke about this at some length with Robert C. Cooper, who created the Ori and wrote and directed *The Ark of Truth*. He started out as a writer and a story editor during *SG-1*'s first season, rising up the ranks to become an executive producer and showrunner. Cooper himself is responsible for much of the mythology of the Ancients and ascension that forms the backdrop to *SG-1*'s story. In what follows, I will offer my own analysis of the show's approach to religion, and the theological perspective that it holds. But the answers to these questions belong finally to the writers, and so included here is Cooper's own perspective – comments shared with me directly in our conversation.

What is clear, upon careful reflection, is that *Stargate* is by no means anti-religious, or irreligious. Religious belief and practice, in fact, are fundamental to its story. But the show's theological perspective is decidedly *humanist*, operating from the conviction that the subject matter of religion – the real object of its inquiry – is not God or the divine but humanity itself. And the ultimate good of any belief system is the positive moral outcome it produces in human behavior. After seeing how this plays out in some of *SG-1*'s memorable stories and character moments, I will end with a brief critique.

False Gods

> You believe in freedom, Teal'c. You believe in justice, in protecting people from false gods. You despise everything Apophis was.
> — Samantha Carter ("Threshold")

The basic conceit of 1994's *Stargate* feature film, written by Dean Devlin and Roland Emmerich, is that Ra – the sun god of ancient Egypt – was not only a real person, but an alien who enslaved people and used their religion as a tool of bondage.

The people of Abydos, including Kasuf and his children, Sha're and Skaara, worshiped Ra in fear, and when Ra was displeased his judgments were swift and harsh. In the film, he set loose a pair of death gliders to shoot up the city of Nagada, simply to keep the people cowering in obeisance.

Stargate SG-1 expanded this mythology through numerous other deities, drawn from many ancient cultures around the globe – Egyptian and Hindu, Babylonian and Greek, Norse, Mayan, and Native American. Some of these aliens who posed as gods were benevolent, including the Asgard and also the Salish Spirits, shapeshifters who played the roles of Xe'ls, T'akaya, and other protectors.

The show's writers usually kept it ambiguous whether the Goa'uld and other alien species came to Earth and found these fully formed religious myths and deities, and only impersonated them, or if in some cases perhaps the Goa'uld themselves were the origin of the myth. Early on in the series, Daniel Jackson speculates that it was the former: the Goa'uld exploited existing beliefs for their own corrupt ends. However, we also know that for a time, Goa'uld such as Ra, Hathor, Seth, Osiris, and others lived and ruled on Earth.

But their patterns of oppression are consistent: the Goa'uld abducted humans from around the world, transporting them to other planets as slaves. Some they took as hosts; others were put to work in naquadah mines, built great pyramids, or were pressed into service as personal attendants. Finally, many humans were forced to take up arms and fight for their "gods" as Jaffa. The Goa'uld used their technology to create pouches within the Jaffa's abdomen in order to incubate larval symbiotes – or prim'tah – making them all the more dependent upon the Goa'uld for their life and good health. From a young age, the prim'tah functions as the Jaffa's immune system, and without it the Jaffa dies.

Because of this unique arrangement, the warriors of the Jaffa armies were often fanatical devotees of the cult of the gods. They were sent out to battle their master's rivals (chiefly other Goa'uld), and while entire cultures of Jaffa people grew up around the gods they served, a resistance movement also steadily grew throughout the centuries. On the television show, the icon of this movement is Master Bra'tac, Teal'c's friend and mentor. Though he could not escape his condition of servitude for more than a century, Bra'tac knew the truth about the Goa'uld, and he quietly cultivated that truth in the hearts of Teal'c and other young Jaffa.

Before Earth began to undermine the System Lords and upset the paradigm within which the Jaffa had lived for millennia, freedom for the rebels was a freedom of the soul and the spirit, though not of the body. The Jaffa rebel who was found out could only fall back resolutely upon their most basic creed: *"Shal kek nemron"* ("I die free").

Religion here is a tool of oppression in the most literal sense. The Goa'uld took on the personae of deities, using their advanced weapons and technology to force others to worship and serve them. To rise up against such an oppressor was to ensure death. But the exploitation of religion in this system was still more insidious: most of the Jaffa, and many among the enslaved worlds of humans, were true believers. The Goa'uld used their religious beliefs to convince those who served them that *they wished to do so.*

In spite of the deceit, though, is there true faith here as well? Is there an inward strength or personal devotion among the Jaffa that could be called "religious," even recognizing that the cult of the Goa'uld was both false and evil? The depth of Bra'tac's own spirituality is evident in "Maternal Instinct," a third-season episode in which he visits the monks of Kheb – forbidden by the Goa'uld, where evidently Oma Desala has helped generations of Jaffa cast off their symbiotes and ascend to a higher plane of existence. Bra'tac looked forward to one day taking that journey, but he knew that the Goa'uld were not worthy as objects of devotion. And it is *this* that Bra'tac rails against in "Threshold," when he challenges a brainwashed Teal'c: "In battle, Teal'c, faith will not save you – blind faith least of all. Rely on your own strength, your own wits, or you are of no use to me."

This is more than mere pragmatism from a seasoned soldier of war. Bra'tac does not believe that faith is worthless, after all – only that *faith in the Goa'uld* is so. Apophis will not save his body, and faith in Apophis will not save his soul. Why? Because Apophis is a *false god*. And Bra'tac's own gospel message is that of self-reliance: stand up for yourself, think for yourself, depend upon what comes from the deepest part of you... and you will be saved.

This is the religion of *Stargate SG-1*, and the writers' own vision of both the source and the ultimate good of spiritual belief. The goodness of a person, and one's worthiness to attain to a higher spiritual plane, come from within one's self. Devotion may be directed toward another, but this is only proper when it is done in truth and for the good of others, and not by the will of a power-hungry false god.

Dead False Gods

> Go tell your people Cronus is dead. If they still think he's a god, have 'em come take a look.
> — Jack O'Neill ("Double Jeopardy")

SG-1's pattern, when faced with these powerful aliens who enslave worlds and who demand worship, is, most decisively, deconstructive. Much of the show is an ongoing military and ideological struggle against the cult of the System Lords and other Goa'uld, and after them against the Ori and their followers. Earth's opposition comes in the form of direct combat – and nothing says "false god" like a body on the deck. After the death of Cronus, the SG-1 team invited the people of Juna to come and see him if they still had doubts ("Double Jeopardy"). Disrupting the System Lords' control over a planet is often enough to begin to convince people to shake off not only the physical but the spiritual and intellectual shackles of slavery, and to begin to think for themselves.

Opposition to the Goa'uld cult also takes the form of reverse proselytizing, often from Teal'c and Daniel, who work to convince local inhabitants that they have been deceived by malicious aliens who simply have more advanced technology than they do. And from Jack O'Neill it takes the form of outright mockery, impudently standing up to Anubis or daring to mock the mighty Baal ("... as in, bocce?"). When Teal'c is brainwashed by Apophis into a fanatical adherence to the cult of his former master, Jack offers him a description of his god as "that scum-sucking, overdressed, boombox-voiced, snake-in-the-head, latest in our list of *dead* bad guys" ("Threshold").

The defeat of Goa'uld figures throughout the show's run serves this important narrative theme, piercing the veil of lies and deceit told by the enemy over thousands of years. There are negative consequences here, too, as the Tok'ra often remind Earth: other Goa'uld can move into the power vacuum created by the death of a System Lord, sometimes leaving enslaved worlds no better off, or in fact *worse* off under the new rulership. The feudal hierarchy at least kept the System Lords somewhat in check, with no one power able to completely dominate the others and enforce their will upon the galaxy... until SG-1 came on the scene and started turning over tables.

Still, on the whole, SG-1's assault on the System Lords helps to liberate countless worlds from servitude (with a little help along the way from the Replicators). Thematically, this is much deeper than good guys defeating bad guys, the triumph of the narrative's protagonist over its antagonists. The series is layered with religious ideas, chief among them liberation from false gods. The Goa'uld are evil not only due to the corruptive effects of the sarcophagus ("Need"), or the base instincts passed on through genetic memory ("Absolute Power"), but because they believe they *deserve* to be worshiped. Most seem to operate under the conviction that might makes right, and so they are "gods" simply by virtue of their power to dominate others.

As it becomes clear, there is no negotiating with this enemy. The Goa'uld cannot be convinced to surrender this power, and they refuse to give up the religious ideology that secures it. The only way to end the oppression of millions of men, women, and children throughout the galaxy is to defeat them – and, in so doing, to expose their true nature. But what happens when Earth encounters a new foe, who also pose as gods and demand worship, but whose claims cannot be so readily disproved? How do you unmask a villain when you cannot simply take off their helmet, seize their technology, or remove a parasitic symbiote? How can SG-1 prove a god to be false when, for all intents and purposes, it really does display godlike powers?

Ori Ascendant

> Any sufficiently advanced technology is indistinguishable from magic.
> — Arthur C. Clarke

In the context of aliens using their advanced technology to pose as divine beings, the writers' choice to introduce ascension was a stroke of genius. It added an important layer of complexity to *SG-1*'s storytelling, not only building out the galaxy with some new players but opening a path to explore the mystical. Ascension in the *Stargate* universe may ultimately be explained by evolutionary science (and by "Prototype" in season 9, progress toward ascension can even be measured), but the higher plane is so far removed from mortal existence that it can never be completely described. Ascension remains a locus of mystery, and of powers beyond our comprehension – not because they are "divine" in a precisely theological sense, but because at our current level of understanding humans lack the power of explanation.

Those ascended existed on another plane as beings of pure energy. Top row: Oma Desala (Mel Harris), Orlin (Sean Patrick Flanery), Daniel Jackson (Michael Shanks), and Anubis/Jim (George Dzundza). Bottom row: Moros/Merlin/Myrddin (Matthew Walker), Ganos Lal/Morgan Le Fay (Sarah Strange), Kasuf (Erick Avari), and Skaara (Alexis Cruz).

"One of the reasons for keeping the Ori and the Ancients a little bit at arm's reach is because it maintains that level of mystery, shall we say, that keeps us all kind of intrigued by what the answers to those questions are," Cooper says. This is why SG-1 encountered so few ascended Ancients, and really only when one defied the wishes of the others to assist mortal beings in direct ways: Oma Desala, Orlin, Merlin, and Morgan Le Fay. "I think that if you ever did [see them], because the Ancients are so 'out there' on a mystical, magical, powerful level, that there's really almost no visual that could do it justice. And I feel like it would have been maybe deflating to the whole concept of who they are if you ever did see them."

As Cooper explains, "Part of the adventure of what it is to be human is to not have all the answers, and to go out into this mysterious universe and go exploring." That is the story of *SG-1*, and it is narratively important to have limits on the heroes' knowledge and ability. They could expose the Goa'uld as false gods, but when it came to ascended beings, they did not have all the answers. After the downfall of the System Lords, the story and the ways in which the team advanced its values were deeply complicated by the discovery of the Ori. These are ascended beings who share a common ancestry with the Ancients, but who are deeply divided from them ideologically. Once they, too, evolved to the higher plane, the Ori's own religious fanaticism led them to assume the role of gods.

Left: The Doci (Julian Sands), the most devout follower of Origin, spoke the holy word of the Ori. Right: Serving the Doci and the Ori were artificially evolved humans known as Priors, who carried the Book of Origin to other worlds and demanded its worship.

The Ori demand the daily worship of mortal beings, not to keep workers in the mines or to support a life of luxury, but (quite literally) for a pseudo-spiritual *power*. As Orlin revealed to the team, this is a real, physical transfer of energy *en masse* to the ascended plane, which the Ori share amongst themselves. How this energy benefits them we do not know, but it is theologically interesting to posit worship itself as a commodity, a positive force that accrues to the benefit of the divine. The religion of Origin is given to structure this mortal devotion, complete with priests and missionaries (the Priors), a holy book, and a daily liturgy (called "Prostration").

Like the Goa'uld, though, the Ori conduct their religious affairs entirely for their own self-interest. Their human followers receive no more benefit than a Goa'uld host. They are promised salvation (that the Ori will one day help them also to ascend), spoon-fed stories and vain practices, only to be left to die a death "of the most meaningless kind."[1]

Practically, then, as Ori missionaries arrived in the Milky Way, they preached a message similar to that of the Goa'uld — but one not so easily disproved. As ascended beings, they actually appeared to be godlike, and they bestowed upon their Priors what looked like supernatural powers: telekinesis and the ability to control the weather, to bring sickness, and to cure it in an instant, not to mention the Ori's own immortality. "What if the person or being taking on that position [of a god] actually had very much more godlike powers?" Cooper asks. "Wouldn't it be much harder to convince people not to follow them?"

In this regard, *Stargate* as a whole, and the Ori storyline in particular, becomes a religiously themed reflection upon Arthur C. Clarke's Third Law: "Any sufficiently advanced technology is indistinguishable from magic."[2] Whether it is the technological gap between the Asgard and the Cimmerians ("Thor's Chariot"), or the evolutionary distance between the ascended and the mortal plane, what is unknown and inexplicable to a people is deified. In the case of the Goa'uld and the Ori, of course, this is due to the actions of malefactors: they are not spontaneously worshiped by people groups in search of an object of honest devotion, but instead they actively *pose* as gods. (Such can also be said of the Asgard, though their intentions and actions appear to be largely benevolent.)

Thus, the Ori provided the show, during its final years, with a villain that was thematically consistent with *SG-1*'s exploration of religion, faith, oppression, and truth, only now made more complex. For Cooper's part, however, the Ori and their own feigned divinity were never the focus of the story. "The gods themselves were never the aspect of the mythology that was as interesting to me, because they are so powerful," he says. Rather the more interesting side for *SG-1* to explore was the people who worshiped these beings, and how they chose to live. "How do the humans who are dealing with that interact? And how are they affected by that? I find that more interesting and identifiable, and more of an analogy to our own existence, because we can't seem to prove one way or the other who's right. And that leads to a lot of conflict. … And I think that's an interesting thing to explore in the milieu of science fiction."

---

[1] "The Fourth Horseman, Part 1," *Stargate SG-1*, 2005.
[2] Clarke, Arthur C. *Profiles of the Future: An Enquiry into the Limits of the Possible*, revised edition (New York: Harper & Row, 1973), 21.

Therefore, the real antagonist is not the all-powerful Ori, but their followers – and by the show's final year the mighty invasion fleet they had assembled, and the character of Adria the immaculately conceived woman who led them. This gave Earth and its allies a visible foe to struggle against, which was more practical for the series (invisible enemies not making for great television). But it is also wholly consistent with the writers' approach to *Stargate*'s basic questions and the values espoused by its heroes: Those who are not merely deceived but who actively choose to do evil in the name of false gods must be opposed and defeated. The truth is a powerful force for good in the world, exemplified by the Ark of Truth as a *deus ex machina* plot device.

The beautiful Adria, also called the Orici, was primarily portrayed by Morena Baccarin (left), with three remarkably similar-looking child actors playing younger versions: Emma Rose (age four), Jodelle Ferland (age seven), and Brenna O'Brien (age twelve).

In a sense, this great confidence in humanity is the real and positive "religion" of *Stargate SG-1*. What the show advocates is not a freedom from *religion* but from *falsehood*, a freedom *for* the truth and for the love of one's neighbor.

Faith in Humanity

> I think, in principle, the idea of bettering ourselves and seeking 'ascension,' in one way or another, is what it's all really about.
> — Vala Mal Doran (*Stargate: The Ark of Truth*)

If Clarke's law is right, and if the enslaved peoples of the galaxy believed the Goa'uld to be divine because they did not understand their technology for what it was, then salvation comes to them in the form of enlightenment. Once the pretender has been exposed for what he is, those who once worshiped him can (in theory) move on to a healthier way of living. We can, therefore, describe

Stargate SG-1 as profoundly *modern*, by which I mean that it is shaped by the values of the Enlightenment of the seventeenth and eighteenth centuries. As Immanuel Kant defined this movement in 1784:[3]

> Enlightenment is man's emergence from his self-imposed nonage. Nonage is the inability to use one's own understanding without another's guidance. This nonage is self-imposed if its cause lies not in lack of understanding but in indecision and lack of courage to use one's own mind without another's guidance. Dare to know! (*Sapere aude.*) "Have the courage to use your own understanding," is therefore the motto of the enlightenment.

What Kant calls "nonage" is the basic, existential problem of most civilizations visited by Stargate Command. Whether they are oppressed by the Goa'uld or are under the benevolent care of the Asgard, they lack the critical pursuit of truth that is the right of all sentient species. The task of liberation is thus not merely to put another System Lord on the deck, but to bring an end to their cult of devotion and free people to think for themselves.

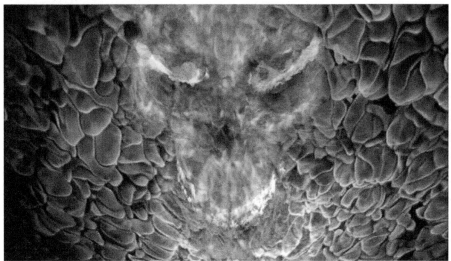

The ascended Ori present themselves as a wall of fire in an ancient temple.

SG-1 and the people of Earth play a unique role on this religious landscape. They visit these worlds and speak into local beliefs from an outside perspective. This point of view proves decisive not merely because they do not share the religious convictions of the indigenous peoples – from the priests of Chulak to Tonane and the Salish, from the fanatics of Bedrosia to those across the Pegasus

---

[3] Kant, Immanuel. "What Is Enlightenment?," trans. Mary C. Smith, accessed 1 Feb. 2022, Columbia University, columbia.edu/acis/ets/CCREAD/etscc/kant.html.

Galaxy who worship the Ancients as their ancestors. More than this, the SG-1 team comes from a world that has evolved without the oppression of the Goa'uld. And so present-day Earth and its representatives on the galactic scene have the benefit of millennia of scientific and technological development, including the Renaissance and the Enlightenment, the scientific revolution, and the advent of the information age.

This does not remove religious faith from their intellectual make-up, like some Gene Roddenberry dystopia,[4] but it does put religious belief and practices into a perspective that most cultures in the galaxy lack. Setting aside the sometimes unsettling motif of the Tau'ri as saviors, this leaves the show's heroes in a middle position: When SG-1 visits a planet controlled by the Goa'uld or the Ori, they are neither the oppressed nor the oppressor but a force for change, disrupting the *status quo* – sometimes for Earth's own benefit (obtaining new technologies, or finding sources of naquadah or trinium), but usually also in the interests of the oppressed.

Indeed, if Stargate Command's standing orders are to secure advanced technologies to defend Earth, SG-1's unstated but equally vital mission is to liberate the oppressed. And while it is true that freeing a population is sometimes secondary to killing a Goa'uld or otherwise disrupting the System Lords, the SGC usually gets around to helping newly freed worlds learn to take care of themselves – and to think for themselves, to pursue the most good for the most people.

If knowledge is power, *enlightenment* is the ethical foundation for the show's writers: Earth can use not only its military might but also its understanding of the universe to benefit others. Importantly, most of these civilizations need this intervention not because of their religious beliefs, or because they are less evolved culturally and technologically, but because they have been oppressed by outside forces. Without the heavy hand of the Goa'uld, they too could have evolved and discovered much in the generations since their ancestors were taken from Earth (as evidenced by more advanced planets where the Goa'uld were no longer active, such as Tollana).

---

[4] As Jean-Luc Picard said of the Mintakans, "Millennia ago, they abandoned their belief in the supernatural. Now you are asking me to sabotage that achievement, to send them back into the Dark Ages of superstition and ignorance and fear? No! We will find some way to undo the damage we've caused." ("Who Watches the Watchers," *Star Trek: The Next Generation*, 1989)

Put in other terms: SG-1 does not simply arrive in a medieval village and tell people that their belief in God is *superstition*, but only that their belief in evil aliens posing as gods is *oppression*. These peoples deserve to be free not from faith in the supernatural, from things beyond the ken of modern science, but from the exploitation of faith as a way to keep them servile. "I think that the moral or the lesson or the side that ultimately *SG-1* has always fallen on is that it's not wrong to believe," Cooper says. "Everybody deserves to believe in whatever they want. And when people misuse power and misuse their position in order to take advantage of other people – or, in the worst cases, kill them – that's just wrong."

Stargate SG-1 thus follows the Enlightenment not only in its insistence upon human rights and individual liberty, but also in its great confidence in humans and their abilities. We can learn, we can grow and evolve, become better than we are today – not merely in terms of scientific and technological advancement but also intellectually and morally. Indeed, this humanist outlook is endemic to much of science fiction, which commonly takes as its starting point scientific advancement, human ingenuity, and speculation of what may be achievable in the future. Cooper identifies this as the "science" in "science fiction." Religion has a place here, yes, but from his perspective it is simply another aspect of human existence.

This is not to deny the reality of the spiritual, of other planes of existence, or even of God. "There was a conversation that [Cameron] Mitchell and [Hank] Landry had at one point where they acknowledged the fact that just because Ancients exist on this higher plane of existence doesn't mean there isn't a plane of existence even higher than that," Cooper says.[5] "[We] never have stated or even suggested that science itself or the universe itself in its existence is not being governed by, or was not created by, a higher power. We never go to that level. We're always operating underneath that level. We're dealing with beings that are – human beings, ascended beings – they're all beneath that structure."

---

[5] This exchange comes at the end of season 9's "Origin," when Landry also states: "Proof of powerful beings is not proof of God." If the universe is infinite, then it is impossible to know everything, and "somewhere in there you gotta fill in the blanks with a little faith." ("Origin," *Stargate SG-1*, 2005)

Oma Desala

> The universe is vast and we are so small. There is only one thing we can ever truly control: whether we are good or evil.
> — Oma Desala ("Meridian")

There is a case to be made that Oma Desala, an ascended being who defies the Ancients to help lower beings ascend, is the central spiritual figure of *Stargate*'s story. She is the first (and one of the few) from the race of gate builders who showed any positive disposition toward Earth and its cause. And when the SG-1 team lost its own heart and soul when Daniel Jackson was exposed to a lethal dose of radiation, it was Oma Desala – "Mother Nature" – who showed up to offer him a measure of salvation.

Ascension as Oma practiced it requires enlightenment, which she described not as mere knowledge but releasing one's "burden." She explained to Daniel that it was not enough for him simply to *agree* to be ascended. This was not a mechanical process for his cells to undergo, nor an intellectual achievement for the wisest among mortals.[6] For her, ascension requires the whole self, freely opening oneself to the cosmos and the limited part we play within it. Daniel approached death with a savior complex, from his opposition to the Goa'uld and his failed efforts to save his wife Sha're to offering up his own life to spare the Kelownans from a cataclysm ("Meridian"). For Daniel to release his burden was to acknowledge that he could not earn salvation by the accumulated weight of his good deeds. Instead, he had to accept that "there is only one thing we can ever truly control: whether we are good or evil."

Cooper (who also wrote this episode) reiterates this value: "What we're saying is 'Be a good person.' At its core, there's more to it than just having the scientific knowledge to become something better. You need to be good at your core. That's the message that Oma gives to Daniel back in season five. I think those are spiritual messages that we've tried to convey." And so the essence of *SG-1*, according to Cooper, is this: "If you are a good person... you are going to 'go to a better place.' You are going to improve the human race and the human

---

[6] See Rodney McKay's failed efforts to "science" his way to ascension in the *Stargate Atlantis* episode "Tao of Rodney" (2007). Anubis, though, could fake his way through the process by deceiving Oma – and later developed a technological way to ascend a human... or at least come very close ("Prototype," *Stargate SG-1*, 2005). This suggests that Oma did not merely function as a guide but was actively engaged in helping people to ascend.

condition. Those are all, if you will, aspects of the fundamental, best aspects of religion."

Oma speaks on behalf of *Stargate* and its humanism when she teaches that, while we can try to do good for others, the outcome and the value of our actions are beyond our control. And so this is not merely a matter of faith in good behavior, salvation by good works in a Pelagian mode. The religion of Daniel's adopted home on Abydos held that a person's heart is weighed in the afterlife, and if its wicked deeds weigh it down more than a feather, then that person cannot join the gods.[7] But Oma insists otherwise:

> The success or failure of your deeds does not add up to the sum of your life. Your spirit cannot be weighed. Judge yourself by the intention of your actions and by the strength with which you faced the challenges that have stood in your way.

Our convictions are important, Oma believes, and the good actions that result from our convictions are important, particularly when they benefit others. But what ultimately matters in the deepest and most existentially relevant sense is "whether we are good or evil." And that, according to *Stargate SG-1*, is finally in our own hands.

Because humanism is so spiritualized in the world of *Stargate*, it amounts to more than just a perspective on the world and on human ability. Humanism itself serves as a sort of *de facto* religion. Like the show's basic optimism regarding human advancement, this is fully in keeping with the spirit of the modern age. The long tail of Christianity's theological response to the Enlightenment is the anthropocentrism of the nineteenth century (and beyond), during which the schools of liberal Protestantism attempted to reinterpret and requalify the nature of religious belief in the scientific age.[8]

---

[7] "If my heart weighs more than a feather, my soul still contains sin. If not, may my soul join the god." ("Forever in a Day," *Stargate SG-1*, 1999)

[8] A key figure among liberal Protestant theologians is Friedrich Schleiermacher, who in his *On Religion: Speeches to Its Cultured Despisers* (1799) and *The Christian Faith* (1830–1831) labored to defend Christianity in the absence of supernaturalism by grounding it in religious self-consciousness (rather than, say, revealed doctrine). The fields of biblical studies and history also saw severe revisions to their methods and standards, following such figures as Ferdinand Christian Baur (1792–1860) and David F. Strauss (1808–1874). Common to these is a willingness to read the supernatural as only the perceptions of ancient peoples, and a corresponding confidence in the practice of philosophical rationalism. For a concise history of

In its subsequent, more atheistic forms, this led to the casting of all religious belief as *merely* a human phenomenon: Ludwig Feuerbach argued in 1841 that God is only a projection of human ideals in order to satisfy human needs.[9] Karl Marx agreed that "man makes religion, religion does not make man" before famously asserting that religion is "the opium of the people" and an illusion from which people must be freed.[10] Though it never makes such a negative estimation of religion writ large, *Stargate SG-1* also orients religion to the human person, that person's spiritual (or psychological) needs, and their moral action in the world. Religion here finally concerns not God, or supernatural intervention in the natural world, or the destination of one's eternal soul, but simply who we are and how we act toward one another. Will our beliefs (whatever content they might have is irrelevant) cause us to do moral good, or evil? Will we attempt to impose our beliefs upon others by force?

This is why the religion of *Stargate SG-1* (if there is any such thing) is humanist. The object at its center, the point of its concern and its reflection, is not the supernatural at all but the natural – not the gods but the people who play them, and the people who worship them. While the team sometimes causes trouble ("Red Sky") or leaves bodies in their wake, on the whole our heroes use their skills and their values for the improvement of human societies. And though religion itself is far from the focal point of most episodes, ultimately the writers reflect upon this disposition in elemental terms of good and evil.

Thus far, to identify *Stargate*'s perspective of religion as humanist, and even to speak of humanism as its own form of religious contemplation, is intended to be an observation and not a value judgment. And so we conclude finally with a brief evaluation.

---

these figures and their place in recasting Christian theological speech see Claude Welch, *Protestant Thought in the Nineteenth Century: Volume 1, 1799–1870* (New Haven: Yale University Press, 1972), 147-160.

[9] Feuerbach, Ludwig. *The Essence of Christianity*, trans. Marian Evans (New York: Calvin Blanchard, 1855).

[10] Marx, Karl. *Critique of Hegel's Philosophy of Right*, trans. Annette Jolin and Joseph O'Malley (Cambridge: Cambridge University Press, 1970), 131. Though Feuerbach affirmed the positive value of religion for the psyche and for human communities, Marx anticipated the secular nihilism of Friedrich Nietzsche and his infamous 1882 proclamation, attributed to "the madman," that *God is dead* because we moderns have killed him. See Nietzsche, *The Gay Science*, trans. Josefine Nauckhoff (Cambridge: Cambridge University Press, 2001), 119-120.

Is *Stargate* Against Religion?

> Do you believe in a god, Major Carter? How would it be if you were punished
> for loving your god as I love mine?
>
> — Teal'c ("Threshold")

Stargate SG-1 is ultimately neutral on questions of the supernatural and the existence of God, which is the result of a deliberate effort on the part of Cooper and the other writers. Its concern instead is with how humans behave based on whatever beliefs they have, and whether those who believe in God will use that as an impetus for moral good or as a cudgel against others.

"We're not saying religion itself is bad," Cooper says. "There's certainly a moral fabric to it. What we're saying is there are people who misuse it. *People*. In some cases, powerful people, who take advantage of other people because of it. And that's just a basic human, good-or-evil story. I think we've always tried very carefully not to judge religion itself, and not to identify anyone's specific religion itself. It's really more of a comment on how you go about practicing your beliefs, and whether you impose them on other people."

What is perhaps the show's most subtle reference to the beliefs of its heroes comes in "Threshold," when a brainwashed Teal'c attempts to equivocate with Samantha Carter. He asks her, "Do you not believe in a god, Major Carter?" Her response is that "It's not the same" – a veiled affirmation that, yes, this heroic woman of science is also a person of faith.[11] This is enough to add texture to the exchange, and to her character, without making an issue of it. And when Teal'c reveals that he has been reading the Christian Bible, Jack quips, "I'm listening to it on tape. Don't tell me how it ends." In these ways, the writers make reference to faith in a neutral way – not dismissively, and not judgmentally, but only to establish that the religious beliefs of our heroes are *not* the same as the religion of deception and death that is imposed by the Goa'uld upon their subjects.

Cooper says of such moments, "I hope that our portrayal has always been, I think, fair and open-minded. I think there have been instances where we've acknowledged characters' beliefs in religion and that that aspect is not wrong, or not the issue. The issue has always been: What are you doing in the name of your beliefs? And is your behavior good?"

---

[11] Carter also readily quotes the first of the Ten Commandments, as though she has come fresh from Sunday School, in *SG-1*'s "The First Commandment" (1997).

Stargate's orientation to religion as a human enterprise, concerned foremost with ethical behavior and irrespective of the actual existence of any supernatural beings, is a more benign and less judgmental form of the critiques of Feuerbach and Marx. But for its part, it is just as "modern." And so it is no surprise that, while carefully avoiding atheistic arguments against God, *Stargate* follows much of science fiction in the embrace of humanism. The common invocation of "spiritual but not religious" in contemporary discourse moves along this same curve: it is a faith directed not at God or higher powers but at a human person's sensibilities, inner convictions, and own actions. Like Oma Desala, the show is simply, single-mindedly, concerned with whether a person is "good" or "evil." Any supernatural or mystical content in that system of belief is beside the point.

That is, perhaps, not much of a religion. As a theologian of the Christian tradition, I would add that it is also *a-theological* – which is not to say that it is atheistic or anti-religious. Rather, the show, as a contemporary exploration of belief through the lens of humanism, simply does not concern itself with any of the matters of traditional theological inquiry. Does God (or do gods) exist? What is God like? How are human persons related to the divine, and how might God be involved in addressing humankind's existential crises?[12] Cooper says that he would hate for the writers of *Stargate* to ever answer such questions, to pull back the curtain on the *higher* higher plane and discover who, if anyone, is above the Ancients. "I think it's OK to bring up those questions and let people answer them for themselves," he says. "But I certainly hope that we haven't ever made that statement, one way or the other."[13]

---

[12] Contemporary religious scholar Steven Prothero suggests, quite helpfully, that all major religions hold to the same basic pattern of identifying humankind's existential crisis (be it the problem of sin, or suffering, pride, exile, disconnection, chaos, etc.) and then proposing the way or ways in which that crisis is remedied. See Prothero's *God Is Not One: The Eight Rival Religions That Run the World – and Why Their Differences Matter* (New York: HarperOne, 2010). Postmodern efforts to characterize all religions as merely different paths to the same god are thus historically and theologically naïve.

[13] One has to wonder, then, how the mystery of *Stargate Universe* would have been resolved. Cooper co-created the spinoff with Brad Wright in 2009, and in its second season *Universe* posited a sign of intelligence in the cosmic microwave background radiation left over from the formation of the universe. The show was canceled after two years of a planned five-year story.

This informs *The Ark of Truth* and its closing scene with Tomin and Vala, who reflect upon the good that remains within the faith of Origin. What does one do with a faith that endures even after "God" really is dead, killed not by modernity but an Ancient weapon deployed through a supergate by self-appointed, righteous do-gooders ("The Shroud")? The end of the cult of the Goa'uld is not the end of religion and spiritual practice for the Jaffa people. And the end of the Ori is by no means the end of Origin. But it does require a Reformation, a new beginning that tests all things, holding on to what is good and rejecting every kind of evil.[14] Tomin will not stay in that small, spartan room on Earth but return home, perhaps as a new Martin Luther, leading the transformation of Origin into a positive force for human flourishing.

Stargate's final answer to religious belief is a positive one because, even in the light of all he has learned and the corruption he has confronted, Tomin's faith remains. "That came out of my wanting to humanize, in some way, the people who believe differently than we did," Cooper explains. "I didn't want them to be just cartoon bad guys who didn't believe the right thing. I wanted them to be human beings, and I wanted you to understand and see why they were doing the things they did."

Is *Stargate* against religion, then? After all, it is a show about a team of modern heroes who slay the false gods of the old world. As with many things in this franchise, matters are more complex when one digs beneath the surface. The better answer comes not from *SG-1*'s mustache-twirling villains but from its heroes, who oppose false gods wherever they are not because they are faithless, but so that all people may be free.[15]

---

[14] 1 Thessalonians 5:21-22.

[15] For a full transcript of my 2008 conversation on religion with *Stargate SG-1* writer and executive producer Robert C. Cooper, visit gateworld.net/religion.

To *Infinity* and Beyond the Pale

by Rich Handley

Every long-running franchise has a film or episode – or an entire series – that doesn't hold a candle to the rest. In the *Star Trek* arena, *The Next Generation*'s "Code of Honor" and *Voyager*'s "Threshold" typically share that title. For *Battlestar Galactica*, it's *Galactica 1980*. For *Star Wars*, it's *The Star Wars Holiday Special*. For *Planet of the Apes*, it's a tie between Tim Burton's film re-imagining and the 1970s cartoon, *Return to the Planet of the Apes*. And for superheroes, it's *Green Lantern*, *Catwoman*, *Batman & Robin*, *Superman IV: The Quest for Peace*, *Ghost Rider: Spirit of Vengeance*, *Howard the Duck*, *Elektra*, *Son of the Mask*, and... well, a lot of other movies.

When it comes to *Stargate*, it's easy to identify the outcast. It's not the theatrical film, which has a lot of fans and inspired all that followed. It's not *Stargate Universe*, the popularity of which justifiably increased over time, or even *Stargate Origins*, which is enjoyable despite its flaws. It's certainly not the much-beloved *Stargate SG-1* or *Stargate Atlantis*... although the episode "Emancipation" might make the cut. Rather, the clear candidate is *Stargate Infinity*, an oft-overlooked animated show from 2002. With apologies to Buzz Lightyear, *Stargate*'s Saturday-morning cartoon took the franchise to infinity and beyond the pale.

Created by Eric Lewald and Michael Maliani, *Infinity* was developed by Mark Edward, Michael Edens, Kaaren Lee Brown, and Phil Harnage as the first television spinoff of *SG-1*, and it was directed by Daytime Emmy nominee Will Meugniot. The show, co-produced by French company DIC Entertainment Corp. and its Les Studios Tex S.A.R.L. subsidiary in association with MGM Television Entertainment, premiered on Fox as part of 4Kids Entertainment's FoxBox Saturday-morning lineup, and its "E/I" status meant it met the Federal Communications Commission's standards for educational and informational programming aimed at young viewers. This is why the episodes provided so many moral lessons. So, so many.

Infinity helped to launch the DIC Kids Network (later rebranded as the Cookie Jar Kids Network), and its single season played on Cookie Jar Toons, This TV's daily and weekend children's programming block, until 2011. Popular animated shows airing in the United States around that time included *Codename: Kids Next Door*, *He-Man and the Masters of the Universe*, *Kim Possible*, *What's New, Scooby-Doo?*, and *The Adventures of Jimmy Neutron: Boy Genius*. Each of these series lasted longer than *Stargate*'s animated adventures, and each retains fans to this day, whereas *Infinity* has been all but forgotten, even among avid *Stargate* circles.

Out of Toon

Dissecting *Stargate Infinity* without dismissing it entirely is no easy feat, as it's a bland dish offering little sustenance. While several essays in this anthology tend toward the erudite and philosophical, that approach wouldn't work with something as juvenile and goofy as *Infinity*. The poorly received series was quickly canceled without resolving its ongoing plot points, and those responsible for *SG-1* and its sequels have indicated that it's not part of their shows' continuity. When asked, during a 2001 interview with *GateWorld*,[1] whether the cartoon should be regarded as official canon or as "an entertaining romp through an alternate universe, which has no impact on the live-action stuff," producer Brad Wright replied, "The latter." Diplomatically, he then added, "By the way, I don't have a problem with it. I'm just not involved." Anyone who has watched even a single episode of *Infinity* would easily figure that out, as the shows are largely incompatible.

---

[1] Sumner, Darren. "Interviews: Brad Wright." *GateWorld*, 2001, archived at web.archive.org/web/20090319011631/http://www.gateworld.net/interviews/bra d_wright.shtml.

Animated spinoffs based on popular franchises tend to be a mixed big. For every highly regarded cartoon like *The Clone Wars*, *Men In Black: The Series*, *Marvel's What If...?*, or *Star Trek: Lower Decks*, there are many more that miss the mark. *Spaceballs: The Animated Series*, *James Bond Jr.*, *Robocop: Alpha Commando*, and the short-lived *Swamp Thing* all come to mind. Sadly, *Stargate Infinity* falls squarely into the latter category. It isn't the absolute disaster many make it out to be, but time has been unkind to *Infinity*, and that's saying something since reactions to it while it was on the air were decidedly dissatisfied. An online search yields a plethora of scathing reviews. Yet beneath its flaws, there are some aspects that can (sort of) provide enjoyment for those willing to find them.

The show is set three decades after the 1994 theatrical film, placing it in approximately 2024, only two years from the time of this anthology's publication. Given the rather dystopian nature of the world these past few years, that might explain a lot. The series follows Gus Bonner (voiced by Dale Wilson), a veteran officer of Stargate Command who has been framed for a crime he didn't commit. Such a setup has been used to great effect on both the large and small screens, notably on *The Fugitive*, *The Incredible Hulk*, *To Kill a Mockingbird*, *The Shawshank Redemption*, *The Green Mile*, *Harry Potter and the Prisoner of Azkaban*, and many more tales. When done well, it can be immensely entertaining. When not done well, it can be *Stargate Infinity*.

Bonner – a character with some depth, to be fair to the writers, as he's branded a traitor yet is the most honorable of the bunch – becomes a fugitive after the lizard-like Tlak'kahn assault Stargate Command to steal an alien chrysalis unearthed in Egypt. Blamed for disobeying orders and sending soldiers into an ambush, Gus jumps through the stargate with his young team to protect the chrysalis, and the group then travels from one world to the next, seeking evidence that will prove Bonner's innocence and expose the true culprit so they can all return home. The show's quick demise, prompted by low ratings, prevented viewers from seeing the story through to its conclusion, but considering how the show had faltered with fans, it's doubtful many were disappointed.

Infinite Regression

Bonner's team includes his niece Stacey (Tifanie Christun), a new recruit who initially believes her uncle opened the stargate so the Tlak'kahn could storm the base. Stacey grew up idolizing Gus, so the thought of him helping the enemy leaves her feeling outraged and betrayed, though she soon comes to recognize his innocence and fights by his side. Frankly, Stacey is rather fickle with her loyalties. Seattle Montoya (Bettina Bush), meanwhile, is an indigenous American from a poverty-stricken New Mexico reservation (a common TV trope known as "The Rez"[2]) who experiences psychic visions enabling her to protect her team from harm. Why does she have this mystical power? For no discernable reason, really, other than to make her stereotypically spiritual, consistent with Hollywood's "Magical Native American" trope.[3]

Neither Stacey nor Seattle are overly compelling characters, and both take a storytelling backseat to the cringeworthy antics of teammate R.J. Harrison (Mark Hildreth), a recent Academy graduate who loves to flirt with women – human women, fox women, fish women, you name it – to the point of being problematic. That's kind of weird when you consider how kid-friendly the show is otherwise, but 2002 was a weird time for children's cartoons. A sarcastic action hero intended to seem "cool" to the preteen crowd, Harrison provides comic relief with his incompetence, though he's not so much comedic as he is annoying – and it's hard to imagine anyone actually viewing him as cool.

Harrison is among the main reasons the show is difficult to sit through, as there is little about him that is admirable. He's the space equivalent of *Top Gun*'s Pete "Maverick" Mitchell and *Fast Times at Ridgemont High*'s Jeff Spicoli, all rolled up into one, but without the former's charm and talent or the latter's humility and likability. In a typical episode, the witless fool will fall into a mud pit, screw up everyone's plans, get himself in trouble with local authorities, and create unnecessary mayhem during a crisis. He's like the titular first mate of *Gilligan's Island*, but with a muscular physique and a predatory nature where the ladies are concerned. The "J" in "R.J." likely stands for "Jar Jar."

Fellow contributor Keith R.A. DeCandido has a different perspective on Harrison, proving Keith has far more patience than I when it comes to children's television:

> The characters are so very stock that you just roll your eyes. In particular, it's frustrating to see that Harrison is so pigeonholed into the dumb lazy guy role that the others constantly make fun of him for it even though *there's*

---

[2] tvtropes.org/pmwiki/pmwiki.php/Main/TheRez
[3] tvtropes.org/pmwiki/pmwiki.php/Main/MagicalNativeAmerican

nothing to support it. He actually *does* a lot of work, *has* a lot of talent, and is a very good officer. The others are making fun of him because that's what they're supposed to do to that character, but it makes no sense.[4]

I respect Keith's opinion, of course. He's a friend and he undeniably makes valid points here... but I'd still toss Harrison out an airlock. I own the *Stargate Infinity* DVD boxset, but thanks to R.J.'s scenes, it took me more than a decade to finish it since I kept stalling out after the first couple episodes.

Meet R.J. Harrison—intrepid adventurer, galactic lothario, and... destroyer of animated shows.

Ec'co and the Not-So-Funnymen

The team features two non-human characters who had the potential to be the show's standouts, though both failed to live up to that potential. Some of *Stargate*'s most intriguing characters have been its aliens: Teal'c, Ba'al, Adria, Thor, and Yu-huang Shang Ti on *SG-1*, for instance, as well as Ronon Dex, the Wraith hive queens, and Todd on *Atlantis*. But on the live-action *Stargate* shows, the aliens are almost always identical to Earth humans, without the functionless nose and forehead bumps often used to depict extraterrestrials on *Star Trek*. Teal'c and other Jaffa look just like Earthers aside from brandings and a hidden symbiote pouch, while Ronon, *Atlantis*'s Teyla Emmagan, *SG-1*'s Jonas Quinn, and *Universe*'s Varro are indistinguishable from Earth humans – and in Quinn's case, he even has an Earth name.

---

[4] DeCandido, Keith R.A. "The *Stargate* Rewatch: *Infinity*." Tor.com, 18 Sept. 2015, tor.com/2015/09/18/the-stargate-rewatch-infinity/.

So, with Draga (Kathleen Barr) and Ec'co (Cusse Mankuma), *Infinity*'s producers had a chance to create aliens who looked, sounded, and acted like non-human species. To their credit, they largely succeeded. Ec'co, a hybrid alien with a human father and a Hrathi mother, resembles a green-painted Terminator endoskeleton with a HAL 9000 eye in the middle of his head. Draga, meanwhile, is rather like a cross between a giant snake and a moth, with massive wings and a long, legless tail that comprises the entire bottom half of her body. More on her in a moment, as there's something unusual about Draga that is fascinating in the writers' clumsy efforts to offer world-building.

With such *alien* aliens among the crew, why don't they work well as characters? For one thing, Ec'co *constantly* talks about his mother. He often laments his tortured childhood, when he was taunted by other kids for being a half-breed. That's not a bad concept, per se — in fact, it's Spock's backstory on *Star Trek*. But it happens in nearly every episode, and since he was raised on Earth and knows nothing about his mother's species, his story is far too terrestrial for him to come off as alien other than in appearance. Ec'co's childhood was no different than that of any human child unable to fit in with the popular kids. If he weren't green, naked, emaciated, and devoid of visible genitalia, he could just as easily be a human character.

One of Ec'co's memories, for example, involves inviting human children to his birthday party, only to have none of them show up, and all for the same fake reason: a toothache. The clichéd "One-Person Birthday Party" trope[5] has played out on far too many feel-good family-friendly shows, so it's painful to see a *Stargate* episode utilize such low-hanging fruit as a plot device. It's not just birthday parties and child cliques that illustrate how kid-centric this show is, though. *Infinity* features characters learning how to swim, overcome their fear of spiders, be responsible for pets, and endure the pain of saying goodbye. Meanwhile, educational lessons explain the nature of storms, DNA, the food chain, nebulas, volcanic eruptions, and other science-based topics. It's *Mr. Rogers' Neighborhood* meets *Bill Nye the Science Guy*, minus everything that was wonderful about both those shows.

Ec'co sometimes provides the lesson of the week, and other times it comes from Harrison or others on the team. In 2002, the aggravating tendency of 1980s and '90s kids fare to talk down to children was still prevalent in Hollywood. Thus,

---

[5] tvtropes.org/pmwiki/pmwiki.php/Main/OnePersonBirthdayParty

the show preachily reinforced the need for kids to face their fears, be kind to friends, remain tolerant of others' opinions, not fear the unknown, apologize when they're wrong, learn from their mistakes, expect consequences when they misbehave, and value teamwork and cooperation. The show never reminded kids to drink their space-milk, eat their space-veggies, do their space-homework, or kiss space-Mommy goodnight, but it might as well have.

Stargate Infinity presented the franchise in a format that neither kids nor adults embraced. The lesson here: TV should never talk down to children.

It didn't end there, either. Young viewers were encouraged to do the right thing even if it was scary, embrace different cultures, not judge a book by its cover, value what's inside a person instead of just admiring superficial beauty, never underestimate an opponent, avoid being greedy, not accuse others without proof, exercise and meditate for good health, never brag or boast, and protect the environment from pollution, along with dozens of other *ABC Afterschool Special*-like messages. All of these are – let's be clear here – *admirable* mottos by which one should strive to live, and children would indisputably be far better people if they internalized all of it. But this is *Stargate*, not *Davey and Goliath*, so such heavy-handed message delivery comes off as hilariously incongruous.

Ancient Her-Story

As for Draga, Kathleen Barr does the best she can with the material she's given, but it isn't enough to overcome the character's conceptual problems. When viewers first meet Draga, she's an alien baby who emerges from the chrysalis. Her people, the Otsorok, exhibit a wide array of mental powers, such as healing abilities, telepathy, telekinesis, image projection, lie detection, and laser vision, not to mention they can activate stargates using their minds. All of this could and *should* have made her the most fascinating new addition to the franchise, because again, she was drawn as something far more alien than most aliens depicted on any live-action *Stargate* show. She could have been the franchise's analogue to Jean Grey... with wings.[6]

However, two things undermined any chance of the audience connecting with Draga. The first was how the character was voiced. Barr is an experienced voice actor with a ton of animated shows to her name, so this is not meant to disparage her talents in the slightest, but Draga's modulated voice gets on one's nerves pretty quickly. In truth, *all* the voices do, though I hesitate to blame the cast for this show's failings since they were just reading the uninspired scripts they were handed – they weren't writing the scripts, nor were they responsible for sound editing. This is compounded by Draga spending the show alternately confused by human idioms and displaying one convenient new mental power after another. The bigger issue, though, is that she is said to be an Ancient, and the Ancients were not flying dragon-moths, nor were they called the Otsorok.

Like most of *Stargate*'s cultures, the original gate builders looked like humans, as shown on both *SG-1* and *Atlantis*. To be fair to *Infinity*'s writers, little about them had yet been revealed in 2002, when the cartoon debuted. Still, *SG-1*'s viewers had already met Oma Desala in 2000's "Maternal Instinct," as well as Orlin in 2001's "Ascension," so the Ancients' human nature had already been established. Yet when the audience first meets Draga, she's a green infant slug inside a 5,000-year-old sarcophagus, after which she quickly grows to adulthood

---

[6] A mutant with vast empathic and telepathic abilities, from Marvel's *X-Men* comics and films.

and then looks like the offspring of Mesoamerican serpent deity Kukulkan and an Ewok hang glider.[7]

It's unfortunate that the writers would choose to jettison the Ancients' established nature when they could have simply kept Draga an Otsorok without connecting her to the mysterious ascendants – kind of like how Benedict Cumberbatch made for a menacing John Harrison in *Star Trek Into Darkness*, but his character fell apart the moment they revealed he was Khan Noonien Singh. (Maybe he was related to R.J. Harrison. It all becomes so clear now.) As with the Khan reveal, Draga's just makes no sense. *Infinity*, as mentioned, is set three decades after *SG-1*, and it's unlikely Stargate Command would forget about its past Ancient encounters.

It's this aspect that primarily knocks *Infinity* out of continuity, though it's not the *only* aspect. There's also the fact that every alien culture has an iris attached to their stargate, just like the one unique to Earth's gate on *SG-1*, indicating the animators based their design of every stargate on the one at Cheyenne Mountain, without realizing the metal gate cover had been created by Stargate Command to thwart unwanted visitors. No one else should have one, yet every planet does. Perhaps Earth has spent the past thirty years making a lucrative bundle selling gate covers around the galaxy.

What's more, the characters utilize military gear never shown on other *Stargate* shows. Stargate Command now equips its personnel with skintight body armor plating, as well as all-terrain vehicles, motorcycles, jetpacks, and laser guns, and everything is so brightly colored. Even taking the three-decade time jump under consideration, the aesthetic is not at all *Stargate*. The team members also sport punk-rock haircuts and random facial tattoos, despite SGC being a branch of the U.S. military. It's *G.I. Joe* meets *Halo* meets *Power Rangers*, with *The Book of Boba Fett*'s speeder bike gang thrown in for good measure. It's not a bad look on its own, but it's bizarrely out of character for *Stargate*.

---

[7] Contributor Keith R.A. DeCandido astutely points out: "Yes, the show aired in 2002, but the lead time between writing and airing on an animated series is much longer than it is for live-action, often upwards of two years or more. So the writers of *Infinity* were lagging behind *SG-1* in terms of continuity, and when they were putting together the stories, significantly less was known about the Ancients (pretty much just the one appearance in 'Maternal Instinct,' which wasn't a lot to go on)." That's an excellent point, so I'm going to cut *Infinity*'s writers a little slack here... but only a little. A millimeter, maybe.

Where Goa'uld Have Gone Before

Infinity's villains vary from one episode to the next, though there are a few who continue throughout the show. First and foremost are the Tlak'kahn, chiefly represented by Da'Kyll (Mark Acheson), a violent commander determined to capture Draga, and his warrior subordinate Pahk'kal (Mackenzie Gray). Da'kyll serves the same function as *The Fugitive*'s Philip/Sam Gerard, *The Incredible Hulk*'s Jack McGee, and *Planet of the Apes*' General Urko, pursuing the heroes from one location to another while never quite managing to apprehend his prey. Also, he's nowhere near as remarkable a character as Gerard, McGee, or Urko.

Modeled after *SG-1*'s Goa'uld, the Tlak'kahn were the primary nemesis of the *Infinity* team... and their species name sounded a little too much like "Chaka Khan."

Though reptilian, the aggressive, antagonistic Tlak'kahn are clearly modeled after the Goa'uld, as they are said to have visited Central America and enslaved the Aztec and Mayan civilizations, forcing them to worship the Tlak'kahn as gods. Like *SG-1*'s resident snakeheads, they travel in pyramid-shaped ships, fight with weapons resembling the Jaffa's Ma'Tok staff, have an apostrophe-split species name, and invade worlds via stargates, subjugating less fortunate species as slaves. It's as though they, like the Lucian Alliance, ran around stealing Goa'uld technology and playbooks for themselves. All that's missing are the serpents and the lavish costumes. And, well, good scripts.

It's worth noting that the show mentions the Goa'uld as having been defeated – pretty much the only future extrapolation *Infinity* gets right – which would explain how the Tlak'kahn were able to steal their shtick, though it would mean the lizards would have had to discover time travel as well, given their conquering of ancient Earth empires. With such appropriation of Goa'uld motifs, coupled with the mischaracterization of the Ancients, it would appear the show's writers may have assumed the audience were too young to internalize the lore of *SG-1* and thus wouldn't notice.

This begs the question of who *Infinity*'s target audience were supposed to be. Was it aimed at children? It would certainly seem so, given the non-subtle good-citizen messaging and the silliness, yet the show utilized serialized storytelling that might have confused young viewers if they missed any episodes, and it contained some mature moments, such as Harrison's lust-filled leering, not to mention Draga's horrific *Aliens*-like emergence from the chrysalis, which might have traumatized little kids. Or was it intended for existing *Stargate* fans? The opening credits montage includes Paul Langford discovering the Earth gate at Giza, which is something only fans of the film and *SG-1* would have understood, yet anyone who'd watched those prior stories would have found *Infinity* off-putting due to its near-total lack of resemblance to what they knew as *Stargate*. It didn't work as *Stargate* and it didn't work as children's fare, so it's no wonder it failed to find an audience.

Talkin' 'Bout Sheftu

In addition to the Tlak'kahn, the series introduced the shapeshifting Sheftu, which have a pair of transparent organ sacks connected by visible nerves, one of which contains their brain. The shifty Sheftu can change their form to that of any other living creature, animal- or plant-based, provided there's an available sample of DNA for them to replicate. That ability is only temporary, however, as they eventually return to their original form unless they have more DNA samples handy. This makes the Sheftu one of the most alien species ever featured on a *Stargate* TV show.

The shapeshifters are a recurring presence on *Infinity* starting with the first episode, "Decision," in which viewers meet a Sheftu spy named Nephestis (Lee Tockar). The manipulative, treacherous Nephestis frequently poses as Arnold

Grimes, a high-ranking member of the U.S. Air Force and Stargate Command, to aid the Tlak'kahn in their schemes. To that end, it is he who frames Gus Bonner in the pilot, setting the show's events into motion.

Nephestis/Grimes is relatively entertaining compared to most other characters, seemingly paying homage to Jonathan Harris's Zachary Smith from *Lost in Space*. Like Smith, Grimes has a thin frame, grey hair, expressive eyes, an insincere smile, a prominent nose, arched eyebrows, and protruding cheek bones, not to mention a sneering voice that telegraphs his untrustworthiness. Both characters are presented as traitors and saboteurs who infiltrate a U.S. military base to help an enemy force – well, before the audience learns Grimes is an impostor – and they even both wear yellow shirts. It's an effective parallel that appears intentional.

Gus Bonner (left), along with Sheftu shapeshifter Nephestis in the body of Arnold Grimes, were two of the show's only *somewhat* enjoyable characters.

The Tlak'kahn and the Sheftu exemplify one area in which *Infinity* scores high marks: in its design of non-humanoid species. This is even true for Draga, despite the misstep of making her an Ancient. On the live-action shows, a typical episode features the cast encountering medieval human peasants in medieval human villages on conspicuously Earth-like planets. But on *Infinity*, the galaxy is populated by an impressively varied array of species, many non-humanoid, and the worlds they inhabit are unlike our own, for which *Infinity*'s creators deserve kudos.

This is due to the makeup, prosthetics, and special effects required to turn actors into aliens, and to create non-terrestrial landscapes, costing more than what it takes to animate it all. Drawing people with six arms, five eyes, and trees for ears, living on the purple mountain range of a planet with twelve moons and three suns, costs little more than drawing humans in Colorado. It's the same reason there was so much more variety among the alien and planetary designs on the 1970s *Star Trek* animated series than there had been on the 1960s show.

For example, the Alteri look like cyclopean punk-rock Yodas, while the Ludan are elf-like. The Makua are multi-colored avians, the Mardan are hulking lizards, and the Mostari have four arms and elongated heads. The Mu'adash sport blue skin and green hair, dwell in swamps, and cover themselves in heavy layers of clay. The aquatic Su'ri have heads with fish fins, the Thorn look like chipmunks, and (naturally, this being a children's cartoon) the Urson are giant teddy bears. Setting aside the cutesiness of these descriptions, the truth is that *Stargate Infinity* beats out the other shows when it comes to representing aliens as, well, *alien*. That doesn't make it a *good* cartoon, but at least it has *that* going for it.

Limp DIC

In any discussion of *Infinity*'s faults, it's important to keep in mind who brought the show to the airwaves. DIC Entertainment was the studio behind such unwatchable pablum as *The Littles, Rainbow Brite, Heathcliff and the Catillac Cats, Care Bears, Hulk Hogan's Rock 'n' Wrestling, The Adventures of Teddy Ruxpin, M.A.S.K., ALF: The Animated Series, Dinosaucers, Hello Kitty's Furry Tale Theater, The Karate Kid, The Super Mario Bros. Super Show, New Kids on the Block, Street Sharks, Double Dragon, Siegfried & Roy: Masters of the Impossible, Mary-Kate and Ashley in Action, Strawberry Shortcake, Trollz*, and the abysmal *Swamp Thing*. Given DIC's lackluster treatment of so many franchises, it's no wonder the company failed to get *Stargate* right.

Giving credit where it's due, though, DIC was also involved with *The Real Ghostbusters, G.I. Joe: A Real American Hero, Captain Planet and the Planeteers*, and *Inspector Gadget*, so the studio did have a few notable hits along the way. Alas, *Infinity* was not among them, for many reasons. In one episode, for example, R.J. Harrison ends up the property of what appears to be a malodorous mud-creature but is really a gorgeous woman wearing a heavy coat, which he discovers upon leaving her service, at which point he wishes he'd stayed. This problematic idiot remembers not to judge people based on appearances – but *only* after realizing he wants her body. (Hey, kids! Cartoons!) In another, the team's pet grows enormous and eats all their equipment, which would have been a far more appropriate storyline for an episode of Lucasfilm's *Ewoks* cartoon.

In what may be the series' most inexplicable oddity, every episode sees at least one character utter an exaggerated and elongated "Huuuuhhhh?" or "Whaaaaaat?" in surprise, as though the group exists in a perpetual state of bewildered befuddlement. In the episode "Who Are You?", in fact, it happens no fewer than 22 times within 22 minutes. (Yes, I counted.) If you have access to the show, check out that episode and see for yourself – once you notice it, it's impossible not to see it, making the viewing experience unintentionally hilarious. Perhaps this was due to how children tended to be portrayed in 2002. If the show were made now, the characters would no doubt spend most of their time typing "huuuuhhhh? lol omg" on their smartphones, and then posing for duck-face selfies.

Stargate Infinity is not an easy show to endure, with its abundance of goofy situations, its message-of-the-week preachiness, the unlikability of most characters, the atrocious theme song from Mike Piccirillo and Jean-Michel Guirao,[8] and the series' incompatibility with the franchise. It may have been fun to watch for children twenty years ago – or perhaps not, given its low ratings – but it's doubtful it would hold the attention of today's viewers, young or old. It's more a weird, lazily made *Wormhole X-Treme!* pastiche than actual *Stargate*, and the fact that there's so little that is *Stargate*-like, other than the presence of stargates, presents a sizable barrier to entertainment. As writer and YouTuber Pug Mugsly so astutely summed up the show:

> If your favorite part of *Stargate* was just the *word* "stargate," and no elements related to plot or characterization or team dynamics or humor or visuals or internal consistency or *plot*, then you might like this show. (You won't. You won't like it.) For the record, I *am* pleased that *Stargate* was considered such a viable franchise by MGM that they made these spinoff shows, like the *Stargate Origins* webseries or the *Stargate Infinity* cartoon. I just wish that they would have done it in a more meaningful and well-constructed way, and maybe consulted some of the original showrunners or the creative team from the series – anybody.[9]

---

[8] youtube.com/watch?v=67E-_SQLVRo
[9] youtube.com/watch?v=PZ9zTR75Q7Q

The Least Pearly Gate

DeCandido, in his online discussion of the cartoon, amusingly quips that its worst episode was "The one where they go to a planet that has aliens who enable the kids to learn a valuable lesson about life..." He also notes the following, with which I readily agree:

> The show had its good points, most notably that it took advantage of the unlimited costume and makeup capabilities of animation to give us a galaxy that is truly filled with aliens. We also get an SGC that is known to the public, to the extent that humans and aliens are interbreeding (as we see with Ec'co). These would've been cool things to see on the live-action shows – especially Ancients who were truly alien like Draga instead of the proto-humans we got. Plus, *Infinity* did follow the *Stargate* credo of doing adventure stories, which is a big part of its appeal.[10]

For those interested in adding the series to their shelves, Shout! Factory distributed the complete set of 26 episodes in 2008 as a four-disc boxset for the U.S. audience, while MGM Home Entertainment offered the show in the United Kingdom under the name *Stargate Infinity: Volume 1*, even though it contained the entire run, ruling out a second volume. At press-time, fans can also view the series for free at the Tubi streaming platform.[11]

There are not many reasons to recommend *Stargate Infinity*. It's the disavowed branch of the family tree, and justifiably so. But those marathoning the full franchise – the theatrical film, *SG-1*, *Atlantis*, *Universe*, *The Ark of Truth*, *Continuum*, and *Origins* – might wish to add *Stargate*'s Saturday-morning cartoon to the mix, if for no other reason than to say they've sat through every single episode and film there is. *Infinity* may pale in comparison to the rest of the saga, but after watching it, you might appreciate the live-action shows even more... because *none* of them feature R.J. Harrison.

---

[10] DeCandido, Keith R.A. "The *Stargate* Rewatch: *Infinity*." Tor.com, 18 Sept. 2015, tor.com/2015/09/18/the-stargate-rewatch-infinity/.
[11] tubitv.com/series/3354/stargate-infinity

Francis Bacon's *New Atlantis* and the Ideals of Modern Science in *Stargate Atlantis*

by Anastasia Klimchynskaya

It is fitting that *Stargate Atlantis* is set in the mythical city of Atlantis, for the conception of scientific endeavor that animates the *Stargate* franchise (and the science-fiction genre more broadly) stems from another canonical text set in that ancient city: Francis Bacon's *New Atlantis*. A revolutionary thinker who, during the Scientific Revolution, contributed to molding scientific practice into the form with which we are familiar today, Bacon lays out in this 1624 utopia[1] his ideals for what science should look like: based in experimentation, material intervention, and an attitude of mastery and control over the natural world that positions humans as quasi-gods. Where previously the world had been a place mysterious and marvelous, full of wonders to be passively observed, Bacon inaugurated a different paradigm: that of a natural world actively dominated, altered, and controlled by humans, as the scientists in his Atlantis prolong life, create new species, and change the natural order of the seasons themselves,

---

[1] Published posthumously, and incomplete, in 1626.

with the goal of "enlarging of the bounds of human empire, to the effecting of all things possible."

Left to right: Sir Francis Bacon's *New Atlantis*, the frontispiece of Bacon's *Novum Organum*, and a portrait of Bacon himself.

This scientific ideal was broadly realized in the nineteenth century due to industrialization,[2] and it forms the basis of science fiction, the emergence of which in that same period[3] reflects this new sense of humanity's power over the world. A genre premised on the idea of humans, for better or for worse, gaining through science and technology the power of magicians or gods, it is the very embodiment of Arthur C. Clarke's Third Law: any sufficiently advanced technology is indistinguishable from magic. This law, importantly, is relativistic, begging the question: advanced in relation to *what*? Science fiction occurs at the moment when humanity traverses the divide between magic and technoscience by rationalizing magic and, in doing so, acquiring through the harnessing of scientific principles those powers that, in our stories, previously only belonged to

---

[2] See Richard Yeo, "An Idol of the Market-place: Baconianism in Nineteenth Century Britain." *History of Science*, 1 Sept. 1985. See also Rosalind Williams, *The Triumph of Human Empire*. Chicago: University of Chicago Press, 2013.

[3] Numerous science-fiction scholars have made the argument that the genre emerged in the nineteenth century, usually with *Frankenstein*. See, for example, Alkon, Paul. *Science Fiction Before 1900*. Aldiss, Brian. *Billion Year Spree*. Tresch, John. "Extra! Extra! Poe Invents Science Fiction." In *The Cambridge Companion to Poe*, edited by Kevin J. Hayes, 113-132. Cambridge: Cambridge University Press, 2001.

gods and magicians. "Science fiction can only exist when it is possible to distinguish in this way between a natural and supernatural as realms,"[4] writes science fiction scholar Paul Alkon.

Thus, the first work of science fiction, Mary Shelley's *Frankenstein* (1818), published at the dawn of the Industrial Revolution, sees a man create life, a power that had previously belonged only to divinity. But he attains this power to "animate the lifeless clay"[5] through scientific endeavor, and this "takes her story over the threshold separating ancient and modern, superstition and science. It takes her book over the border from fantasy to science fiction."[6] This inaugurates a tradition: the invisibility cloak becomes the cloaking device, ghosts and spirits turn into holograms and artificial intelligence, magical portals into wormholes, reflecting the marvelous possibilities that a newly industrialized world seemed to open up to humanity in the nineteenth century.

This Baconian ideal remains the primary framework through which we understand both scientific endeavor and our relationship to the natural world to this day. When we speak of modern science, we do so in terms of mastery and discovery, exploration and control: disease is a thing to be overcome, the genetic code something to be cracked; despite the dangers, we seek to delve progressively further into the "final frontier" of space and build colonies on inhospitable planets, to construct buildings that reach ever higher into the sky and machines that "think" faster and better. We have a whole vocabulary and set of references to articulate the idea of scientists playing god, whether by drawing on *Frankenstein* to express concerns about the CRISPR gene-editing technology[7] or by referencing J. Robert Oppenheimer's apocryphal "I am become death, destroyer of worlds" upon seeing the results of harnessing the atom's power toward destructive purposes.[8] In other words, one of the prevalent ideologies

---

[4] Alkon, pg. 2.

[5] Shelley, Mary. *Frankenstein.* Edited with a foreword and notes by Leslie S. Klinger, W.W. Norton and Company, 2017, pg. 80.

[6] Alkon, pg. 30.

[7] See, for example, Anne Mellor, "Mary Shelley's *Frankenstein* and Genetic Engineering," in *Frankenstein,* edited with a foreword and notes by Leslie S. Klinger, W.W. Norton and Company, 2017, pg. 279-289.

[8] Both are referenced in *Stargate*, as we'll see below: "Michael" is essentially a version of *Frankenstein*, while references to the Manhattan Project abound, especially in the episode "Trinity."

governing our existence today sees the natural world as a thing to be dominated and ourselves as the quasi-gods capable of doing so through technoscience.

This leads neatly into the interpretation of the *Stargate* franchise, and particularly of *Stargate Atlantis,* that I offer in this essay. The idea of humans as quasi-gods through technoscience implicitly underlies most science fiction, but in *Stargate* this ideology is foregrounded and repeatedly made explicit. Centering on alien beings who were or are worshipped as gods due to their advanced technologies, it sees humanity pursuing that same godhood (metaphorically speaking) – until, gaining mastery of those same technologies and scientific principles, we realize the dream and the ideal of modern science by proving ourselves equally capable of such divinity. In *Stargate SG-1,* this is made apparent via the Goa'uld and the Asgard, whom humans across the galaxy worship as gods possessed of magical powers until that belief is rationalized: on Earth, they were the Egyptian and Norse gods, belief in whom gradually falls away and is transformed into an understanding and, progressively, through jerry-rigging, backwards engineering, and inventiveness, the acquisition and replication of the technologies through which they wielded such power.

As Carter says upon seeing a dial home device (DHD) in a since-cut line from "Children of the Gods," "It took us fifteen years and three supercomputers to MacGyver a system for the gate on Earth." But MacGyver it they did, taking their first steps into the galaxy. Consequently, Thor predicts that humanity will one day become the Fifth Race ("The Fifth Race"), taking its place in an alliance that includes the Asgard and the Ancients – who, although benevolent, were once worshipped as gods due to their technological supremacy. And with help from the Asgard, the Tau'ri (humans) do eventually become that Fifth Race ("Unending").

Stargate Atlantis, meanwhile, proves humanity's claim to being the Fifth Race by allowing them to take the place – literally and metaphorically – of the Ancients. As we learn, the Ancients, not unlike the Goa'uld, were (and sometimes still are) worshipped as gods because their technologies were so advanced as to be indistinguishable from magic by the less advanced societies of the Pegasus Galaxy. Thus, the Brotherhood of the Fifteen worshipped the Ancients as the Ancestors, considering the stargate a sacred portal, its symbols religious icons, and the Zero Point Module (ZPM) – which the Lingara call a *Potentia* – a sacred artifact ("Brotherhood"). The Athosians, too, refer to the Ancients as the Ancestors, and believe Atlantis to be a sacred place. This is not without basis, for the Ancients seeded the galaxy with humans, performing the fundamentally divine act of creating life in their image ("The Gift," "Michael"). They then watched over these societies as benevolent gods, even influencing their development by setting themselves up as "Oracles" whose instructions must be followed ("The Game") – once again enabled by technology, including the arrays of satellites that allowed them to surveil these civilizations and communicate with them.

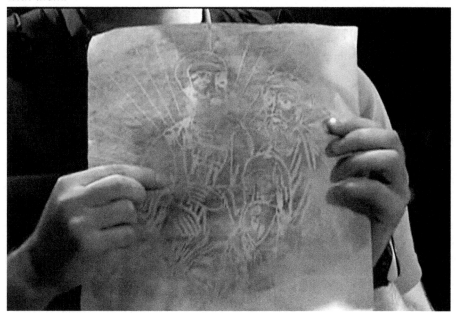

This rubbing of a religious image containing the *Potentia*, or Zero Point Module, appeared in "The Brotherhood."

This godlike role is one that, both intentionally and unintentionally, the Atlantis expedition takes up when they step through the gate, due to their unique position in Atlantis and their mastery of Tau'ri and Ancient technologies that render them the most advanced beings in the galaxy, and which had once made the societies of Pegasus view the Ancients as gods (though the fact that the Wraith cull any society that promises to become too advanced helps, too). When the expedition first arrives in Pegasus, they receive pushback on this from the people of the galaxy. As Halling tells Teyla Emmagan, "They may reside here, Teyla, but they're not the Ancestors, no matter how much you wish them to be" ("Hide and Seek"). Allina of the Brotherhood, too, once she finds out that the expedition has only recently arrived in Atlantis, refuses to hand over the ZPM, stating "You live in Atlantis, but you are not the Ancestors" ("Brotherhood").

And yet, the Tau'ri progressively acquire a stunning amount of competence in understanding and using Atlantis and its many treasures. They're able to initialize the city's key systems, access its databases, use its defensive systems, fly the city, and even succeed at completing and using a wormhole drive – a technology the Ancients themselves abandoned due to its instability and high power requirements ("Enemy at the Gate"). Dimas of the Coalition admits as much, saying "You possess technology and military power beyond the scope of most of the indigenous peoples of this galaxy" ("Inquisition"). In other words, if Atlantis was the Ancients' greatest creation, then the Tau'ri's ability to take the Ancients' place within it – and even surpass them, in some regards – truly marks them as an equal of the Four Great Races who had once been worshipped throughout multiple galaxies.

As the Ancients watched over the humans they had created, so too do the new Atlanteans (there is no Prime Directive in the Pegasus Galaxy, it seems). Taking on the Ancients' godly role of protectors of Pegasus's humans, they maintain the ZPM-powered device that serves as a shield on M7G-677 ("Childhood's End," "Critical Mass"), rescue innocents from an erupting volcano ("Inferno"), protect the Balarans when the Wraith come to demand the survivors of a Wraith plague ("Outsiders"), share their biomedical technology to help the Hoffans develop their anti-Wraith drug ("Poisoning the Well"), and protect and evacuate the Athosians, among many other instances. Most importantly, because they woke the Wraith, they find themselves compelled to protect the people of Pegasus from that threat. Doctor Elizabeth Weir states as much to General George Hammond in "Home," noting their "responsibility to the other humans who live there":

> We did wake up the Wraith – and while, yes, that would have happened eventually without our interference, our access to Ancient technology puts us in a unique position to help those people. We can't just walk away.

This is reiterated in "The Seer," when Richard Woolsey, John Sheppard, and Samantha Carter debate their responsibility to the humans in the Pegasus Galaxy:

> **Woolsey:** It's a pretty safe assumption. Right now, we're not a target.
>
> **Sheppard:** No, no. But the rest of the humans in this galaxy are, *and* it's our fault.
>
> **Woolsey:** Nevertheless, our priority remains the safety of this expedition, and you know as well as I do the Wraith can't be trusted.

Carter and Sheppard then have another conversation away from Woolsey:

Sheppard: Look, technically Woolsey is correct. The safety of this city is our first priority and, based on that, there is only one decision: take out both the hive ships as soon as possible.

Carter: But...?

Sheppard: But what the hell's the point of being out here if we're not gonna help people? We're gonna be safe and sound while the rest of the galaxy gets slaughtered?

Carter: So, play it safe, or take a chance with the Wraith and maybe save millions of lives.

Through necessity, then, they fight the same war against the Wraith as the Ancients did to protect the humans of the Pegasus Galaxy, and the parallels are numerous. "Now we know how the Ancients must have felt," Rodney McKay quips in "The Siege," an episode that in many ways reenacts the first siege of Atlantis.

Many of the episodes of *Stargate Atlantis*, particularly during its first season,[9] reiterate this through a plot trajectory within which the supernatural is rationalized. In these episodes, rituals, magic, prophecy, or divinity believed in by the native peoples of Pegasus inevitably turn out to have a rational, scientific, or technological explanation, one usually discovered by McKay – who, as a scientist, is invested in and represents the idea of a knowable, material world. This plot trajectory of rationalization reinforces the idea that the universe is not a place of inexplicable, supernatural marvels, but of rational, natural phenomena, subject to fixed laws – and which can consequently be understood and mastered by our human heroes.

Through their scientific knowledge and methodologies, their empiricism and skepticism, and their technological prowess – in short, all the things that make up modern scientific practice, many of them dating back to Francis Bacon and the Scientific Revolution – they can not only comprehend but also wield the technologies that seem to be as magic to the locals. Thus, *Stargate Atlantis* repeatedly emphasizes the paradigm of modern science: that any magic is just sufficiently advanced science, and that humanity, once it advances sufficiently, can harness its principles, wield that "magic," and (should they wish) become as gods. The credulous native societies of Pegasus, meanwhile, serve as stand-ins for a less advanced Tau'ri of prior ages, the ones who would have worshipped the Goa'uld and the Asgard before taking on that divine mantle themselves.

---

[9] Which, in my opinion, is the best – and I am prepared to fiercely defend this point.

In "Childhood's End," for example, the locals believe that sacrificing themselves before they reach the age of twenty-five keeps the Wraith at bay and ensures their safe passage into the Eternal Rest. The Atlantis team is understandably skeptical, and McKay deduces that there is, in fact, a more rational explanation: the sacrifices are a means of population control that keeps the locals within the area protected by a ZPM-powered electromagnetic field, which the Wraith cannot penetrate. It thus becomes the Atlantis team's duty to bring that revelation to the locals and demystify their beliefs. In "Hide and Seek," when an unknown source wreaks havoc on the systems of Atlantis, Halling believes it is the ghosts of offended Ancients, offering a prayer: "If you are angry that we have unrightfully inhabited your great city, we humbly apologize." The Atlantis expedition entertains no such beliefs, however, isolating the source of the malfunctions to an energy being that had escaped containment.

In "Sanctuary," meanwhile, the local people believe that the goddess Ithar looks to their every need, and they have never known illness, want, or war. Ever the scientist, McKay again refuses to accept divinity as an explanation, and he is unsurprisingly proven right: there is no divinity, only deeply advanced science and evolution at play, as "Ithar"'s priestess, Chaya, turns out to be an ascended Ancient. And in the aforementioned "Brotherhood," what to Atlantis is a power source that "generates vacuum energy derived from a self-contained region of subspace time" ("Rising") is, to the Brotherhood of the Fifteen, a sacred artifact, portrayed in religious or devotional paintings. The juxtaposition is striking: whereas the Brotherhood, which McKay describes as being "at a Renaissance level of development," sees divinity and its trappings, the much more technologically advanced humans of Atlantis see a natural phenomenon they can understand and harness.

Finally, in "The Seer," the expedition is confronted with the possibility that there exists a prophet who can see the future, an idea that again leaves McKay incredulous. But this, too, turns out to have a rational explanation: just as ascension itself is a question of evolution and of brain activity, so the brain of the "seer," Davos, has "abnormally high synaptic activity," recalling McKay's when he encountered the ascension machine ("Tao of Rodney"). Even the inherent unpredictability of the future due to the realities of quantum physics – McKay's main argument against the possibility of such a prophet – is incorporated into the episode, making the seemingly supernatural impossibility coherent with modern-day scientific understanding:

I realized that quantum uncertainty doesn't necessarily preclude the possibility of seeing probable futures. It's like blackjack: you never know exactly what's gonna happen next, but a card counter can certainly increase the odds in his favor – and frankly, this feels like hitting on an eighteen.

As Brooks Landon writes, "Discoveries in quantum physics have more and more challenged science fiction's early identification of science with certainty and its positivistic optimism that everything could be known and all problems solved if only we thought long enough and well enough."[10] *Stargate* firmly goes against the grain on this, however, insisting on a world that can be known, predicted, and therefore controlled by our human heroes, despite the unpredictability inherent in quantum physics.[11]

The line between being as gods in the natural world through technoscientific preeminence and playing god through those same means, however, is a blurry one. In the Western imagination, exploration, discovery, and mastery of the natural world are difficult to disentangle from conquest and domination, and for Francis Bacon, the ideal of dominion over the natural world was inseparable from power and empire. His other seminal scientific text, the *Novum Organum* – which lays out the modern scientific method, arguing for empiricism – sports a famous frontispiece showing ships sailing off beyond the horizon, presumably toward the New World, symbolizing the seeking of new knowledge through discovery, exploration, and experimentation at a time when European explorers were bringing back new flora, fauna, knowledge, techniques, and ideas from that new continent. That knowledge was, for Bacon, inextricable from power – it is to him we attribute the phrase "knowledge is power" – as he believed a mastery of the natural world and the harnessing of its possibilities leads to political and social power that enables the construction of a society according to one's principles.

The science-fiction genre is a particularly apt tool for investigating these ideas, as its formal qualities allow it to take possibilities to an extreme and, through that process of exaggeration, to work out consequences and

---

[10] Landon, Brooks. *Science Fiction After 1900,* pg. xv.

[11] The only exception to this within *Stargate Atlantis* is "Trinity," in which exotic particles enter our universe due to an experiment run by Rodney McKay. "You cannot predict the inherently unpredictable," Radek Zelenka warns McKay, and he turns out to be right. No matter how smart Rodney is, or how good his calculations may be, this impossibility cannot be overcome or rationalized. It can only be worked around by putting those particles in an alternate universe ("McKay and Mrs. Miller"), and even that turns out to have dire consequences.

implications to the fullest degree. Thus, as the expedition takes the place and the mantle of the Ancients and plays God in the Pegasus Galaxy, *Stargate Atlantis* allows us to see the positive aspects, the dark sides, and the implicit assumptions within the ideals of modern science. Made during or immediately in the aftermath of the 11 Sept. 2001 World Trade Center bombing and the subsequent Iraq and Afghanistan wars, it possesses a much more ambivalent attitude than its predecessor toward the relationship between knowledge and power, military intervention, science and technology's entanglement with warfare, and the consequent potential for "playing god."

Most notably, the expedition's mandate is to seek knowledge, resources, and technology (particularly weapons) in the Pegasus Galaxy, both in the name of exploration and discovery *and* because it may help with the war against the Goa'uld. Even Weir, despite the concern she voices that "This country's history of manifest destiny cannot be continued out to the rest of the galaxy" ("Lost City, Part I") – and, presumably, other galaxies – insists in "Home" that "We need to continue to explore the opportunities for technological advancement Pegasus Galaxy has to offer."

These opportunities for technological advancement have the potential to help mankind fight the Goa'uld *and* to solidify Earth (and the United States, in particular) as a military power, and the show frequently questions this dangerous entanglement of knowledge and war within the expedition's underlying mandates. Often, this is done through a painfully familiar reference: the Manhattan Project, a go-to example of the danger of such entanglements in the American consciousness. As the leaders of the expedition discuss tactics for the impending Wraith siege, for example, Sheppard mentions that science has often changed the tide of war by evoking the atomic bomb, prompting Zelenka to reply, "Not exactly our proudest moment" ("The Gift").

In "Trinity," too, McKay advocates for continuing the Ancients' research on the Arcturus Project by referencing Harry Daghlian, a scientist on the Manhattan Project who accidentally irradiated himself and continued his research for the thirty days it took him to die. McKay casts this as a heroic feat, in terms of a search for pure knowledge: "He tried until his last breath to understand what had happened to him so that others could learn from the tragedy, so that his work, his death, wouldn't be rendered meaningless." But there is much more than theoretical knowledge at stake: the unlimited power yield of the project is truly frightening. As Colonel Steven Caldwell describes it:

A weapon that could effectively eliminate the Wraith threat is very attractive to me, and to the people that I work for. I'm not hiding that fact. But there's more to it, isn't there? No more hunting for ZPMs; the shield at full strength; faster, more powerful ships. How 'bout a power source that could provide the energy needs for an entire planet? No more fossil fuels.

More than winning a war against the Wraith, then, this limitless power source has terrifying implications: providing for the energy needs of a whole planet and more could easily turn to warfare and set humans up as the next imperial power in two galaxies. It would render it possible for them to become the next Goa'uld or Wraith, a power that could never be argued with. No wonder references to the Manhattan Project abound: Project Arcturus's destructive potential, the episode continually signals, has the possibility to lead to numerous other scenarios that, like the A-bomb, we might later call "not our proudest moment."

Furthermore, it is not insignificant that most of the major challenges the expedition faces are of their own creation, allowing the show to interrogate whether a foreign, quasi-military force that acts as arbiters and peacekeepers in a foreign land have a right to do so, regardless of their technological supremacy. The Ancients were flawed, imperfect gods who left behind a galaxy in disarray, at the mercy of an enemy they had created, and the Tau'ri repeat many of their mistakes while avoiding some others only to invent their own – evoking, again, familiar imprecations against using science and technology to play God. It is they who awaken the Wraith (a parallel, possibly, to the Ancients' initial accidental creation of the Wraith); it is they who alter the Replicators' programming to fight the Wraith, resulting in their destruction of human worlds; and it is they who create Michael and repeatedly betray him, creating one of their most formidable enemies.

Thus, when Weir makes the argument to Kolya that "The city of Atlantis holds many secrets which will help us win [the] war [against the Wraith] – but only if my team are here to discover them" ("The Storm"), because many among said team possess the Ancient gene (and expertise in Ancient technology), Kolya rightly pushes back on that presumption:

> You believe your people – who are not even of this galaxy – are closer to the Ancients than we are? Your arrogance is astounding. We will take this city, we will mount a defense, and we will win – with or without your help, Doctor Weir.

Equally unsurprisingly and fairly justly, the expedition is put on trial for "crimes against the peoples of [the Pegasus] galaxy," because, "According to [the

Inquisition's] calculations, the Atlantis expedition is responsible – directly or indirectly – for the deaths of over two million people in this galaxy" ("Inquisition") as a result of the divine role they have taken on.

In particular, the story arcs involving Michael offer a rich example, recalling the tale of Frankenstein, which, alongside the Manhattan Project, has become an oft-evoked parable about the dangers of using science to play God. Frankenstein, termed "the modern Prometheus" in partial reference to the Titan who breathed life into inanimate clay, made a being by bestowing "animation upon lifeless matter."[12] The Ancients, too, created a monster in their quest to create life by seeding the galaxy with humans – at the expense, it must be noted, of any other form of (potentially sentient) life that may have otherwise developed on these planets – and inadvertently seeding a planet that played host to the Iratus bug, which eventually evolved into the deadly predators ("The Gift," "Michael").

Left: the story arc of the Wraith-human hybrid known as Michael paid homage to Mary Shelley's 1818 novel *Frankenstein; or, The Modern Prometheus*. Right: the steel engraving frontispiece for the novel's 1831 edition, published by Colburn and Bentley.

The Tau'ri do likewise, inadvertently creating a new species when they attempt to turn a Wraith into a human ("Michael"): as we later learn, Michael might very well be considered a new species, for the Wraith do not accept him as one of their own, but rather as a hybrid, "unclean" ("Vengeance") – a different, fundamentally *other* being between human and Wraith – a perverse echo of

---

[12] Shelley, *Frankenstein,* pg. 77.

Frankenstein's godlike dream that "a new species will bless me as its creator."[13] And, like the Ancients seeding the galaxy and Frankenstein making life, this new species, too, is initially made in their image: a human, created via retrovirus that removes the Iratus bug elements from a Wraith.[14] Like Frankenstein's creature, he becomes monstrous, turning against his creator-gods because they rejected him and going on to wreak revenge by experimenting on and destroying humans, a perverse emulation of the very human creators who played God in making him.

The *Daedalus,* with vast horizons of exploration before it, was one of several BC-304 battlecruisers – the successor to Earth's first interstellar vessel, the *Prometheus.*

And yet, not all is hopeless. *Stargate Atlantis* can also be read as a parable about the triumph of humanity, writ large. In many ways, it is a celebration of the power of knowledge, intelligence, ingenuity, resourcefulness, and creativity, with science playing just as significant a role as brute force in overcoming the challenges and dangers posed by a vast and unknown galaxy. It is the scientists who help defend Atlantis in the siege, from fixing an Ancient defensive satellite to building nuclear bombs to transforming the city's shield into a cloaking device ("The Siege"), and it is McKay and Zelenka's calculations that enable a wormhole drive that allows Atlantis to save Earth ("Enemy at the Gate"). It is science and engineering that saves the day when McKay fixes the hyperdrive of an Ancient

---

[13] Ibid, pg. 78.

[14] The fact that they do so through genetic engineering, one of the technologies most frequently likened to playing God in contemporary discourse, and one most often discussed via allusions to *Frankenstein,* is striking.

starship, allowing them to escape a planet with an erupting supervolcano ("Inferno"), harnesses the energy of a storm to power the city's shield ("The Storm," "The Eye"), finds a Wraith virus hidden on the *Daedalus* ("Intruder"), invents a way to destroy the Asurans ("Be All My Sins Remembered"), and changes the very timeline by inventing a new math to prevent Michael's domination of the galaxy ("The Last Man"). Time and again, McKay, Zelenka, Carter, and the other scientists save the day with their brains.

Furthermore, what most significantly distinguishes the humans of the Atlantis expedition from the Ancients is that they share their knowledge and resources, insistent on helping other societies progress as they have. The Ancients, we are led to believe, took no issue with – and perhaps even encouraged – being worshipped as gods by more "primitive" societies, raising the question of how that might have affected those societies' development. Upon their arrival in Atlantis in "The Return," they insist that the expedition vacate the city, refusing access to its wonders and scientific riches to any other humans.

The expedition takes a much different approach. They consistently demystify what Pegasus societies believe to be the supernatural, prompting the end of ritual self-sacrifices on M7G-677 ("Childhood's End"). They offer to help the Genii build atomic weapons to protect against the Wraith ("Underground"), lend their technologies to the Hoffans ("Poisoning the Well"), cure rebel Genii of radiation poisoning ("Coup d'Etat"), form an alliance with the Travelers, leaving them in possession of an Ancient starship activated by Sheppard and cooperating with them to destroy the Asurans ("Travelers," "Be All My Sins Remembered"), and show Geldar and Hallona that they are but people at the other end of the Oracle ("The Game"). McKay, in particular, is adamant about helping Geldar develop once he learns that it's a real society in "The Game." As he explains to Nola:

> It is not about winning or losing. Look, the information I gave you and your people is very real, very useful. I've set you on a course that will allow you to develop into a modern society. I mean, what were you two years ago? You were a primitive, disparate cluster of villages stalled in development. Now you're making dirigibles. Do you have any idea how momentous that is?

McKay is animated by the desire to help the Geldarans progress as the Tau'ri once did – and unlike the Ancients, who knew they were manipulating real societies and presumably continued to do so, the expedition, once they realize there are real people at the other end of the "game," try to give them agency. "You and your people need to start thinking for yourselves," Rodney says firmly.

Thus, although the Tau'ri are set up as the ones with the most knowledge and firepower in the galaxy, the former, at least, is something they are willing to share, helping other civilizations understand magic as simply advanced technoscience and affirming the idea that *any* human population can progress to a position of mastery and divinity over the natural world.

To describe the emergence of science fiction as a transition from a supernatural to a rationalistic paradigm, I often cite the words of science popularizer Michio Kaku:[15]

> Our destiny is to become like the gods we once worshipped and feared. But our tools will not be magic wands and potions but the science of computers, nanotechnology, artificial intelligence, biotechnology, and most of all, the quantum theory.

To this list might be added wormholes, hyperdrives, and cloaking devices – which, in addition to the technologies Kaku lists, quite literally give human beings within the world of *Stargate* the power of the gods themselves. Thus, as the franchise's stories progress, we fulfill our destiny, rationalizing a world full of impossibilities and attaining the powers of those gods – Goa'uld, Asgard, or Ancient – whom we once worshipped and feared.

---

[15] Michio Kaku. *Physics of the Future: How Science Will Shape Human Destiny and Our Daily Lives by the Year 2100,* 2011.

Lonely at the Top: The Underused Leaders of *Atlantis*

by *Keith R.A. DeCandido*

Traditionally, in an action-adventure story, the person in charge is often a supporting character. Whether it's cops or the military or even teams of superheroes, it's the people out in the field who are the main characters. The ones who direct the action or give the orders or dole out the assignments are generally not the focus. Charles Xavier is not the main character in Marvel's *X-Men* stories – the actual team of X-Men are. The detectives are the leads in *Law & Order* and *Homicide: Life on the Street*, not the lieutenants in charge of their shifts. And the leads of *Stargate SG-1* are the members of the SG-1 team, not General George Hammond.

This would also apply to *SG-1*'s first live-action spinoff, *Stargate Atlantis*. The main characters are the team of military and support personnel who go on missions through the stargate. The person in charge of the expedition is truly a secondary character. On *SG-1*, this formula works: Hammond is the general on his way to retirement who finds himself thrust into a position of greater-than-expected authority. He takes to it quite well, but he was never intended to be anything other than the guy who keeps the base running – an important task, but not one that would ever be the focus of the show beyond the occasional spotlight.

But *Stargate Atlantis* put three different people in charge of the Earth occupation of the city of Atlantis: Doctor Elizabeth Weir for the first three seasons, then Colonel Samantha Carter in season four, and finally Richard Woolsey in the fifth year. All three had established backstories on *SG-1* (and, in Woolsey's case, also on *Atlantis*), and those backstories pointed toward a much stronger role than any of them actually had once they got there.

The highly competent Doctor Elizabeth Weir was portrayed by Jessica Steen (left) on *SG-1*, then by Torri Higginson (middle), Holly Dignard (top right), and Michelle Morgan (bottom right) on *Atlantis*.

Weir had been introduced on *SG-1* as a crack negotiator and a valued diplomat, whom Doctor Daniel Jackson cited as one of the people who'd inspired the language used in the treaties that Stargate Command (SGC) negotiated on Earth's behalf with alien nations. As played initially by Jessica Steen and then by Torri Higginson,[1] she came across as compassionate, rational, friendly, easygoing, and decisive. Weir handled herself beautifully when negotiating with the Goa'uld in "New Order," which seemed to be setting the tone for how she'd handle being in charge in the Pegasus Galaxy.

Thus, Weir should have been at the forefront of speaking to the aliens they met in Pegasus – in other words, she should have had the Daniel Jackson role. Instead, they put her in the General Hammond role, doling out assignments and sitting in the base fretting and worrying about John Sheppard and his team while they travelled through the gate to have adventures.

---

[1] As well as, briefly, by Holly Dignard ("Before I Sleep") and Michelle Morgan ("Ghost in the Machine").

What makes this even more frustrating is that they very occasionally remembered that Weir was supposed to be a rock-star negotiator. Probably the character's best moment in the entire series is in "The Siege, Part 2," when she goes to see the Genii for a couple of nuclear warheads. Weir is tied to a chair and blindfolded, yet she *still* negotiates from a position of strength. It's a crowning moment of awesomeness for the character, but it is also the sort of thing she should have been doing *all the time*.

The other source of storytelling potential that having a civilian in charge of an expedition with a large military presence offers is the conflict between those two aspects. Unlike *SG-1*, which was pretty much a pure military operation, *Atlantis* was about equal parts civilian and military in terms of personnel, and the oversight was handled by both as well, with the base reporting to Generals Jack O'Neill and Hank Landry, as well as to the International Oversight Advisory. This conflict was brought into sharp relief by the expedition being the catalyst of the Wraith's early reawakening, thus necessitating a much stronger military presence than had originally been anticipated.

"Hot Zone" does a lovely job of setting up a rather nasty rift between Weir as the head of the expedition and Sheppard as the head of the military contingent. Indeed, the ingredients were already in place for a lot of difficulties, not just because the need for military force was so much greater with the Wraith going around sucking the life out of people, but also because Sheppard was only the head of the military by default, since Colonel Sumner had been killed in "Rising" and Sheppard was the highest-ranking military officer left. When there is an outbreak in the city, Sheppard violates lockdown against Weir's explicit instructions (not to mention common sense and standard medical procedure during an outbreak) because, basically, he is bored and he is the male lead on the show, and he wants to *do* something.

The episode ends with a rift between Weir and Sheppard... which is *never followed up on*. In fact, at the top of season two, when the expedition is finally back in touch with Earth and they resupply and restaff, Weir argues to keep Sheppard as the head of the military, which *makes no sense*. Sheppard is insubordinate, doesn't always make the best decisions, and has been shown to put his own preferences above those of the expedition. Weir's bitching him out in "Hot Zone" is completely justified, but the show just forgets about that in order to justify Joe Flanigan's place at the top of the opening credits.

Perhaps the worst thing the writers did with Weir was to have her be responsible for the rather awful thing that happens to Michael toward the end of season two. Michael is a Wraith on whom they'd experimented to remove the Iratus bug DNA and make him human, and the way the Atlantis expedition treats him is appalling, to say the least. It is Weir who signs off on the plan and approves its execution.

The nature of how Michael's story is told obfuscates his origin – we first meet him as a human who seems to be amnesiac, and we don't find out the truth until Michael does. Because of this very effective storytelling technique, the actual genesis and execution of converting Michael happens off-camera before the episode begins. While this makes for a very good episode of television on its own, it also avoids having to deal with how Weir could even have *considered* doing such a *horrible* thing. This is a ghastly violation they've committed upon Michael, and nothing in the Elizabeth Weir to whom we'd been introduced on *SG-1* and had watched throughout the first two seasons of *Atlantis* had indicated she would tolerate being party to such an atrocity.

Frustratingly, another of Weir's best moments came after she had already been written out of the show at the top of the fourth season. Having had her life saved by Replicator nanobots, she uses this connection to get the Replicators to fight the Wraith, and to also steal a Zero Point Module for Atlantis. She winds up being captured by the Replicators, thus enabling her to be written out, but before that happens, she does a beautiful job of distracting Oberoth, the head of the Replicators, giving Sheppard and the gang time to do what they need to do.

Weir should have been at the forefront of Atlantis's mission to explore the Pegasus Galaxy, but instead she was relegated to sitting in her office and furrowing her brow a lot. With Amanda Tapping still having a year left on her contract (due to time she'd taken off for her pregnancy during season nine of *SG-1*), and with Higginson and the producers unable to be on the same page with regard to the character, it was decided to bring Tapping's Carter over to the spinoff for its fourth season. Reportedly, Higginson was offered a chance to remain a recurring character, but she only actually appeared in four episodes – and in one of those, she isn't really Elizabeth Weir, just a Replicator duplicate of the real Weir.

On the face of it, Carter was the perfect person to run Atlantis. She had both the military and scientific chops to deal with all the crap Atlantis had thrown at it. Even more so than *SG-1*, *Atlantis* was a show on which scientific knowhow was often necessary to save the day. The brains of not only McKay, but also Radek Zelenka, Carson Beckett, and Jennifer Keller, were far more beneficial in getting our heroes out of jams than the brawn of Sheppard, Aiden Ford, Ronon Dex, and Teyla Emmagan. Carter had spent ten years on *SG-1* as both a military badass and, most especially, a scientific badass – including two different occasions ("48 Hours" and "Redemption") when she showed up one Doctor Rodney McKay, and another when the two were, at the very least, on equal footing ("The Pegasus Project").

Amanda Tapping introduced Captain Samantha Carter on *SG-1*, before the brilliant scientist received a promotion to colonel and a reassignment to *Atlantis*.

Yet once Carter is assigned to Atlantis, she, too, is relegated to the background. With military personnel, this has a certain amount of realism – officers are promoted and eventually find themselves in supervisory positions. The *Stargate* franchise, in general, has been very good about this, with Hammond being promoted to head of Homeworld Security, and then retiring (and then, sadly, passing away when actor Don S. Davis did); O'Neill being promoted to general and head of the SGC, and then taking over from Hammond as head of Homeworld Security (a position he still holds as of *Stargate Universe*); Sheppard's promotion to lieutenant colonel in season two; and Carter herself going from captain in *SG-1*'s first season to full-bird colonel by the time she takes over Atlantis.

While Carter, as the head of the expedition, wouldn't be expected to go on many field missions, she still should at least be somewhat involved in the science-based storylines. But her participation in either is vanishingly rare. In fact, only two stand out from after she assumes command: in "Reunion," when she leads the rescue, and in "Be All My Sins Remember'd," in which she makes the scientific leap that leads to the final victory. Carter comes across as a strong leader, and the expedition thrives during her one year in charge, but there is still a sense that more could have been done with the character in that setting.

In particular, Carter should've been diving right in with McKay and Zelenka to work on the science stuff – she is one of the top astrophysicists extant, after all, so that's a talent that needed to have been put to more use. The worst offender is "Trio," in which Carter, Keller, and McKay fall down a hole and have to get back out. Throughout the episode, it feels like this is an older script written for Weir, Beckett, and McKay that had been hastily and clumsily rewritten for the newer characters, with Carter talking and acting nothing like the character we'd seen since 1997.

The producers wanted to bring Tapping back for the fifth and final season, but her web series *Sanctuary* had been picked up by Syfy as a series, and since she was both the executive producer and star of that show, she understandably chose to do that instead of filming another season of *Atlantis*. One cannot fault Tapping for that decision in the slightest – and *Sanctuary* was an excellent show – but it left *Atlantis* with the need for another commander. The writers went with Woolsey.

First established as a lawyer assigned to investigate the SGC in "Heroes," Woolsey proved to be a hardass, but also someone who believed in being fair. As played by the always-delightful Robert Picardo, Woolsey was an interesting mix of well-meaning support and obdurate bureaucrat. In some ways, he was the perfect person to run Atlantis, but completely differently from how Carter had: he was put in by the IOA, and he was exactly who they wanted in charge. He was a stickler for the rules, he understood the IOA's agenda because he'd been working for them since they'd been formed, and he was much less likely to act entirely on his own authority, the way both Weir and Carter had.

In addition, you could see the evolution of the IOA's outlook on things. Weir was their hand-picked leader, but as her tenure went on, her relationship with the agency became increasingly more contentious. At the top of season two, she could count on the IOA backing her no matter what, but by the time the Ancients temporarily took Atlantis back in season three, she was on much less firm ground with her superiors.

Indeed, Woolsey was put in place as oversight for Carter — notably in "The Seer," in which he questions a lot of her decisions — but he also proved himself unable to handle the pressure of violent situations, such as in "The Return," when he and O'Neill are menaced by the Replicators. He would seem not to have been a good person to lead the expedition in a crisis, and indeed Sheppard ends up handling most of the leadership duties.

Robert Picardo's bureaucratic but well-meaning Richard Woolsey also made the leap from *SG-1* to *Atlantis*.

One of Woolsey's more problematic portrayals is in "Inquisition." On the one hand, this episode makes good use of Woolsey's legal background, as he is put in the position of defending Atlantis in a court of law. A Coalition of Planets has formed, and rather than welcoming Atlantis as an ally, they instead treat its new occupants as the enemy for waking up the Wraith prematurely. Woolsey uses a lot of dirty tricks to manipulate events — which is very much true to the stereotype of lawyers and bureaucrats, but contrary to how Woolsey had been established on *SG-1* as firm but fair. In much the same way that the experimentation on Michael had been out of character for the compassionate Weir, and how playing second-banana to McKay in matters scientific had been out of character for the brilliant Carter, so is being all skeevy and underhanded wildly out of character for the very rules-oriented lawyer Woolsey.

Had Woolsey – or someone like him – been the one in charge from jump, the whole thing might have worked better. This theoretical bureaucrat could have been in charge of running the expedition, thus freeing Weir up to do what she was best at: negotiating, communicating, and committing acts of diplomacy. Indeed, Woolsey's role in season five is more in keeping with what you would expect anyhow – he is completely absent from some episodes, and he is the fifth-billed star (as opposed to second-billed, as both Higginson and Tapping had been). Plus, he isn't somebody whose skills are suited to either military field work or scientific theory, so his being absent from those aspects doesn't stand out the way it had for his two predecessors.

Atlantis's three leaders each had their moments, certainly, and they were played by three truly magnificent actors. However, the show could have and *should* have done so much better by all three of them.

A Wolf in Sheep's Spacesuit: Nicholas Rush and the Dark Side of *Stargate Universe*

by Robert Jeschonek

What kind of person lies at the drop of a hat to suit his own purposes... hides vital information from his shipmates to maintain power and control at all costs... and turns a mission commander into a murder suspect because he doesn't "believe in the mission?" His name is Doctor Nicholas Rush, and his trickery and manipulations keep life unpredictable – and exciting – aboard the starship *Destiny*, as featured on the TV series *Stargate Universe*.

Paging Doctor Troublemaker

From the beginning of *Universe,* Rush, played by Robert Carlyle, serves as a catalyst for conflict. He always believes he knows what's best for the ragtag crew stranded aboard *Destiny*, and he doesn't hesitate to act to make things happen the way he thinks they should. Rush would argue it's an approach that makes perfect sense. After all, no one else aboard *Destiny* has his level of expertise when it comes to Ancient technology, and no one shares his deep commitment to achieving *Destiny*'s mission. Getting to *Destiny* is the culmination of his life's work and dreams, so why would he be expected to let others get in the way of facilitating the great ship's epic journey?

To Rush, the ends *always* justify the means, no matter how messy things get along the way. According to his dodgy moral compass, doing whatever it takes to keep the ship flying toward its ultimate goal – which turns out to be nothing less than solving the fundamental mysteries of the universe itself – is perfectly acceptable, no matter the cost to himself or others... and the others in the picture don't always agree.

Popularity Challenged

Pushy and abrasive, Rush is *not* one to suffer fools gladly. He doesn't waste time on tact and couldn't care less what other people think of him unless it directly impacts his plans. Needless to say, this is exactly the kind of personality that puts people off fast, especially in the pressure-cooker environment of *Destiny*.[1]

When the castaways first arrive onboard the ship, and the ranking military commander, Colonel Everett Young, loses consciousness from his injuries, Rush claims that none other than Lieutenant General Jack O'Neill[2] put him in charge and proceeds to start barking out orders.[3] It's a power play that doesn't get a lot of support. Right from the beginning, Rush's shipmates instinctively distrust him, and the more likeable – and heavily armed – Lieutenant Matthew Scott has better luck at taking a leadership role.[4]

It's the kind of popularity gap that haunts Rush in various ways throughout the 40 episodes of *Universe*. He's just not a sweetheart of a guy, able to easily sway others to his cause with sheer charisma... though he can be persuasive and win supporters under trying circumstances, especially when his Ancient technology expertise could tip the scales. For example, when Rush launches a coup to seize control of *Destiny*, he's able to enlist a civilian faction in opposing Young and the other military personnel.[5] Such successes don't diminish the fact

---

[1] See this author's other essay, "Same Gate Time, Same Gate Channel: Resurrecting the *Stargate* Brand (Twice) with a Serial Flair," elsewhere in this volume.

[2] Hero-in-chief of the original TV series, *Stargate SG-1*.

[3] "Air, Pt 2," 2 Oct 2009.

[4] Until Colonel Young recovers and awakens.

[5] "Divided," 9 Apr 2010.

that Rush has a blunt, bristly personality and lacks charm (or perhaps he simply chooses not to bother employing it).

Throughout most of the series, Rush is dysfunctional to the point of being antisocial, tending to view and treat others as obstacles, expedients, or outright threats. He doesn't seem to care how he comes across, either, though he recognizes similar traits in others. When a shipmate is murdered, for example, Rush recalls that the victim was "involved in several confrontations."[6] He says he doubts many tears would be shed over the man and asks if he had "one single friend aboard this ship." No one can say that he did – and no one points out the irony, either, that the same could be said of Rush himself (though you just *know* they're all thinking it).

"Jerk" Is an Understatement

It's safe to say that Nicholas Rush acts like a jerk in *Stargate Universe*, though his actions exceed the jerk archetype. He does much worse than flout a bad attitude and irritate those around him on a daily basis. Plotting and attempting a coup to take over the ship is just one example. Rush's proclivity for taking dangerous actions can also be seen when he jeopardizes the life of shipmate Doctor Jeremy Franklin by persuading him to try using the ship's Ancient interface chair.[7] The test leaves Franklin catatonic.

Later, when Rush discovers *Destiny*'s bridge and cracks the vessel's master code, he hides it from everyone else as he tries to figure out how best to put his new discoveries to use. His concealment takes a tragic toll when Sergeant Hunter Riley dies in a shuttle crash that could possibly have been prevented if Rush hadn't insisted on keeping the control center and master code to himself.[8]

When it comes to high-stakes, morally questionable actions that endanger others, however, the attempted takedown of Colonel Young for a crime he didn't commit is at the top of the list. Convinced that Young is the wrong person to lead the *Destiny* mission, Rush tries to make the crew suspect he might be guilty of Sergeant Spencer's murder.[9] As he explains later: "I knew there wouldn't be any real evidence against you. The idea was to create just enough doubt to get you to step aside."

---

[6] "Justice," 4 Dec 2009.
[7] "Life," 20 Nov 2009.
[8] "Aftermath," 5 Oct 2010.
[9] "Justice," 4 Dec 2009.

Colonel Everett Young (Louis Ferreira) emerged as a foil to Nicholas Rush's plans, which sometimes ran contrary to the well-being of the *Destiny* crew.

It's an extreme measure, to say the least, but the fact that Rush tries it at all shows the lengths to which he's willing to go in defense of his agenda. To hear him tell it, though, he did it all for the greater good because Young is an incompetent leader:

> You don't believe in the mission. You resigned your position as S.G. leader because you didn't want to make the hard decisions, the life-and-death decisions. Well, that makes you a liability. I'm not proud of what I did, but I did it for the benefit of everyone on board.

Rush makes his rationale seem noble, but the result would be the same even if nobility weren't part of the equation. His single-minded determination to achieve his dream at any cost has led him to try to ruin an innocent man. At least, that's how it might seem at first, as the truth emerges during a furious confrontation with Young on the surface of an alien planet. Until this time, the colonel's only apparent crimes were disagreeing with Rush and not backing his every play... but that quickly changes.

When Rush admits to casting blame on him for Spencer's murder, Young goes ballistic. The two men brawl aboard an abandoned alien ship, with Young finally coming out on top – and taking Rush's measure. "Are we done?" he asks. Rush's answer is unequivocal: "We'll *never* be done." At this point, the colonel makes a dramatic choice, knocking the scientist unconscious and marooning him on the alien planet. Returning alone through the gate to *Destiny*, he then neglects to explain the full truth about Rush's absence to the crew, simply saying, "He didn't make it."

Just like that, the victim becomes the victimizer. Young, who had been innocent of Spencer's murder, has now condemned Rush to death, effectively becoming a murderer after all. Was the tendency within him all along? Was Rush right about him and correct in trying to push him out of a leadership role for the good of the crew and their mission? Or does Rush simply bring it out in him, turning a good man bad in furtherance of his own dark desires?

Rush soon returns, but the answers to these questions remain as murky as fundamental human nature. Only two things are clear: Rush and Young will continue their battle of wills, and *Stargate Universe* will be all the more interesting because of it.

Never Fear, Rush Is Here

Universe would not be as exciting without Rush in the mix. Characters like him, in the grand tradition of Machiavellian schemers sabotaging things from within, have a history of making strong impressions in science-fiction TV shows and films. They add color and spark to what might otherwise be a drab palette of earnest do-gooder types. They provide a contrast that makes the heroes seem more heroic – and the power conflict that keeps the story dynamic and unpredictable.

The film *The Empire Strikes Back*, for example, introduces Lando Calrissian, who cuts a dashing figure while betraying his old pal Han Solo and company. The HAL 9000 computer turns against the crew of *Discovery One* in *2001: A Space Odyssey* and is most memorable for the mellow personality he exhibits while killing his human colleagues. In *Alien,* crewman Ash turns out to be a traitorous android who sacrifices his shipmates to the xenomorph lifeform on orders from his corporate masters. And on both versions of *Battlestar Galactica*, the revered Baltar (whether intentionally or not) ends up betraying humanity to the Cylons.

The prime example of this character type, perhaps, is Doctor Zachary Smith from the original TV series *Lost in Space*, which aired from 1965 to 1968. A stowaway aboard the *Jupiter 2* spacecraft, Smith, portrayed by Jonathan Harris, is taken in by his shipmates yet never misses an opportunity to turn against them in service to his own agenda. Time and again, Smith betrays the Robinson family to all manner of alien beings, always acting out of selfish motives, chief among them greed and self-preservation.

Doctor Smith's schemes routinely backfire, often because he is betrayed in turn by his supposed alien allies. Inevitably, Smith ends up desperately seeking salvation from the Robinsons and their robot (Smith's eternal frenemy, the one member of the crew who, along with Major Don West, most consistently sees through him). The good-hearted Robinsons triumph and have a good laugh at the expense of the callow and cowardly Smith, and life aboard the *Jupiter 2* resumes its usual course.[10]

Never fear, Rush is here! Nicholas Rush served as *Stargate*'s analogue to *Lost in Space*'s Zachary Smith – minus the campy antics and robot frenemy, and with a great deal more intelligence and bravery.

The Doctor Smith template certainly has its similarities to Doctor Rush in *Universe*. Both men have what might be called difficult personalities that often put them at odds with their shipmates. They also have big egos and a belief in their natural superiority. At one point, for example, Rush says, "Some are better than others, and it's those who recognize and exploit that who succeed."[11]

Another similarity is that both Rush and Smith put their own agendas ahead of others' needs and wishes, acting according to what they think best instead of

---

[10] The implied bravado of Smith's oft-repeated catchphrase, "Never fear, Smith is here," is a joke in the face of his abject cowardice.

[11] "Resurgence," 30 Nov 2010.

following the agreed-upon consensus. Neither man puts much stock in the opinions of others, and they each tend to function as opportunists, seizing advantages when they present themselves. They often do so by lying freely and without guilt, a tactic Rush justifies thusly to Eli Wallace, *Stargate Universe*'s "young genius" Will Robinson analogue: "The grownups do that sometimes."[12]

The genius of Doctor Nicholas Rush (Robert Carlyle) and Eli Wallace (David Blue) kept those aboard the *Destiny* alive, though Rush's motives were not always altruistic.

Despite all the similarities between Rush and Smith, the two men have obvious differences. For example, Rush isn't a coward, even though he's accused of being one when he hesitates at first to test the interface chair on himself.[13] Though Smith's intellect never seems as formidable as he thinks (not even close), Rush's mind is his most powerful weapon.

Perhaps most noteworthy of all, when it comes to motivations, is that Rush is not a selfish man, for the most part. Almost everything he does is for the good of *Destiny* and its mission – or, at least, what he considers to fit that category. For example, when personnel are being selected to leave *Destiny* and start a new

---

[12] "Water," 30 Oct 2009.
[13] "Life," 20 Nov 2009.

life on an alien world, Rush gives up his spot,[14] ensuring that someone else will have the opportunity to start over. It's a generous gesture... though it turns out Rush's motives also have a selfish component in this case. As he explains: "This ship... coming here... was my destiny. My life's work was to be *here*, not trying to survive on some rock with a bunch of strangers."

In a later adventure, when *Destiny* is infiltrated by tiny alien lifeforms, and the acting leadership asks Rush for his advice, he tells them, "Always consider the greater good."[15] In another episode, tellingly titled "The Greater Good,"[16] Rush battles and finally establishes a détente with his nemesis, Colonel Young, despite their mutual distrust and animosity, "for the sake of the crew." Yes, it's a complicated relationship, far more so than any of the relationships between Zachary Smith and his perpetual victims/protectors, the Robinson family. Rush is a complex man, a fact confirmed by a glimpse of his past before the coming of *Destiny*.

Cracking the Code

Observing Rush's extreme actions and abrasive behavior during his time on *Destiny*, it's only natural to wonder if he has always been the same. Before arriving on his ship of dreams, was he a perpetually demanding and manipulative jerk who'd do almost anything to direct events in his favor? Back on Earth, did he lie and conceal and maneuver to get his way, rationalizing his self-serving actions with what could have been delusional thinking as much as sound, logical reasoning? The answers – some of them – lie in visions of the past.

While trying to crack *Destiny*'s master code, Rush links with the interface chair and flashes back to his life on Earth. Even as he fights to crack the code, he relives a traumatic time in his life: the decline and death of his wife, Gloria, due to cancer.[17] Through these memories, we see that Rush was flawed even then, letting himself be consumed by his work (cracking the secret of the ninth chevron) instead of being there for Gloria as he should have been. When Daniel Jackson recruited him for the Icarus project, that provided a relief as well as a challenge, an excuse to avoid dwelling too long on the terrible impending loss of his wife.

---

[14] "Light," 23 Oct 2009.
[15] "Water," 30 Oct 2009.
[16] "The Greater Good," 9 Nov 2010.
[17] "Human," 23 Apr 2010.

Rush's wife Gloria (left) died of cancer, while his lover Amanda Perry (right) was murdered but survived as a disembodied mind.

In real life, Rush never solved the ninth chevron problem... but in the simulated memory-scape, he figures out the key to the master code based on a clue from his dying wife. He then exits the simulation victorious, again leaving behind the pain of loss in favor of the pursuit of knowledge. Rush, it turns out, was a bit of a bastard before he ever boarded *Destiny*... but his behavior was motivated as much by love and grief as a selfish quest for exploration. He closed himself off to mitigate the pain of losing Gloria, which made him colder.

Yet, perhaps, it also prepared Rush for his trials aboard the Ancient vessel. As he tells her in his vision, "I always had it in me... to make the hard decisions. I have reasons... good reasons." To this, Gloria replies: "To hurt people? Are you sure? You tell yourself my death gave you courage. In truth, it made you callous. You're not the man I loved."

Does reliving his tragic history make Rush more aware of his flaws and better equipped to change his ways in the present day? Does he finally see the light, gain internal equilibrium, and become a more humane and compassionate presence aboard *Destiny?* His next major confrontation with Colonel Young, another high-stakes brawl between alpha males with everything on the line, shows he hasn't come so far after all... or maybe he has.

Rush vs. Young, Round Two

Open warfare erupts between Rush and Young despite a truce that keeps them from going after each other's throats for a while. The truce begins when Rush returns to *Destiny* after being marooned by Young on the alien world; rather than escalate further, the two men agree to put their differences aside for the sake of the crew. Maybe their conflict could have ended there, but Rush goes on to help a civilian contingent stage a mutiny against the colonel.[18] The mutiny ultimately fails, and the two sides agree to work together again, but the bad blood never really goes away. All it takes for the war to flare back to life is for Rush to screw up again, which he does in spades.

When Rush discovers *Destiny*'s bridge, he keeps his shipmates in the dark about it. Instead of looping in Young and the rest, he works solo on the bridge, alone except for lifelike visions of people he knows. To make matters worse, when he cracks the ship's master code, he keeps that to himself as well. When Young finds out the truth, he is *not* a happy camper, especially because one of his soldiers died in a shuttle crash that could perhaps have been avoided if Rush had given others access to the code and the bridge. The colonel doesn't mince words about this when he faces off with Rush over the discovery. He tells him, in no uncertain terms, "I should have killed you when I had the chance."[19]

Hand-to-hand combat erupts between them, but Young has the power of sheer rage on his side. He beats Rush into submission, leaving him bruised and bloody as the scientist tries to explain himself:

> Look, when I unlocked the code, the amount of information it revealed was overwhelming. I had to make sure I had a proper handle on this stuff before letting anyone have access to it.

When Young insists that Rush could have told him the truth, Rush counters by saying, "I couldn't trust you – and I'm not the only one who feels this way." The scientist tells him, further, that Young is unfit for command:

> Come on, Colonel, look at yourself. You can hardly get out of bed in the morning, never mind make command decisions. It's a heavy burden to carry, I know, but you have to ask yourself this question: 'Am I fit to lead these people?' Well, maybe at one time, yeah, but not now. I couldn't tell you about the code, Colonel. How can I trust you when you don't even trust yourself?

None of this seems likely to win over Young. Rush has pushed Young too far, as he has in the past; he's practically begging to be marooned again. But... that isn't what happens. Rush tries a different tack, one that suggests he has a deeper understanding of the situation and a willingness to try something different if it might help to further his goals. He tries using *the truth*. Instead of playing games

---

[18] "Divided," 9 Apr 2010.
[19] "The Greater Good," 9 Nov 2010.

or resorting to more verbal attacks, Rush opts for full disclosure. He tells Young what he's discovered in *Destiny*'s computers – the secret behind her mission and his passionate support for it:

> A long time ago, the Ancients made a discovery. They found evidence of a structure buried deep within the [cosmic] background radiation. They believed that, at one time, this structure had genuine complexity, coherence, and therefore could not have occurred naturally.

When Young asks if the structure represents some kind of message, Rush explains further:

> Well, that's the very question they sought to answer when they launched *Destiny*. That is the mission. We're talking about a mystery rooted in the foundation of reality, a puzzle with pieces scattered across the length and breadth of the universe itself.

Rush then suggests he and Young work side by side to solve this great mystery, forming an alliance "for the benefit of everyone" – and, amazingly, Young agrees. Even after everything that has happened between them, the strategy works. Not only will Rush survive Young's fury, but his chances of continuing his work and fulfilling *Destiny*'s mission improve significantly.

By taking this new path, Rush demonstrates maturity and a willingness to enlist the help of others – not qualities he was known for at the start of his journey on *Universe*. Unlike his partial antecedent, Zachary Smith, Rush is capable of evolving, not locked into a set of dead-end behaviors that doom him to the repetition of endless try-fail cycles. It's a good thing he manages to grow a bit, too, as he faces a parade of new menaces and challenges throughout the rest of his travels aboard *Destiny*.

The Perils of Nicholas Rush

Stargate Universe's remaining onscreen adventures put Rush through a meat-grinder, pushing him to his limits and beyond. He loses the woman he loves, Amanda Perry, then vengefully executes her killer in cold blood on the surface of an alien planet.[20] He faces off with a duplicate from an alternate timeline and watches him go down with an alternate *Destiny*.[21] He becomes trapped in a simulation in *Destiny*'s computers with dead Mandy's consciousness.[22] And his

---

[20] "Malice," 16 Nov 2010.
[21] "Twin Destinies," 14 Mar 2011.
[22] "Seizure," 27 Feb 2012.

rash decision to investigate an energy signature puts the vessel in the crosshairs of a fleet of relentless drones[23] – an unstoppable threat that signals the end of the ship's great mission unless drastic steps are taken.[24]

To survive the drones' onslaught, *Destiny* must flee to another galaxy, and her crew must enter cryo-stasis – all except for Eli, who will remain awake throughout the three-year journey. Until that final, desperate twist, Rush proves again and again that he is a match for any danger, setback, or emotional upheaval. His dedication to the mission of the Ancients drives him onward, and his intellect enables him to think his way through almost any problem. He might be a difficult person with more than a few sharp edges, and his nature might force him to keep most people at arm's length, but he has a habit of coming through in a pinch.

Ultimately, that's what makes Rush a figure worthy of redemption... and someone we want to see at the core of a show like *Stargate Universe*. Like other such snarky, devilish characters, he stirs the pot, drives the action, triggers conflict, and keeps things interesting in the process. The goodness and light of more conventionally heroic figures are heightened by their interplay with this shadowy anti-hero.[25] They appear brighter in comparison... but Rush is still the one we enjoy the most.

Nicholas Rush knows what he wants, he tells it like it is, and he refuses to let anyone or anything get in the way of his dreams – though he is also capable of affection for his colleagues, in his own way. In the final episode of *Universe,* for example, just as Rush is about to enter a stasis pod to hibernate through the long trip to the next galaxy, he gives Eli some parting words in his own inimitable style:

> You know, maybe I haven't said this often enough, Eli, but you do have... tremendous potential. I'd hate to see you throw it all away. You've come a long way from that video game slacker I discovered a year ago.

In that moment, said with just the right inflection, Rush's words come across as almost affectionate, while yet again getting in some digs and asserting his own superiority. He comes as close as he ever has to expressing warm feelings for Eli,

---

[23] "Resurgence," 30 Nov 2010.
[24] "Blockade," 2 May 2011, and "Gauntlet," 9 May 2011.
[25] Though it's true that *Stargate Universe*'s characters, in general, tend to be complex and flawed.

who has had a tendency to rub him the wrong way (and vice versa).[26] Rush has a heart after all, doesn't he?

Then again...

During the same conversation, Rush admits to manipulating Colonel Young one more time, volunteering to stay out of stasis because that was what he *didn't* want to do, and he knew Young wouldn't trust him to be the one watching over the rest of the crew while they slept. Once again, Rush has proven himself to be a master of deceit in support of his own agenda.

Let's face it, we wouldn't want him any other way.

---

[26] After all, Eli had solved the problem of activating the ninth chevron, a puzzle Rush himself was unable to work out on his own.

Ch-Ch-Ch-Ch-Changes: *Stargate*'s Revolving Cast of Characters

by Joseph Dilworth Jr.

I think I can do more this way. It's what I want. I have to go now.
— Doctor Daniel Jackson, "Meridian"

A major key to any story's success, perhaps the most important one, is its characters. One could craft the most adventurous tale ever told, but without believable, relatable people navigating those experiences, there is no hook to bring an audience along for the ride. Ask anyone who has watched even a handful of episodes of any series who their favorite character is, and you'll get a definitive answer – even if they don't yet know the character's name or possibly even the show's premise. And despite who *you* might personally choose, every character on a series is someone's favorite.

But what happens when a main character leaves a show, especially when that character is part of an ensemble or a crew and fulfills a specific function, and especially if that function is vital to the show? Every franchise has experienced this at one time or another. *Star Trek: The Next Generation* replaced Beverly Crusher with Kate Pulaski for its second season, then replaced Pulaski with Crusher the following year. John Doggett replaced Fox Mulder on *The X-Files*. And

The Three Stooges replaced Curley with Shemp. That last one may have been the other way around, but you get the point.

Stargate SG-1 was no exception to this, though it did enjoy nearly five seasons with a stable cast of main and recurring characters. *Stargate Atlantis*, on the other hand, almost seems to have had a revolving door as far as its cast was concerned, but it wasn't quite *that* unstable. *Stargate Universe* weathered its short run fairly unscathed, except for one technical exception. More on that later; first, let us first look at how things played out on *SG-1*.

During the production of *SG-1*'s season five, Michael Shanks felt that his character, Doctor Daniel Jackson, had strayed too far from how he was originally portrayed, and that he was being woefully underutilized. For these reasons, Shanks decided he was ready to leave the show. Doctor Jackson was thus written out in the season's penultimate episode, "Meridian."

In that episode, the SG-1 team visits the planet Langara and discovers that one of its nation states, Kelowna, is developing a bomb with a more powerful and unstable form of the mineral naquadah, called naquadria. The Kelownans are in a Cold War with two other nations and plan to use this bomb in the inevitable impending war. While observing an experiment with naquadria that goes awry, Jackson saves the day but in so doing is exposed to a lethal radiation dose. At the end of the episode, he ostensibly dies – however, this being science fiction, he is given the opportunity to ascend to a higher plane of existence, thereby leaving the door open to future guest-star appearances.

Introduced in this episode is Jonas Quinn, portrayed by Corin Nemec, an actor already known for his roles on *Parker Lewis Can't Lose* and in the ABC miniseries *The Stand*. The native Kelownan (Quinn, not Nemec, who is from Earth) is a man of conscience who would rather work toward a peaceful resolution to the growing conflict. Unhappy with the weapon his people are developing, as well as their public scapegoating of Doctor Jackson as the one who'd caused the accident that had been detected by the rest of the planet, Jonas steals a quantity of naquadria and defects with it to Earth.

Season six began not only with the series on a new broadcast station (Sci-Fi Channel, as Syfy was then known, had rescued the show from its cancellation by Showtime), but with a change in the opening credits. Within the narrative, the SG-1 team was still mourning the loss of Daniel Jackson while Jonas Quinn was doing his best to prove that he would be a worthy addition to the team. Quinn had the ability to learn far more quickly than a human, and since he'd absorbed all of Jackson's research, he seemed to be the logical fit.

The original *SG-1* lineup underwent several cast changes, including the temporary replacement of Daniel Jackson (Michael Shanks) with Corin Nemec as Jonas Quinn for season six.

However, Jack O'Neill, Samantha Carter, and Teal'c still harbored ill feelings toward Quinn due to his people's misrepresentation of the events that had led to Jackson's death. Eventually – and, not coincidentally, by the end of the season premiere – O'Neill, after auditioning eight other potential team members (nine if you count the two hours Captain Matheson lasted in the job), accepts Quinn as an official member of SG-1. The fact that O'Neill was going to be forced to take on a delegate from Russia may have played into his decision. Maybe.

In the same way that the character felt the need to prove himself to the other members of SG-1, so too did the actor playing him have a challenge in proving himself to the audience, who'd come to adore Shanks as Jackson. Fortunately, both Quinn and Nemec acquitted themselves admirably. Perhaps ironically, the character was strong in the very traits that Shanks felt had been diminished in the writing of Jackson: namely, his research and his advocacy for peaceful solutions.

And then, just as Quinn was finally accepted by other characters on the show, as well as by the fanbase, it was announced that Michael Shanks would be returning full-time as Daniel Jackson the following season. He had appeared in three episodes of season six, including the finale, and the season-seven premiere featured Jackson's reintegration, the defeat of the current big bad, and a suitable sendoff for Jonas Quinn as the latter returned home. While there were promises that Nemec would be back on a recurring basis, Quinn returned in only one more episode, then was never heard from again. A later episode made mention of his planet falling to the Ori with his fate unknown, then a second-season story on *Stargate Universe* took place on Langara, but with no mention of Jonas or whether he survived the Ori takeover.

The seventh season enjoyed a period of relative cast stability... until about two-thirds of the way through, when Doctor Janet Frasier was killed during a volatile offworld mission. While Teryl Rothery may not have been in the opening credits, her Doctor Frasier was a mainstay of Stargate Command and frequently played a major role in the proceedings. Frasier was very briefly replaced by Doctor Brightman (Alisen Down) the following season, but that character only appeared in a single episode, "Lockdown," before a permanent staff physician was introduced in season nine. Brightman would later feature in a few episodes of *Stargate Universe*, making her the only *SG-1* character to have appeared on *Universe* but not on *Atlantis*.

The real-world illness and passing of actor Don S. Davis, and thus of his much-beloved character General George Hammond, led to the arrival of Beau Bridges as the equally likable Hank Landry, shown here with Gary Jones as Walter Harriman.

Season eight further shook up the cast when Don S. Davis left the show for health reasons. At the same time, Richard Dean Anderson had been gradually reducing the number of episodes he shot each year, so it was natural to have the newly promoted Brigadier General O'Neill take the chief spot at Stargate Command. Davis had several more appearances on the show, including in the final TV movie, *Stargate: Continuum*, before passing away just prior to that film's release.

At the end of season eight, Anderson decided he was no longer able to commit full-time to the series, and so season nine brought about the biggest cast shakeup. Meanwhile, Amanda Tapping had been going through the last part of a pregnancy when shooting for the season began, necessitating her being absent for the first five episodes, except for a couple very brief appearances. To fill these two vacancies, four new cast members were introduced – two regular and two recurring.

To cover for Tapping's absence, Claudia Black returned as Vala Mal Doran. She had guest-starred in an episode of the previous season and her character was very well-received. Vala was an uninhibited and unapologetic thief who injected over-the-top humor into nearly every scene in which she appeared, and she was a much-needed breath of fresh air. She left just after Carter returned, then came back for the season finale. Ironically, Black was pregnant at that time, but *her* pregnancy was written into the storyline. Vala would become a permanent member of the cast and team for the final *SG-1* season and would also appear in the two TV movies, *Continuum* and *The Ark of Truth*.

The other new recurring cast member was Lexa Doig as Doctor Carolyn Lam, introduced in "Avalon, Part 2" as Stargate Command's new doctor and the permanent replacement for Doctor Frasier. What's more, she had some sort of close yet strained connection to the new head of the base, Hank Landry. General Landry, played by veteran actor Beau Bridges, had big shoes to fill, but he quickly established himself as a tough but fair commander and developed the same relationship with SG-1 as his predecessor, Hammond, who had been fiercely loyal to and protective of his charges. It turned out that Doctor Lam was his estranged daughter, and there was an ongoing storyline regarding them patching up their relationship and reestablishing their bond.

The final new addition was Colonel Cameron Mitchell, played by Ben Browder. Black and Browder had previously starred together on the series *Farscape*, and their amazing chemistry there carried over to *Stargate*, even though both were portraying very different characters than they had on the earlier show. Mitchell's career ambition had been to be a part of SG-1, but since the season began with Jackson, Teal'c, and Carter moving on from Stargate Command, he had a rather amusing struggle getting the band back together.

The cast would remain unchanged for the rest of the series and through the two movies that concluded *SG-1*'s storyline. However, *Stargate Atlantis* was airing by that time, and it was no less immune to cast shakeups. *Atlantis* went through its first season without any major changes, though it became apparent that the writers weren't sure what to do with Lieutenant Aiden Ford, portrayed by Rainbow Sun Francks. Ford was part of the military side of the Atlantis expedition, reporting directly to Colonel John Sheppard, played by Joe Flanigan.

Interestingly, Sheppard was somewhat of a replacement himself, as his commanding officer, the expedition's original military commander, had been killed during *Atlantis*'s opening story. That may be a bit of stretch since the show was written that way, but it's allowed in on a technicality. At any rate, having two affable, likeable military characters meant there was only enough story space for one – and, well, Flanigan had top billing in the credits. Going into the second season, it was decided to take Ford in a different direction by having him become unstable due to an overdose of an enzyme from the Wraith, the series' main antagonists.

The *Atlantis* cast also experienced a high turnover, including the departure of Rainbow Sun Francks as Aiden Ford and the arrival of Jason Momoa as Ronon Dex—and, later, of Jewel Staite as Carson Beckett's replacement, Jennifer Keller.

This development reduced Ford to a recurring character, and he only made a couple more appearances in that capacity without fully resolving his storyline. This left Sheppard without a trusted sidekick, but not for long. In the episode "Runner," which kicked off Ford's unfulfilled storyline, viewers were introduced to Ronon Dex, played by some actor you may or may not have heard of, Jason

Momoa.[1] Ronon is the titular runner, hunted by the Wraith for sport. He hates the Wraith and wants to see them eradicated from the galaxy. Plus, he's irreverent and an exceptional warrior, and he has little use for playing strictly by the rules. Naturally, Sheppard instantly likes the runner and adopts him as a member of his team.

The show would get through the rest of its sophomore run and most of the third season before the next departure. Toward the end of season three, in the episode "Sunday," Doctor Carson Beckett (Paul McGillion) was killed off. If you're experiencing a little déjà vu, that's to be expected, for three years earlier, Doctor Frasier had been killed off over on *SG-1*. It would seem to be a coincidence, except that both deaths were deliberately written to shake things up on each respective series – and both characters were doctors. Any inferred dislike of physicians by the franchise's producers is left for you, the readers, to interpret.

Rodney McKay (David Hewlett) and Carson Beckett (Paul McGillion) enjoyed a special friendship, making the physician's unexpected demise heartbreaking not only for the audience but also for Rodney.

---

[1] For those living under a rock, Momoa has become a household name since his *Stargate* days, thanks to the TV show *Game of Thrones*, as well as the films *Aquaman*, *Justice League*, and *Dune*.

At any rate, *Firefly*'s Jewel Staite was introduced in the season finale as Doctor Jennifer Keller, and she would continue as a recurring character throughout season four before being promoted to a regular for the final run of episodes. Keller proved immediately popular (who doesn't love Jewel Staite?) and was brilliant, kind, and compassionate. That she become romantically entangled with Rodney McKay is beyond belief, but that's where she ended the show. Oh, and Beckett was brought back, albeit as a clone of the original. Remember that bit at the beginning about how every character is someone's favorite? Well, *Atlantis*'s producers had *vastly* underestimated the number of viewers who had Carson Beckett as their number-one, and they realized it only too late. At least they kept Keller around after he came back, so it wasn't another Jonas Quinn situation.

Season four saw the cast remain stable throughout the rest of the show's run. Wait, no, that isn't true at all. What had been apparent with Aiden Ford during the first season of *Atlantis*, just as with Kate Pulaski on *Star Trek: The Next Generation*, was becoming crystal-clear with Elizabeth Weir, the civilian leader of Atlantis. Weir had originally been portrayed by Jessica Steen in the season-seven finale of *Stargate SG-1*, then Torri Higginson took over the role in the arc that launched the eighth season. She even briefly replaced General Hammond before leaving things in O'Neill's hands and moving on to take the lead role in the Atlantis expedition.

As discussed elsewhere in this anthology,[2] Weir was intended to be *Atlantis*'s analogue to General Hammond. This became frustrating for the actor, who was either relegated to the background or merely reacted to things and gave the other characters their marching orders. Eventually, the producers decided to do to Weir what hey had done to Ford, except this time involving an infection of replicator nanites. Basically, she became a threat and fled the city, with the promise that she would be a recurring character thereafter. As Higginson declined to return, however, Weir made a final appearance with a new face and... that was pretty much it.

Weir was replaced by Amanda Tapping's Samantha Carter for a season. Then, when Tapping left the franchise to write, produce, and star in her own series, *Sanctuary*, Richard Woolsley (Robert Picardo) stepped in for the final season. All

---

[2] See "Lonely at the Top: The Underused Leaders of *Stargate Atlantis*," by Keith R.A. DeCandido.

three characters were underutilized, which seems to have been due to the nature of the position they held. It could be said that it's a *good* problem to have an overabundance of strong characters and gifted actors, but part of a television show's development process should be to clearly define how each character fits within your story's framework.

What of *Stargate Universe*? During that show's two seasons, no major cast shakeups occurred. A couple recurring characters were killed, but none were replaced due to the nature of the show's "cut off from everyone" premise. The cast did expand during the second season, but not due to any actors leaving the lineup. Honorable mention could be awarded to the episode "Twin Destinies," in which, due to some timey-whimey shenanigans, both David Telford and Nicholas Rush are killed, with the former replaced by an alternate version of himself from twelve hours in the future, and the latter death being the Rush from that same near-future. It's complicated but makes for a neat take on an old science-fiction trope.

The webseries *Stargate Origins* lasted for only a single season, chronicling the untold story of young Catherine Langford. Had that show continued beyond its freshman storyline, it would apparently have taken on an anthology format and would have featured major cast changes from one season to the next as the writers delved into different characters' pasts – in other words, it would have epitomized the very essence of this essay. Regrettably, viewers never got to see those other stories or meet the other casts. As for the animated series, *Stargate Infinity*, that show never underwent any cast changes... unfortunately.

David Bowie, on his 1971 album *Hunky Dory*, included the following lyrics: "Ch-ch-ch-ch-changes / Turn and face the strange / Ch-ch-changes / There's gonna have to be a different man." The following year, the musician introduced his famous alter-ego Ziggy Stardust, an alien rock star worshipped as a prophet due to his predictions about the coming of a savior from the stars. It would appear Bowie himself was a prophet, for "Changes" reflects the *Stargate* franchise's revolving cast door despite its release a quarter-century before the show's debut.

What's more, Ziggy's "starman" prophecies match how the peasant populations in both the Milky Way and Pegasus Galaxies typically view the SG-1 and Atlantis teams every time they arrive through the local ring to save the day. Perhaps Bowie should have called his alter-ego Ziggy Stargate.

Stargate Merchandise: Why Isn't There More Stuff?

by Mark L. Haynes

When, in the spring of 1997, I first heard there would be a new TV show based on the film *Stargate*, it would be hard to describe how uninterested I was. Furthermore, when I found out it was going to star the guy from *MacGyver* (who also happened to be a producer) as Colonel Jack O'Neill (two L's? WTF?), I swore I'd never watch it. How in the world could they possibly improve on what I thought had been a kick-ass movie that had landed solidly in my "watch it anytime it's on" list?

Kurt Russell *was* Colonel Jack O'Neil (one L, like it's supposed to be), and James Spader *was* Doctor Daniel Jackson. Plus, Dean Devlin and Roland Emmerich were nowhere to be found and had nothing to do with the new show. Brad Wright? Never heard of him. How could this possibly be a worthy *Stargate* without their involvement? The answer was simple: it couldn't. Therefore, I swore I would accept no substitutes. Then I saw it. And I was blown away.

It was one of those free week/weekend previews that the premium cable channels used to offer to drum up subscriptions before streaming became the way humans consumed on-demand entertainment. During that weekend, Showtime (*Stargate*'s home at the time) was running a marathon of *Stargate SG-1*. I was gobsmacked. Not only was this show a worthy successor to the film, but it took the elements of that story and elevated them exponentially, beginning with the basic question of why someone would build a device like the stargate to visit only one other place.

From that humble starting point, Wright and his writing staff built out a universe that felt as real as the one in which we were living, except the relatable contemporary human (and later alien) characters in that universe traveled to other planets and defended ours as part of their day job. In effect, five years before Joss Whedon arrived with *Firefly* and blew people's minds with the idea that science fiction could also be funny on a regular basis, Wright created what could conceivably be billed as the first science-fiction workplace dramedy. Brilliant.

After that weekend, I was hooked. This was in the days before streaming, so if you wanted to see your favorite shows, you had to either videotape them or wait for DVD season sets to come out (which was just starting to become a thing at that point). I looked and looked but couldn't find *SG-1* on video anywhere. It seemed DVDs were available overseas but not here in the U.S. of A. What the what?!? Little did I realize at the time, this was my first encounter with a lack of licensed consumer products based on *Stargate SG-1* (and subsequent *Stargate* series), even though it would turn out to be for different reasons than we'll get into here.

That issue notwithstanding, I had become and still am a loyal fan – a "Gater," as some like to be called. Like most genre series fans, I not only like my shows, I also enjoy collecting things to remind me of my shows, especially when they're no longer being produced. *Stargate*'s genre cousins had done admirable jobs with this. *Star Trek* had a lot of stuff and, of course, *Star Wars* was the OG of modern licensed products, with its creator, George Lucas, famously giving up part of his director's fee for the original *Star Wars* film in favor of retaining the merchandising rights. Granted, both of these franchises had a head start, but that didn't change the fact that there just weren't many officially licensed *Stargate SG-1* products available – either when the show was still on the air or even now, years after *Stargate Universe* was cancelled.

I didn't think much about it after that, until I was approached to co-write *Stargate Atlantis* and *Stargate Universe* comic books for American Mythology. I had worked with other licensed producers by that point, having published Universal's classic *Battlestar Galactica* line under the Realm Press label from

1999 to 2001[1] and then writing an original comic series based on the Fox television show *24* for IDW Publishing from 2004 to 2006. In both instances, I and others involved developed decent working relationships with the studios behind those projects. We didn't get everything we wanted, to be sure, but we were able to do some things that were not only creatively satisfying (like bringing back the reptilian Cylons mentioned in the original *Galactica* pilot) but also greatly enhanced the enjoyment of those books for readers since they knew the writers and publishers were fans, too.

Beyond that, while I was working in and around licensed products as an employee of Diamond Comic Distributors, it became very clear to me that the most successful licensed collectibles where those for which the licensors and licensees collaborated on the final product. In this case, of course, collaboration doesn't mean the hand-in-glove involvement of a partner but more a willingness to let the licensee explore its area of the property to the extent that its creativity would allow, while the licensor kept the brand protected from going too far afield and damaging the intellectual property (IP). Ultimately, what it meant was that both parties wanted the licensee to succeed, so the licensor's brand managers stayed engaged and tried to figure out how to allow the licensee's creative vision to proceed. For most brands, this is not rocket science.

Before we delve too much further, we should establish what a licensed product actually is so we're working with the same definition. Loosely, a licensed product is one for which a manufacturer (like IDW, BOOM! Studios, or American Mythology) has entered into an agreement with an intellectual property owner (in this case, MGM Consumer Products) for the right to create and sell a specific product (or series of products) based on that IP. This agreement usually involves an initial payment (which can be many thousands of dollars, depending on the IP's popularity and the owner's plans for it), to be paid by the manufacturer along with a promise to pay additional royalties if the royalties on the product's sales exceed the initial advance payment.

---

[1] *Ed. note:* Co-editor Rich Handley provided editorial assistance on Realm Press's *Galactica* line as a favor to writer James Kuhoric. Neither Rich nor essayist Mark Haynes realized this connection until Rich read Mark's author bio submitted with this essay and said "Hey... I used to work for you!" For more information about Realm's efforts, as well as all other *Galactica* lore, see *Somewhere Beyond the Heavens: Exploring Battlestar Galactica*, co-edited by Handley and Lou Tambone (Sequart, 2018).

For example, when I was publishing comics based on *Battlestar Galactica*, I entered into an agreement with Universal Consumer Products by which the advance was $5,000 against a small percentage of net profits (I don't recall the exact figure). This would allow my company to publish a comic book line for two years and, if net profits grew to exceed that $5,000 amount, I'd start paying royalties. Most comic publishers will tell you the chances of reaching that figure in an increasingly congested marketplace, then or now, were and are exceedingly slim.

Of course, this was before the wave of nostalgia swept the industry and allowed companies that specialized in licensed material to rise. Either way, it seemed like a good deal to me at the time. I would later find out this was not the case, when I was asked to pony up an extra $10,000 once the property was moved from "library" status to "active" status due to a renewed interest in *Battlestar Galactica* – thanks, primarily, to the late Richard Hatch's seven *Galactica* novels then being released, as well as the first rumblings about new TV shows being developed for that franchise, including one by original series creator Glen A. Larson. Small-press budgets being what they are (exceedingly slim), I had no choice but to stand down and stop publishing.

What does any of this have to do with *Stargate* products or the lack thereof? With its history of only moderately successful licensors (with the exception of Fandemonium, the second licensed *SG1* and *Atlantis* publisher, which commissioned and produced *Stargate* novels steadily for more than a decade), it goes directly to both a manufacturer's ability to pay the advances required, as well as how easy a licensor is to work with. In the case of *Stargate*, most licensed manufacturers or publishers looked at the franchise, which had three series on the air consistently throughout a span of fifteen years, as a pretty safe bet. By all measures they had, it should have been, and for many it was. Diamond Select Toys, for example, offered a very successful line of collectible *SG-1* and *Atlantis* action figures in the mid-2000s, with nearly fifty variations of the major characters issued. I still have a few mint-on-card *Atlantis* figures tucked away somewhere.

Story-based products like comics, novels, audiobooks, and games had a harder time of it, however, and there are several reasons for that, including two that helped to make the series on which the products are based a fan favorite: continuity and canon. For the various *Stargate* TV shows, this powerful combination created a rich, lived-in universe in which characters were knowledgeable about their own history and developed relationships with each other, as well as with the audience. This ended up creating some of the most devoted and knowledgeable fans in the history of fandom. For licensed fiction products set in the *Stargate* franchise, this has been both a blessing and a curse.

Continuity, in television or film production terms, is defined as "the principle of making sure that all details in a film or TV show are consistent from shot to shot and from scene to scene."[2] In simpler terms of creative writing aspects of a television series, it means making sure that nothing (or almost nothing) that comes later in a series contradicts anything that may have come before. For the purposes of licensed *Stargate* fiction, it presented a creative hurdle for authors and editors in finding a place in a multi-series continuity, spanning more than 350 episodes across 14 consecutive years, in which to insert a story that would still have stakes for the characters but that wouldn't likely run afoul of whatever might come later.

That's not to say it can't be done. It has been, to great effect, by the team at Fandemonium, the official *SG-1* and *Atlantis* novel publisher, which has managed a nearly continuous run of novels lasting longer than the original series itself. My own publisher for the *Atlantis* and *Universe* comics would later have similar success, though it had the advantage of then-active *Stargate* television programs in production that could retroactively undermine one of its stories.

Canon, however, is a separate but related challenge for story-based licensees and, in my humble opinion, is far more problematic when it comes to the success or failure of a story-based licensed product. While an actual definition of canon remains a hotly contested subject in some online forums (and in real-world ones, too), for the purposes of this essay, canon, when applied to licensed products based on a film or a television series, means that the "official record" of the fictional universe portrayed is anything recorded on film.

Recently, some have suggested that it could also encompass anything written by the creator of the IP, although the argument against that notion, at least as far as television goes, is that many writers contribute to what becomes canon, at least under the prevailing definition. One of the best examples of this is *Star Trek*, created by Gene Roddenberry. His original outlines and scripts contained much of what the series would become. What they didn't contain were things like Klingons, created by John D.F. Black, and just about all of Vulcan

---

[2] masterclass.com/articles/how-to-maintain-continuity-in-film; Sept 2021.

culture, which was created by Shimon Wincelberg (who developed the mind meld in the classic episode "Dagger of the Mind") and D.C. Fontana (who created just about everything else for "Amok Time" and "Journey to Babel").

That combination of continuity and canon can be a double-edged sword, not only for story-based licensed products but sometimes for the series itself. About two-thirds of the way through the initial run of *Stargate SG-1*, a Hollywood writer and former mentor of mine, who had extensive writing and producing credits in genre television, was approached about pitching or contributing a script to the series. Not being a regular watcher of the show, he asked for reference material to be sent.

When the boxes (yes, *boxes* – plural) arrived, he was daunted to find about a dozen binders covering everything you ever wanted to know about the fictional world of Stargate Command, its frontline team, and the geopolitical state of the Milky Way (this was pre-Ori). Overwhelmed by the material, my friend had to pass on the assignment. I was sad to hear that, because this person is an amazing writer and would have done wonders with an episode. At the same time, though, I was curious about what had happened to the reference material (for research purposes, of course) and was disappointed to learn the producers had sent a messenger to retrieve it.

Similar challenges can be faced by creators and publishers of story-based licensed *Stargate* products. With a continuity woven so tightly, it can be difficult to find a place to continue a story, or to insert a new story into the existing storylines across the three shows, and still come up with something that's compelling for the reader, rather than just a small type of side mission. Further, mixed with *Stargate* fandom's devotion to canon, which can exceed even that of fans of larger or more well-established franchises, the slightest misstep can alienate the very fans a publisher or creator is trying to reach.

It's not impossible, however, and based on fan reaction, it's safe to say Fandemonium, Big Finish Productions, and American Mythology have each created new stories that overcame the continuity-canon double jeopardy. In fact, one online reviewer, while discussing American Mythology's *Stargate Atlantis: Gateways* #1, described it as "one of the absolute best renditions of [a] television show converted to comics that I've had the pleasure to read."[3]

---

[3] readingwithaflightring.weebly.com/reviews/stargate-atlantis-gateways-1; Dec 2016.

Another early success story that avoided both continuity and canon pitfalls saw publisher Penguin Books going back to the original feature film as its basis for licensed products. Beginning with an adaptation of the movie by Dean Devlin and Roland Emmerich (with Stephen Molstad on ghostwriting detail) published in 1994, *Stargate* officially entered the prose media tie-in world. From there, Penguin proceeded with a series of five novels by Bill McCay, published between 1995 and 1999. The first three books, *Rebellion*, *Retaliation*, and *Retribution*, formed a trilogy that had been developed using consulting notes from director Emmerich regarding where he would have gone if additional films had been commissioned.

The books dug deep into the aftermath of Earth's first successful trip to another planet through the stargate, with military, political, and commercial interests on Earth hungry to get their hands on the mineral (not yet named) being mined by the Abydans (as they were then called) while also facing off against powerful new associates of Ra who were angry that the status quo had been upset. Although McCay's books were generally well received, they would also be the franchise's first brush with brand confusion, as some fans didn't realize they were based on the original film and not the new television series, with one online fan commenting, "[I] didn't know there had been book tie-ins with the TV series, [but] *Rebellion* [is] a rollicking adventure ride." Another reader, who had recognized the novels were based on the movie and not *SG-1*, posted, "Very different from the TV series. But it's entertaining and the writing is good."[4]

McCay would return to the writer's seat for two more volumes based on events from the film, titled *Reconnaissance* and *Resistance*. Serving mainly as follow-ups to the above-mentioned trilogy, these books dug deeper into the ramifications of Earth's first mission through the stargate and were the first to suggest the gate could bring travelers to more planets than just Abydos, though it would be far fewer than the thousands suggested on *SG-1*. Indeed, Devlin would later confirm that he and Emmerich had consulted with McCay, telling the *Dial the Gate* podcast that "We worked with him on those original [novels], and I'm real proud of those and I support those entirely." He added, "McCay is a really good writer. He's really engaging."[5]

---

[4] amazon.com/Rebellion-Stargate-1-Bill-McCay/dp/0451455029/
[5] gateworld.net/news/2020/10/mayan-stargate-dean-devlin-reveals-original-stargate-trilogy-plans/

Author Bill McKay's highly regarded *Stargate* novels focused on the concepts introduced in the theatrical film.

A lot of *Stargate* spinoff fiction, such as McCay's novels, has been quite good. However, when it goes bad, it *really* goes bad — and as buying fans, we tend to have long memories. One of the first *Stargate SG-1* novels, *The Morpheus Factor* by Ashley McConnell, published by ROC in 2001, managed to be written, edited, approved by MGM Consumer Products, and finally published with Samantha Carter being referred to as Amanda Carter (mixing actor Amanda Tapping's name with that of the fictional person she portrays) at various points throughout the book. Beyond the technical mistakes like this one, one Amazon reviewer summarized the book this way:

Seldom do you get such a clear idea of why a series of books has been discontinued. The author not only got several key details wrong (calling Daniel a blonde, at one point referring to Amanda Carter), but the story was convoluted and pointless. How did they get home? How'd they get past the aliens? We don't know and, I believe, neither does [the author]. If they plan to make more *Stargate SG-1* books, perhaps they could find someone who has actually seen an episode or two.[6]

The *Stargate* novels and short stories have continued the television casts' exploits. The first book shown, *The Morpheus Factor*, resulted in the author's deal being canceled, but Fandemonium later rescued the franchise's licensed publishing.

---

[6] amazon.com/Stargate-SG-1-Morpheus-Ashley-McConnell/dp/0451458168; May 2002.

While this book was an epic failure for the publisher and for the franchise – and resulted in the author's contract being cancelled because of simple mistakes that should have been caught – the bigger issue is that fans were burned. For three years, at that point, all they had wanted was more and deeper information and interaction with characters they already loved and wanted to know better. This book promised that but fell far short, which made fans gun-shy going into subsequent novels until Fandemonium took over from ROC in 2004. Fandemonium would go on to become one of the most durable and prolific licensees, and it continues with new entries to its line of more than 60 novels, novellas, and short stories.

Fandemonium publisher and editor Sally Malcolm discovered the "secret sauce" to making story-based *Stargate* products viable: make sure the writers and creators were fans of the franchise first, because the knowledge of the franchise, combined with their joy at doing what they're doing, comes through in the work. As Malcolm said in an interview conducted for this essay:

> When we first started publishing *Stargate* novels, we never imagined we'd still be going strong eighteen years later. As *Stargate* fans, we started our business with the objective of bringing the perspective we have as fans of the show into the novels we publish, and I believe that's been a big part of the success of Fandemonium Books. We love being part of the *Stargate* community, meeting fellow fans at events and conventions around the world, and to still be here, creating original *Stargate* stories thirteen years after *Stargate Atlantis* came to an end, is a real honor.

The success of the Fandemonium novel series paralleled the production and release of *Stargate SG-1* and *Stargate Atlantis* audio adventures from British company Big Finish Productions. Produced and released from 2008 through 2012, these enhanced audio dramas were unique in that they featured one main member of the original cast both narrating the episodes, as well as reprising their roles alongside a special guest character. The episodes were further enhanced by the use of familiar musical scores and sound effects from the shows.

Several actors from both *SG-1* and *Atlantis* participated in the Big Finish audio dramas, including Michael Shanks (Daniel Jackson), Claudia Black (Vala Mal Doran), Cliff Simon (Ba'al), Teryl Rothery (Janet Fraiser), Gary Jones (Walter Harriman), Paul McGillion (Carson Beckett), Torri Higginson (Elizabeth Weir), and many more. Later, the audios evolved from being traditional audio book-style productions to full-cast audio plays.[7] While no longer available directly from Big

---

[7] en.wikipedia.org/wiki/List_of_Stargate_audiobooks; Feb 2022.

Finish due to what its website terms a "rights issue," these stories are worth tracking down on eBay or elsewhere online, if for no other reason than to hear your favorite actors in character once again. Listening to a clip that I was able to find online resulted in my buying a couple for myself!

Audiobooks featuring cast members have further expanded the world of licensed *Stargate* literature.

On the comic book front, things proved to be a bit more challenging. After one miniseries and a handful of one-shot stories from Entity Comics based on the original *Stargate* feature film, Avatar Publishing entered the arena with the first comic books based on the television series, releasing the *Stargate SG-1 Convention Special* in 2003, followed by ten issues distributed between one-shots and miniseries. Avatar's *Stargate* work, like many licensed and non-licensed books coming from small to mid-size comic publishers, became the victim of a minimal marketing budget, which resulted in the issues not receiving much attention outside direct-market comic stores.

Furthermore, problems arose during production, when intricate pencil art that exquisitely captured the actors' likenesses (even in smaller panels) was almost completely obliterated by a substandard coloring job. I recall seeing both the before and after and was devastated, not just because I wanted to see these characters in action again, but because a friend of mine had written the book. It was so bad, in fact, that one page featured characters with teeth so white they wouldn't have needed locator beacons to be beamed up to the *Daedalus* – they could've just looked up and smiled, and they would have been visible from orbit. However, while the comics didn't gain the traction Avatar would have liked, fans were generally positive about what they were reading and were happy to see their favorite characters back in new adventures. One GoodReads reviewer noted, "This was a short *Stargate* comic, but it still really gave me the feels at the end."[8]

Several comic publishers have charted new adventures for the mythos, based not only on the 1994 movie but also its televised continuations, some scripted by this essay's author.

After Avatar stood down from publishing, the license moved to Dynamic Forces, a company well-known for its extensive line of licensed comics and variant-cover special editions. Two miniseries released in 2010, *Stargate: Vala Mal Doran* and *Stargate: Daniel Jackson*, saw Brandon Jerwa (a fellow writer with an essay of his own in the volume you're reading[9]) and Doug Murray, respectively, take over as *Stargate* scribes. Regarding *Vala Mal Doran*, fans were

---

[8] goodreads.com/book/show/52053180-stargate-sg-1; Aug 2019.
[9] See Jerwa's "Fear and Loathing in Cheyenne Mountain," elsewhere in this volume.

generally pleased with Jerwa's fun romp through Vala's infamous past as she organizes a massive caper ("Vala doing what Vala does best: shenanigans"), even though some felt, based on fan reviews, that the visual aspect of the comic (many non-humanoid aliens) had been inspired more by *Star Wars* than by *Stargate*.[10] Less well received was Murray's *Daniel Jackson*, which some readers enjoyed but which many felt didn't capture any of the characters well in terms of their behavior, relationships, dialog, or appearance — which is an important consideration in licensed comics featuring original artwork.[11]

Following Dynamic Forces' turn with the license, BOOM! Studios announced in 2014 that it would publish a four-issue miniseries based on *Stargate: Extinction*, the script for a *Stargate Atlantis* television or direct-to-DVD movie that had been written by Joseph Mallozzi and Paul Mullie. As reported by *GateWorld* owner Daren Sumner (represented with his own essay in this volume[12]), the rights for the script rested with MGM. Comic industry insiders familiar with the issues have mentioned to me that an agreement couldn't be reached with MGM on how to proceed with the rights or with a production and approvals schedule that would allow BOOM! to meet commitments to comic book retailers. After a somewhat enthusiastic announcement from BOOM! about the creative teams, as well as a small teaser of the story, nothing further was heard about the project.

After several years, American Mythology was the next publisher to try its hand at comic book versions of two of the shows in the franchise. The company hired me and noted comic writer J.C. Vaughn[13] to relaunch comic book versions of *Stargate Atlantis* (with a series of four three-issue miniseries) and *Stargate Universe* (with a six-issue series). Originally intending to license all three shows with an eye toward the types of crossover events that were fan favorites of the live-action series, MGM withheld the license for *Stargate SG-1* for undisclosed reasons, only suggesting it first wanted to see how well American Mythology did with the other two.

---

[10] amazon.com/Stargate-Doran-Dynamite-Brandon-2010-12-28/dp/B01FIZ8SI2; June 2017 and Mar 2012.

[11] amazon.com/Stargate-Daniel-Jackson-Doug-Murray/dp/1606901982/; Apr 2011.

[12] See Sumner's "Faith and False Gods: Religion in *Stargate SG-1*," elsewhere in this volume.

[13] Vaughan had written for Realm's *Battlestar Galactica* line as well.

Once again, fan response was warm and, in some cases, enthusiastic – with regard to both our portrayals of the characters and our adherence to established continuity – but there was a critical mass of fans who were not interested in something that was not considered canon. This, of course, translated into somewhat lackluster sales, even thought it was among American Mythology's best-selling titles for the years in which these comics were published.

Since this was my first time "on the inside" when it came to licensed *Stargate* products, I can tell you it was an eye-opening experience. I had long been curious about why there wasn't more *Stargate* merchandise. As you've read, there were several unfortunate "perfect storms" of circumstances that had caused fans to be less than interested in licensed products from the franchise. Indeed, I feel one of the main reasons licensed *Stargate* products, especially story-based ones, had a hard time getting traction in any significant way was that the shows on which they were based were still on the air and fans could get plenty of *Stargate* from their screens.

By way of example, *Star Trek* didn't really take hold in the licensed product arena until the original show had entered syndication. *Star Wars*, meanwhile, had diminished considerably in mass-market consumer awareness by the early 1990s, when the publication of Timothy Zahn's novel *Heir to the Empire* and Tom Veitch's and Cam Kennedy's *Dark Empire* comic miniseries were released.[14] After that, the respective licensors of those properties saw the power licensed product could have to keep awareness of series in the public eye, so they leaned into it, developing robust licensing programs.

MGM, on the other hand, has chosen a much smaller focus for its consumer products development strategy, at least with regard to the *Stargate* franchise. Speculation suggested it may have had something to do with a deal negotiated by MGM's hedge fund owners[15] at the time, which may have led to the cancellation of both *Atlantis* and *Universe* on television, contrary to published reports from Syfy that the decisions were based on ratings. In either case, MGM Consumer Products has been much less aggressive about finding and supporting licensees than its competitors at CBS Viacom and Lucasfim/Disney.

---

[14] Despite high-quality storytelling from Marvel Comics, including from writer Jo Duffy, also featured in this anthology – see her essay "The Furlings: From Paradise Lost to Lost Opportunity."

[15] hollywoodreporter.com/business/business-news/why-mgm-choosing-spyglass-over-26627/; Aug 2010.

Another important behind-the-scenes element that, in my experience, was a contributing factor to the success (or lack thereof) for some *Stargate* licensed products was the relationship between the licensors and MGM Consumer Products. Generally, such relationships were always professional and cordial, but it also brought into sharp relief the difference in budgets and economics both were used to, as well as issues involved in the legalities behind three shows that an audience might view as a single franchise, while those on the inside must deem them three separate legal entities.

For example, as we were developing the stories for both comic lines, we thought of a great idea that would allow some characters from *Atlantis* and *Universe* to appear in the opposite comic. From our perspective, character crossover events were a hallmark of the series, and we wanted to bring that to the comics. Instead, we ran headlong into actor contracts and other legalities covering the characters and the IP to which they "belonged," and we were denied multiple requests of this nature. As a businessperson, I understood that – it's the nature of business, and MGM has to protect itself legally, according to the contracts it had signed with the casts of these shows. As a creator and fan, however, I found it maddening.

Whenever things like this cropped up, Vaughn and I liked to think we could find clever ways to work around it in our stories. For instance, when we began working on the *Stargate Universe* comic, our plan was to have our story pick up right where the show had left off. The idea was that we could bring some closure to that series, as well as set up future writers who may follow us on the American Mythology book. MGM Consumer Products, however, let us know that the *Universe* actors had control over their likeness rights (unlike the two previous shows, with the exception of Richard Dean Anderson, since those rights were included in the license), and that David Blue, who had played Eli Wallace on TV, wished some changes made to how his character was drawn.

You see, between the time the TV show had ended and when we had started writing the comic book, Blue had hit the gym hard, had changed his diet, and had completely transformed his body. Being justifiably proud of his work, he wasn't super-enthusiastic with the comic version of Eli looking like he did on television. In order to proceed without needing to get new artist character model sheets for approval, we wrote Eli getting into shape into our story, as a way to think about solving the problem. David was happy and signed off on this, and we were happy since we could celebrate his accomplishment while adding an interesting element to the adventure. It worked out well, but we did gnash our teeth when we were first told about it.

Anyone who has worked in or around licensed products will likely have similar stories to tell, but even as tough as it may get, they keep coming back, not only because they are fans who want to see more, but because they know there are other fans out there who do, too. Going forward, the prospects for the *Stargate* licensed products seem bright. Amazon has acquired MGM and its entire library, greatly increasing the chances of a new *Stargate* television series.[16] Fandemonium has recently renewed its license, so new *SG-1* and *Atlantis* prose fiction is already in the pipeline. And American Mythology is in negotiations to resume publishing both *Atlantis* and *Universe* comics, and it will, hopefully, be able to add *SG-1* to its lineup as well.

In addition to returning licensees, new companies continue to develop ideas, too. Wyvern Games recently released an *SG-1* roleplaying game, which includes a beautiful, full-color manual with in-depth information on *Stargate* characters, history, species, planets, technology, and more. This is the successor to Alderac Entertainment Group's *SG-1* RPG, released in 2003. Drawn to the company's convention booth by the nearly full-sized stargate that dominated that space, I recently saw (and bought, naturally) Wyvern's product, and I'm not even a gamer — it's *that* good! Along with the game's core rulebook, there are episodic adventures that further expand the available offerings of *Stargate* fiction, and plans are currently underway to expand the RPG to include elements from both *Atlantis* and *Universe*.

Fans continue to woo major manufacturers to take a look at *Stargate* through unique and innovative ways. One fan recently created his own custom Lego set, replicating Stargate Command and SG-1 in all of their blocky, barefoot-murdering glory.[17] MGM, Lego, the other licensees mentioned, and those we haven't yet heard from all look at and count on fan support through both social media and, more importantly, sales to measure how much time, energy, and money they'll put toward a product. Going online and letting them know that you want more through your purchases, your comments, your likes, and your shares could mean more *Stargate* for us, and for future fans.

---

[16] syfy.com/syfy-wire/stargate-revival-latest-news; Nov 2021.
[17] youtube.com/watch?v=2u02R1JnF6M

Fear and Loathing in Cheyenne Mountain

by Brandon Jerwa

Working on the *Stargate* comics for Dynamite Entertainment was an interesting – and, at times, wildly unpredictable – experience for me as a writer. When the opportunity first came my way, there was a plan for multiple comic projects in a larger universe of titles connected to the various incarnations of the franchise. Things changed drastically along the way, however, and when all was said and done, the only *Stargate* comic material out there with my name on it ended up being a 2010 five-issue miniseries about Vala Mal Doran, which I had a heck of a lot of fun writing.[1]

I had been working on Dynamite's *Battlestar Galactica* comics based on Ron Moore's rebooted television series, and that was proving to be a perfect match.[2] I had grown up in the 1970s and '80s, so science-fiction television had been a regular part of my nerd upbringing, as common as action figures and colorful, sugary breakfast cereals.

The original *Stargate* theatrical movie was very enjoyable, but I felt that it got lost in the science-fiction action shuffle that was happening at the time. So

---

[1] *Stargate: Vala Mal Doran*, illustrated by Cezar Razek.

[2] See my essay "Sticking With Dynamite: A Tale of Two *Galacticas*," published in Sequart's *Somewhere Beyond the Heavens: Exploring Battlestar Galactica*, edited by Rich Handley and Lou Tambone (2018).

many movies were trying to be the next big thing in that arena. I liked it, but I honestly didn't think about it too much after I saw it. When *Stargate SG-1* came along, it was a better fit for my tastes. I was a late adopter, but I found a lot to love once I got my feet wet.

When I was a child, my uncle was in the U.S. Air Force. He was a communications officer aboard *Air Force One*, and that was just one of the cool and very classified jobs he had. I found everything he did incredibly fascinating. Cheyenne Mountain and NORAD were things that existed in my immediate childhood reality; I was familiar with them beyond basic cultural awareness, all thanks to my uncle's service. Even as a kid, I assumed the government had to have been hiding all sorts of strange things in their massive mountain facilities, ranging from UFOs to high-tech weapons to giant robots.

Stargate offered a cool balance between fantastic science fiction and the sort of military action that I grew up loving, thanks to *G.I. Joe* and a wide array of military-themed action movies and TV shows. Plus, it totally proved out my suspicions about Cheyenne Mountain! The other big point of appeal for me was the show's sense of humor. *Stargate* knows that it doesn't have to always take itself seriously, and that's why it's so fun. The heroes recognize that their lives and careers are slightly absurd, and it makes them a little more relatable. I love truly grim science fiction, but things don't have to be dark all the time.

It's fair to say that I was never a diehard *Stargate* fan, at least not in comparison to most of the other contributors in this anthology. In fact, I'm still not. (Gee, I hope that announcement doesn't get me thrown out of this book!) Don't misunderstand me, I loved *SG-1* – but while I've definitely watched all of the episodes, I never dug much into the various spinoffs at any significant length. That's completely about me, not a commentary on the quality of the shows; you can only *watch* so many things, especially when you have to *do* so many things because you *write about* so many things.

In doing my research for this essay, I had to go back and revisit the entire affair. My memory of it is so clouded in places that I had to find articles, press releases, and interviews regarding my own role in the *Stargate* universe. There were projects I was supposed to be involved with that never came about, most notably *Stargate* #0, a one-shot that had been meant to serve as a teaser for Dynamite's then-new comics universe. In addition to material by other creators, this preview issue would have featured an *SG-1* story by yours truly.

Alas, Dynamite's intended *Stargate* #0 one-shot was never published, as it would have featured characters from *SG-1*, *Atlantis*, and *Universe*.

I found an interview online in which I had discussed having a year-long plan for storylines, and I even provided a preview of some of the details, yet I had forgotten almost everything about it! That's often how it goes (for me, at least) in the world of freelance licensed comics, especially if you're lucky enough to work on multiple books at once – you put everything you have into the effort, but it turns into vapor and floats away if the project goes south. You file it, you forget it, and you go about getting the next gig.

In looking over the short teaser script, I can tell you that Daniel Jackson does a lot of eating in it. I am also reminded that my attempt to name a character "Dilworth" (after my good friend Joe, whose name you may have noticed on this book) was shot down by whoever was reviewing my scripts on the *Stargate* side, as they asked me to pick a different name that "wasn't so silly." Sorry, Joe.

The truth is, I have no recollection of these lost storylines, and I am completely mystified as to what the bigger picture might have been. I lost a lot of early comic pitch files and outlines in a massive computer crash a few years ago, and *Stargate* was clearly a casualty. I'm sure I have copious notes somewhere, lost forever on the digital frontier. Perhaps future generations will unearth them and reboot *Stargate* in 2095, guided by my creative genius. Maybe they'll name a character Dilworth.

One personal observation from my trip through the archives: I don't think the comic universe had much of a chance as originally planned. This is no reflection whatsoever on the quality of the team involved, but there was a definite push to make a comic that tied closely into the events of the TV shows, expanding upon long-running storylines and filling in gaps between specific episodes. I can't speak for every element of the plan, but even my own material seems to have been lacking any kind of welcome mat for a comic reader who was not fully up to speed on the details of the franchise.

This is not an uncommon approach to licensed books, mind you; one could make the argument that we were doing exactly the same thing with our *Battlestar Galactica* stories. I would defend those books as having been enjoyable for readers with a general knowledge beyond the basic concept and character types of the source material, but full of subtle rewards and payoffs for hardcore fans. In the case of *Stargate*, there were certainly discussions about being far more specific and episode-level continuity-driven.

Whatever happened with the various *Stargate* projects that were initially on the table, it was eventually decided that I would be handling a character-specific miniseries as my first proper outing as a *Stargate SG-1* writer. Just as the company had done with *Galactica*, Dynamite offered me a list of characters for potential starring roles. As soon as I saw Vala Mal Doran on that list, I sent an email to make sure she wouldn't be snapped up by anyone else. Portrayed to perfection by Claudia Black, Vala Mal Doran was the ideal kind of character for me to write about: clever, sarcastic, and not afraid to raise an eyebrow at, or to point and laugh at, the absurdity of her own fictional universe. Vala's reactions to the world(s) around her often synched with my own reactions as a viewer. She was the classic fly in the ointment, the rogue with a sense of honor and loyalty to the people she cared about. She was, in short, a character ripe for storytelling, and she lived in a universe that allowed for a wide variety of science-fiction riffs. What could be more fun than pushing that to its limits? It was also a good chance to build a story that I could take outside of the TV plots, hopefully making it fun and understandable for anyone who read it. Admittedly, you can see me going full *Star Wars* in some scenes. I'm not ashamed.

I got caught up on *SG-1* just before all of this started, so the timing had been perfect. The parameters of the solo story allowed me to stay focused on my character and how she related to the rest of the universe, rather than having to tackle the entire universe all at once. There are really two stories in this miniseries, although they are tied closely to one another. The first half of the book is about Vala on a mission before her *Stargate* days, rounding up an *Ocean's Eleven*-style heist crew of weird aliens to steal something from a crime lord. There are deceptions and double-crosses all over the place, and I tried to have fun with it. The second half moves into the world of *SG-1*, with Vala now a valued team member. Unfortunately, her actions in the first half come back to haunt her and her friends in the second, in ways bigger than she could have imagined. It's a familiar trope for *Stargate* fans, because Vala's checkered past came back to haunt her fairly frequently on television.

Dynamite Entertainment's *Stargate: Vala Mal Doran* miniseries, written by this essay's author, was illustrated by Cezar Razek.

The comics further explored Claudia Black's wonderfully unpredictable thief, con artist, ex-Goa'uld host, and SG-1 team member, Vala.

The miniseries was an open-and-shut story that wrapped up and required no connectivity to any other possible *Stargate* comics we might have been working on – but it could have been, if needed! While the story of my actual contribution to the universe is fairly short, I'd like to tell you a couple of fun anecdotes about my interactions in and around the franchise that happened as a result of my involvement with the comics. There was one point, pre-*Vala*, when I was supposed to work on a comic that was tied to a particular component of *Stargate*. I'm not going to be specific about this at all, concealing the names to protect the guilty and all that. What I *can* tell you is...

The person reviewing my previous work in licensed science-fiction comics really went for the throat during a telephone meeting with me and my editor. They didn't feel that my *Galactica* work – offered as samples for consideration – qualified me for *Stargate* because, as this person noted, "There's a lot of violence and sex in this: why would you make such a choice?" I explained that I had made that choice because those were very common threads and concepts within the reimagined *Galactica*. Then I assured this person that I would never do anything like that in a *Stargate* book.

My editor defended me, confirming that I had his full trust in being able to understand the difference between two separate franchises. This particular person was not content, however, and continued to rail on me throughout the phone call. I hadn't written anything for this project yet, as this was our first meeting on the subject. This person simply felt that my *Battlestar Galactica* story was not a very good *Stargate* story at all. And I couldn't agree more... because it wasn't *supposed* to be!

Strangely, the person on this call, whose job it was to have an everyday understanding of *Stargate*... seemed to be the one who had the hardest time not understanding that *Stargate* wasn't *Battlestar Galactica*. In any event, this phone call is in my personal history book, because it was the first time I'd ever had a licensor more or less directly insult my intelligence, and also the first time an editor ever asked me to leave a meeting because he wasn't going to allow me to be subjected to verbal abuse any further. It was *not* a normal experience. OK, I suppose that story wasn't as fun as advertised, but this one from the 2009 San Diego Comic-Con will be...

Stargate Universe had been announced and there was a party at a hotel rooftop bar near the convention center. I attended the party with the above-noted Joe Dilworth. There, we made a couple of friends and begin to enjoy the festivities. I saw actress Ming-Na Wen across the room, and my head started to spin a little. I'm a huge fan, from long before she became the queen of geek heroes across multiple franchises, and her presence cannot be ignored. So much power and grace and absolute radiance. That's the only way I can describe it.

The people I was sharing a table with were laughing at me. I was clearly starstruck by this actor who was halfway across the room. Joe and I decided to get some food. We ended up next to Robert Carlyle at the buffet; we paid him just a few of the compliments he deserves for the whole of his work, and he was incredibly kind and friendly in return.

Just as I returned to the table after my short moment away, I felt a hand on my shoulder. A distinct woman's voice said, "Excuse me." I turned around, and it was *her*. Talk about an unauthorized offworld activation. I cannot overstate how bizarre it was to be in that moment. Before I finish the story, let's pause so I can prove that it really happened with this photo from the encounter. Please note that one of us is a beautiful and immensely talented actress, and the other is a slovenly comic writer in a daze. I'll let you figure out which one is which.

The experience becomes a blur at this point in my memory. Therefore, I reached out to Joe Dilworth to find out what he recalled – which, it turns out, wasn't much. With his trademark thoughtful analysis, Joe offered one memory that may clarify our lack of clarity: "It was an open bar." Ever in search of my personal *Stargate* truth, I turned to a far more reliable participant in the night's events, former Dragon*Con *Stargate* content track director and exceedingly

While writing comics based on *Stargate Universe*, Brandon Jerwa, a longtime fan of actor Ming-Na Wen, was delighted to meet her at last.

pleasant person Jen Baker, who recalled the following:

> So, it was July 2009, at SDCC, the night of the *Stargate Universe* launch party. I met you and Joe for the first time in the bar while we were waiting to go up to the hotel roof for the party itself. We discussed my affection for Amanda Tapping and your hopeful excitement to meet Ming-Na Wen. Once we got up to the party, you and I and Joe and my mom grabbed one of the tables and chatted with passersby, as well as some of the mingling actors from the new *Stargate* show.
>
> At one point, Ming-Na came by, much to your shocked happiness, and said "hi" to me for reasons yet unbeknownst to you, and then looked at you and said, "Wait a minute, aren't you Brandon Jerwa? Didn't you write some of the *Stargate* comics?" To which you completely went blank-faced, about 16 shades of pale and red all at the same time, and rapidly looked back and forth from me to Ming-Na to me, told me adamantly that you hated me, and she burst out laughing and so did I. You got hugs, I got pictures, and forever The Great Prank lives in blessed infamy.
>
> The piece you were missing at the time is that I had actually met her on the other side of the roof while discussing with her which drink to grab off the passing tray. I pointed you out to her across the crowd, and asked her to come by and say hello, telling her you were a huge fan. She was an

absolutely amazing human and I wish we could hang out again, but alas, she got a thousand times more famous.

I'm glad *someone* did! I may not have gained fame and fortune from my strange and unpredictable time in the *Stargate* universe, but I came away with a fun miniseries that I'm proud to have my name on, and a handful of interesting – if slightly cloudy – memories and encounters that I'll treasure for... well, for as long as I remember them, in any case.

I'd love to see *Stargate* make a return in some form. There's clearly still a devoted fanbase out there, and the premise is eternally overflowing with potential. If the franchise is ever looking for characters with silly names and multiple scenes featuring Daniel Jackson eating, I'm available.

The world of licensed comics is a bizarre wasteland; you may find yourself freelancing for a tyrannical overlord or being left in charge of a sweet vintage ride with marching orders no more specific than "Don't scratch the paint." *Stargate* left me with a stack of weird stories, and I'm far more appreciative of that than I could ever be of fame or a paycheck. Maybe someone will crack the *Stargate* comic code to great success someday, but I'll be damned if I have the million-dollar idea. Like the secrets within Cheyenne Mountain, it remains tantalizingly elusive.

Gates, Galaxies, and Globalization: *SG-1* and Science Fiction in the Digital Age

by Val Nolan

One of the more obvious advantages of science fiction as a genre is its capacity to offer a version of the present in allegorical form, a vision of the world which "sends back more reliable information about the contemporary world than an exhausted realism."[1] Read in this fashion, the *Stargate* franchise has profound things to say not about distant planets or alien overlords, but about the highly globalized digital age in which we live.

The franchise's central conceit, the existence of a fictional stargate network which, through the transformation of physical matter into data, provides instantaneous travel across interstellar distances, reduces the galaxy itself to an analogy of the global village. Indeed, the prevalence of actual villages depicted on the majority of planets visited by the protagonists of *Stargate SG-1* (1997–2007) and *Stargate Atlantis* (2004–2009) pleasingly conflates Marshall

---

[1] Jameson, Fredric, "Fear and Loathing in Globalization," *New Left Review* 23 (2003): pp. 105-14 (p. 105).

McLuhan's twin metaphors of "Global Village" and "Gutenberg Galaxy" into something new: the Galactic Village, a constant reminder of exactly how stargate travel collapses distance, and, on occasion, time.[2]

This collision of globalization and digitality is, moreover, a dramatization of the kinds of time-space compression, cultural flattening and associated U.S.-centrism brought about by the increasing pervasiveness of the Internet in people's lives. Indeed, one of the more surprising elements of *Stargate SG-1* is how literally it manifests the concerns of the millennial moment, how it predicts and engages with technological change as well as the accompanying economic unease, and how it suggests the manner by which these upheavals were received and processed by its original audience.

Stargate SG-1's longevity and cultural impact has earned it comparisons with series such as *The X-Files* (1993–2002), *Buffy the Vampire Slayer* (1997–2003), *Babylon 5* (1993–1998), and *Farscape* (1999–2003): "Only the UK's apparently immortal *Doctor Who* and Gene Roddenberry's constantly reincarnated *Star Trek* franchise have exceeded the staying power of *Stargate SG-1* and its offspring."[3] Extant critical work on the *Stargate* franchise has critiqued how it utilizes the "alien as ancient god" imagery and how it draws upon the "pseudoarchaeological theories of Erich von Daniken."[4] Some, like Jan-Johnson Smith, have examined the show's "clear militaristic leanings" while others have engaged with episodes in intriguing if niche fashions, such as reading them as objects of mathematical curiosity.[5] Yet only rarely does the development of late 1990s digitality appear in criticism of the franchise and, when it does, it is primarily in connection with real-world production issues or online fan communities.

Smith's discussion of digitality is concerned solely with matters of special effects and commuter-generated imagery, while Rachel McGrath-Kerr dwells upon the interaction of female viewers with the character of Samantha Carter

---

[2] McLuhan, Marshall, *The Gutenberg Galaxy*. Toronto: University of Toronto Press, 1962: p.31.

[3] Beeler, Stan, and Lisa Dickson, eds. *Reading Stargate SG-1*. London: I.B. Tauris, 2006: p. 2.

[4] Hiscock, Peter, "Cinema, Supernatural Archaeology, and the Hidden Human Past," *Numen* 59.2/3 (2012): pp. 156-77 (p. 169-170).

[5] Smith, Jan-Johnson. *American Science Fiction TV: Star Trek, Stargate, and Beyond*. London: I.B. Tauris, 2005. p. 9. See also Evans, Ron, and Lihua Huang, "Mind Switches in *Futurama* and *Stargate*," *Mathematics Magazine* 87:4 (2014): 252-262.

"through fan fiction and online discussion."[6] Jo Storm acknowledges the show's production during a time of increasing "inclusion (some might say intrusion) of the Internet in our lives," and how online culture was important to the development of *Stargate* fandom, leading to a way "of looking at television series that has never before been possible."[7] That said, while *SG-1* is framed as "not only an escapist adventure series, but also a kind of mirror," Storm's discussion of the show's engagement with digitality limits itself to how episodes such as "Ascension" (2001) were written in response to "fans on the Internet [...] asking to see more about the characters' personal lives."[8]

Nonetheless, the origins and development of the *Stargate* franchise's core themes, and those of *SG-1* in particular, are impossible to separate from the collision of digitality, the Internet, and online culture with the forces of globalized capitalism in the late 1990s and early 2000s. In that respect, the franchise is proof of the widely held maxim that science fiction is always about the time in which it is written, for "what is perhaps most interesting about the series is that it is set in the present."[9] Its protagonists are "ordinary humans, not emotionally advanced, future humans with better education and technologies."[10] The creators behind the show have stated that this was a deliberate decision. As executive producer Brad Wright says:

> As wonderful as the *Enterprise* is as a means of transporting the characters and the audience from adventure to adventure, [the] stargate is capable of doing that for the audience in *the here and now* [my emphasis]. It's people from our world in the 20th–21st century, simply stepping into the gate and embarking on an adventure to another world.[11]

---

[6] McGrath-Kerr, Rachel. "Female Fans' Interaction with Samantha Carter through Fan Fiction and Online Discussion," in *Reading Stargate SG-1*, eds. Stan Beeler and Lisa Dickson. London: I.B. Tauris, 2006. pp. 200-17 (p. 200).

[7] Storm, Jo. *Approaching the Possible: The Worlds of Stargate SG-1*. Toronto: ECW Press, 2005. p. 100.

[8] Ibid. p. 100, p. 301.

[9] Holloway, Samantha, "Space Vehicles and Traveling Companions: Rockets and Living Ships" in *The Essential Science Fiction Television Reader*, ed. J.P. Telotte. Lexington: University Press of Kentucky, 2008. pp. 177-91 (p. 186).

[10] Ibid. pp. 186-187.

[11] Quoted in Garcia, Frank, and Mark Phillips, *Science Fiction Television Series, 1990-2004: Histories, Casts and Credits for 58 Shows*, Jefferson, N.C.: McFarland, 2009, p. 310.

SG-1's narrative is of global capitalism in conflict with a philosophy rooted in digitality, with stargates carrying opportunistic explorers to distant feudal villages.

Much like the user of the early Internet sitting in front of their computer screen, stargate technology allows the show's characters to "encounter a wide variety of civilizations, both primitive and technologically far advanced – situations that also challenge them to respond humanly even as the franchise heavily employs the genre's emphasis on wonder to reflect on our cultural attitudes toward the other."[12] *Stargate*'s creators thus draw not only "upon the audience's underlying cultural knowledge" but on their day-to-day experience of digitally transformative technological change, as well as the accompanying economic ramifications which were only becoming apparent at the time.[13]

The overarching narrative which *SG-1* ultimately presents is one of global capitalism in conflict with a philosophy firmly rooted in digitality, that being the condition of living in a digital culture. Throughout the series, the residual elements of feudalism inherent in capitalism inform the actions of the parasitic Goa'uld System Lords (and, for that matter, several hostile elements of

---

[12] Telotte, J.P., "Introduction: The Trajectory of Science Fiction Television," *The Essential Science Fiction Television Reader*, ed. J.P. Telotte, Lexington: University Press of Kentucky, 2008, pp. 1-34 (p. 25).

[13] Beeler, Stan, "Stargate SG-1 and the Quest for the Perfect Science Fiction Premise," in *The Essential Science Fiction Television Reader*, ed. J.P. Telotte, Lexington: University Press of Kentucky, 2008, pp. 267-82 (p. 279).

humanity). However, the ultimate hegemony of these aliens is repulsed by the influence of the Ancients, the benevolent civilization who originally constructed the stargate network before learning how to "ascend" to a state of pure energy where they share "knowledge and information, understanding on a level" well beyond that of humanity or the Goa'uld.[14]

That this is, in effect, the central conflict underpinning *SG-1* is evidenced not just by such notable episodes as "Absolute Power" (2001), and flashpoints such as "Full Circle" (2003) and "Lost City" (2004), but by the climax of season eight's "Threads" (2005), in which, as the title implies, the writers and producers concluded "almost every story thread that wasn't wrapped up" with the semi-ascended Goa'uld Anubis locked in eternal struggle with the ascended Ancient Oma Desala.[15] The effect of "Threads" is to emphasize just how Goa'uld and Ancient ideologies are polar opposites: globalization, embodied by a cackling madman bent on galactic domination, is a form of evil; digitality, represented by an intelligent woman roused to the use of her astronomical potential, is an expression of wisdom and virtue.

Given its origins in the earliest stages of contemporary digitality, it should come as no surprise that the *Stargate* franchise offered viewers a commentary on and a means of understanding the breakneck infiltration of the physical by the digital, which defines the contemporary information economy. With the *SG-1* pilot airing just eight weeks before the domain name for Google was registered, and a little more than two years after Nicholas Negroponte coined the term "digitality" in his study *Being Digital* (1995; only a few months after the release of the original *Stargate* film upon which the series was based), the franchise is enviably placed among recent popular cultural phenomena to reflect the ongoing changes digitality has wrought throughout society, technology, and communications (according to IMDb.com, *Stargate* is, in fact, the first film to have had a promotional website).

Certainly, it is possible to discern the unique combination of factors responsible for digitality's success at the most basic level of *SG-1*'s construction. For instance, Manuel Castells describes the Internet as having been born through the "unlikely intersection" of science, military, and libertarian cultures, with

---

[14] DeLuise, Peter, dir. "Reckoning," *Stargate SG-1*. USA: Sci-Fi Channel, 2005.
[15] Mikita, Andy, dir. "Threads," *Stargate SG-1*, USA: Sci-Fi Channel, 2005.

"libertarian" used by Castells in its European tradition of "a culture and ideology based on the uncompromising defence of individual freedom" and not, as in the U.S. context of "a systematic distrust of government."[16] In the pilot episode of *SG-1*, this intersection occurs with the first meeting of astrophysicist Samantha Carter (Amanda Tapping), decorated Air Force special-ops officer Jack O'Neill (Richard Dean Anderson), and gifted archaeologist and linguist Daniel Jackson (Michael Shanks).

It is only through the intersection of the scientific, the military, and the libertarian – through the *cooperation* of Carter, O'Neill, and Jackson – that they and the viewer encounter a paradigm-changing perspective, that of fourth regular Teal'c (Christopher Judge), an augmented human with superhuman abilities and a knowledge based upon experiences from across the globalized galaxy. He is, in effect, the killer app (or, to paraphrase the show's parlance, the *warrior* app) though which the other characters fully utilize the seemingly limitless possibilities of the stargate network.

The success of the series has long been ascribed to how "the different backgrounds and goals of the SG-1 team allow for significant innovation, as they react differently to the common dilemmas presented each week."[17] However, such synergy is better read as a direct analogy of what Castells called the "Network Society": a digital economy with "the capacity to work as a unit in real time, or chosen time, on a planetary scale."[18] The impact of stargate travel further conforms to a condition whereby "the flows of information, and the handling, assessments and decisions made on the basis of information, decisively alter previous ways of life."[19] Such a notion, even as *SG-1* premiered in the mid-1990s, was still unbelievable enough to many people that it could offer a means "for exploring the novum" of the Internet, and so provide the foundation of a successful science-fiction series.[20] Digitality's novum, experienced in early

---

[16] Castells, Manuel, *The Internet Galaxy*, Oxford: Oxford University Press, 2001, p. 17, p. 33.

[17] Beeler, p. 272.

[18] Castells, Manuel, *The Rise of the Network Society*, Oxford: Blackwell, 2nd edition 2000, p.60, p. 101.

[19] Webster, Frank, "A New Politics?" in *Culture and Politics in the Information Age*, ed. Frank Webster, London: Routledge, 2001, pp. 1-14 (p. 5).

[20] Suvin, Darko, *Metamorphoses of Science Fiction: On the Poetics and. History of a Literary Genre*, New Haven and London: Yale University Press, 1979, p. ix.

episodes of *SG-1* as a sense of bewilderment by travelers passing through the stargate, further gestures toward the "intense phase of time-space compression that has had a disorientating effect and disruptive impact upon political-economic practices" identified in postmodernity.[21]

Thus, throughout the first few years of *SG-1*, processes we take for granted nowadays, such as conducting "a timeline Boolean search" (a straightforward search engine query employing Boolean operators such as "AND/OR") are depicted as so unbelievable that they could be little else but science fictional in nature. Equally, the occasional instability of the stargate wormhole speaks to the cultural insecurities of the era: can the new technology which networks the world together truly be relied upon? Do its operators have any idea what they are doing, or are they just learning how to use it as they go along? In that way, at least, the technobabble of *Stargate* – remarkably consistent throughout the development of the franchise (as compared to, say, that of *Star Trek*) – makes clear and consistent reference to the digital networks beginning to transform the globalized world.

Take, for example, the primary characteristic of digitality: a transition from the delivery of atoms, meaning physical products, to the "movement of weightless bits at the speed of light."[22] In practice, the stargate provides almost exactly this kind of communications technology, albeit one which has overcome the disparity between atoms and bits for, in the case of the *Stargate* franchise, there is a conflation of matter and information. Stargates are "dialed," following which a "connection" must be made. Those traveling through a gate's event horizon are then dematerialized, their physical form converted into information, even being held momentarily in a "memory buffer" by the receiving gate before their "ones and zeros" are "reconverted back into the matter's original form."[23]

As Carter explains, "the stargate has massive amounts of memory inside"; it stores the pattern of anyone or anything entering, "to make sure it has all the information before it reassembles the object or, in our case, a person."[24] Atoms become bits, which become atoms again and, in this manner, an individual can journey from one side of the galaxy to the other in an average time of 3.2

[21] Harvey, David, *The Condition of Postmodernity*, Oxford: Blackwell, 1990, p. 284.

[22] Negroponte, Nicholas, *Being Digital*, New York: Vintage, 1995, p. 12.

[23] Woeste, Peter F, dir. "48 Hours," *Stargate SG-1*, USA: Showtime, 2002.

[24] Ibid.

seconds.[25] Like the Internet, the stargate network is also an incredibly flexible system. Any gate "can act both as source and sink"; it can be "where the signal comes from" and "where the signal goes," and so the system eschews outdated distribution hierarchies in the same way digital culture does.[26] With the journey from one world to another usually depicted as stepping through the wormhole's event horizon, the buffer aspect of stargate technology is not often labored ("48 Hours" [2001] being a notable exception); however, it is implicit in every episode and is, as Jackson describes it, "gate travel 101."[27]

Seen in this light, the protagonists of *SG-1* are at the forefront of a digital revolution sweeping through a universe which runs on capitalist, globalized principles; the tension resulting from this provides the *Stargate* franchise with much of its distinctive flavor. For though it is clad in the generic guise of military science fiction, the conflict between the humans and the Goa'uld is an information war, a consequence of inequality between the initially information-poor humans – known galactically as the Tau'ri – and the information-rich Goa'uld System Lords, the latter with an understanding of the stargate network, knowledge of hyperspace travel, and access to advanced technologies scavenged and plundered from around the galaxy. On an immediate level, this disparity mirrors that between the rich and poor nations in the early decades of the digital age, the "global digital divide" which exists as a result of how "the Internet has developed unevenly throughout the world."[28]

A surprisingly subversive interpretation of *SG-1* emerges when one reads the series protagonists – a U.S. military unit – as an information-poor party in "so far over our heads that we can barely see daylight."[29] The most powerful nation on Earth represents a world which, throughout much of *SG-1*'s run, is numbered among the undeveloped civilizations of the galaxy, an inferiority reinforced by the constant reference to the Tau'ri as "young," "primitive," or "technologically infantile" by cultures such as the Nox, the Tollan, and the Tok'ra. At its most basic

---

[25] Ibid.

[26] Negroponte, p. 180.

[27] Woeste.

[28] Guillen, Mauro and Sandra Suárez, "Explaining the Global Digital Divide: Economic, Political, and Sociological Drivers of Cross-National Internet Use," *Social Forces* 84.2 (2005): pp. 681-708 (p. 681).

[29] Azzopardi, Mario, dir. "Children of the Gods," *Stargate SG-1*, USA: Showtime, 1997.

level, much of the narrative of *SG-1* depicts an effort to bridge this "gap of development" through the acquisition of "scientific and technical information."[30] In the process, the series touches on a great many aspects of technological progress and the way modern communications systems seem to "banish distance," the most obvious of which is the wormhole network itself.[31]

Paired with each gate is a Dial Home Device that serves not just as an elaborate keyboard but also as a sophisticated router capable of processing vast amounts of data.

As explained in the original film, determining the address of a stargate is analogous to finding "a destination within any three-dimensional space; you need six points to determine the exact location," with a seventh point, "a point of origin," necessary to "chart a course."[32] In the highly interconnected narratives of the *Stargate* universe, galaxies themselves are information spaces, and traveling through them via wormhole is essentially a hypermedia experience. It, therefore, comes as no surprise that early metaphors for stargate operations are drawn squarely from the language of telecommunications: "What happens when you dial your own phone number?", Daniel asks in the episode "Solitudes" (1998) as a means of describing the difficulties of connecting to one's own stargate

---

[30] Sweeney, Gerry, "Information, Technology, and Development," *Information Society Journal* 2.1 (1983), pp. 1-3 (p. 1).

[31] Connell, Liam and Nicky Marsh, eds., *Literature and Globalisation: A Reader*, New York: Routledge, 2011, p. xiv.

[32] Emmerich, Roland, dir. *Stargate*, USA: Metro-Goldwyn-Mayer, 1994.

address from one's home planet.[33] Equally, adding another symbol to the six-symbol address will contribute "a new distance calculation to the existing points, kind of like dialing a different area code" and thereby allowing intergalactic travel.[34]

Paired with each gate is a Dial Home Device (DHD), and though it may appear to be nothing more than an elaborate keyboard, various episodes of *SG-1* and *Atlantis* have demonstrated DHDs to be sophisticated routers capable of processing vast amounts of data and even of "interstellar call forwarding."[35] Systematized gate addresses used to travel the network are, essentially, a fictionalized form of IP addresses, and though gates are dialed with pictorial representations of constellations rather than with recognizable alphanumeric symbols (a touch of exoticism suggesting the pictographic texts of the ancient Middle East), it is revealed in "Lost City" that "each symbol on the stargate has a corresponding sound so that it can be spoken aloud."[36] In this way, a gate address such as the one below can be shared more easily as "Proclarush Taonas," the real place and the virtual space collapsing in a way which prefigures the manner in which websites are now thought of as destinations in their own right, and in which a dot-decimal IP address – a string of numbers and periods – is more familiar to us as a human-readable, human-sharable address such as, for example, google.com (or simply just "Google").[37]

Expanding from this, the *Stargate* franchise frequently draws plots and conflicts from exaggerated concerns of the Digital Age, offering an oblique comment on the frenzy with which identity theft and computer viruses are often dealt with by the media and the less tech-savvy members of society. Personnel assigned to Stargate Command have, for example, often found that identity theft is a quite literal problem (including in the episodes "Cold Lazarus" [1997], "Tin

---

[33] Wood, Martin, dir. "Solitudes," *Stargate SG-1*, USA: Showtime, 1998.
[34] Warry-Smith, David, dir. "The Fifth Race," *Stargate SG-1*, USA: Showtime, 1999.
[35] DeLuise, Peter, dir. "Prototype," *Stargate SG-1*, USA: Sci-Fi Channel, 2005.
[36] Wood, Martin, dir. "Lost City," *Stargate SG-1*, USA: Sci-Fi Channel, 2004.
[37] Ibid.

Man" [1998], "Foothold" [1999], "Double Jeopardy" [2001], and "Fragile Balance" [2003]).

Meanwhile, the interconnectivity of the stargate network, though generally portrayed as a strength, also hides vulnerabilities such as those which occur in the episode "Avenger 2.0" (2003). In that episode, taking advantage of the "correlative update" subroutine in the network's DHDs – a program which enables the stargates to communicate with each other and share new coordinates to compensate for stellar drift – System Lord Ba'al (Cliff Simon) introduces a computer virus into the system which scrambles the entire Milky Way gate network, in much the same way as real-world malware has been used for cyber-sabotage against foreign nations.[38]

One of the few aspects of digital maliciousness which *Stargate* has not dealt with is the issue of spam, though the Goa'uld have occasionally conducted what we might term "denial of service" attacks on Earth's stargate (manipulating the protocols associated with communication requests as Apophis did when his ships brought a second gate and DHD to Earth's coordinates in "Within the Serpent's Grasp" [1998], or overloading the system, such as Anubis's attempt to detonate the gate through a destructive build-up of energy in "Redemption" [2002]).

This metaphorical indebtedness to developments in real-world information processing and communications capabilities is continually hinted at throughout *SG-1*. For instance, although scientists have been working on the mysteries of the gate for many decades (dramatized in episodes such as "The Torment of Tantalus" [1997] and, more recently, in the webseries *Stargate Origins* [2018]), it is only the advent of sophisticated computer technology in the mid-1990s that makes exploration of the stargate network a viable endeavor. Additionally, the "iris" of Earth's stargate, just like the shield protecting that of Atlantis, is the epitome of a firewall, a "gatekeeper of sorts" controlling the flow of information – in this case digitalized travelers – from one world to another.[39] Crucially, *SG-1*'s search for "technologies we can use to defend ourselves" also charts a societal change in Earth's attitude regarding the increasing presence of digitality in our

---

[38] McElroy, Damien and Christopher Williams, "Flame: World's Most Complex Computer Virus Exposed," *The Daily Telegraph*, 28 May 2012, telegraph.co.uk/news/worldnews/middleeast/iran/9295938/Flame-worlds-most-complex-computer-virus-exposed.html (accessed 10 May 2014).
[39] Negroponte, p. 45.

lives, something which the contemporaneous setting of the series makes difficult to ignore.

In early episodes, such as "The Gamekeeper" (1998), digitality is portrayed as a kind of menace or trap, an "advanced creation being pumped into our minds" with the characters' brains "hooked up like computers to some kind of network."[40] By the time of "Avatar" (2004), however, the virtual world of "The Gamekeeper" has been back-engineered for human use in an excellent example of how Stargate Command acquires alien technology and hybridizes it with that of Earth. In this case, the storyline focuses – as much mainstream media did at the time – on digitality's potential to empower and educate undeveloped areas in response to the threat presented by the show's agents of capitalist globalization, the Goa'uld. "Avatar" presents a combat simulation developed by SGC scientists in order that personnel might better prepare for a Goa'uld incursion.

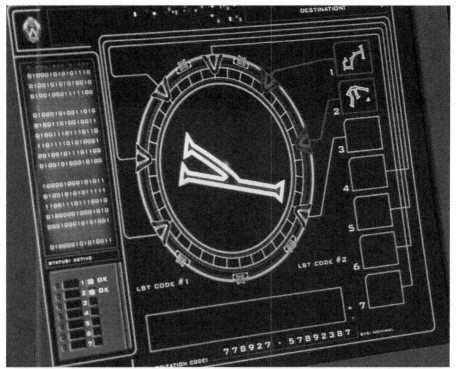

Stargate Command's computers combined symbols from the stargate, the cartouche, and other sources to create a digitized database of dialing destinations.

---

[40] Wood, Martin, dir. "The Gamekeeper," Stargate SG-1, USA: Showtime, 1998.

Whereas "The Gamekeeper" treated the consciousnesses of people themselves as "software," "Avatar" is, relatively speaking, a more realistic depiction of immersive computer environments as "a viable, virtual reality training tool" with a "graphic representation" analogous to contemporary video games such as (to use Teal'c's example) *Def Jam Vendetta*.[41] O'Neill's first words to Teal'c as he emerges from the latter's initial VR experience, repeatedly referred to as "just a game," are "Was it fun?"[42] Nevertheless, even mature digitality is not without its attendant risks, specifically Teal'c's refusal to give up and stop playing, something which serves as an oblique comment on the kind of extreme video game usage which can actively interfere with a gamer's daily life.[43]

Yet while the "Gamekeeper" device is a firmly digital experience, the clearest instances of *SG-1* attempting to bridge the information gap between humanity and the Goa'uld occur in the sphere of military hardware. The new and superior technologies which the team acquires in this field are intended to be effective against what might be thought of as the current "capitalist hegemony over space" in the globalized galaxy.[44] The effect of this is to problematize many of the protagonists' actions and goals, rendering their most conspicuous success stories at least notionally antithetical to the ideology of digitality which underpins the very existence of the stargate network. Storylines such as Earth's quest to construct interstellar vessels are illustrative of a central tension throughout the middle period of the series in particular, an anxiety generated by residual globalist energies within the heart of emergent digitality during the timeframe of the show's production. Manifesting as a response to the malign influence of the Goa'uld, this tension ensures that not all technological progress on the series is necessarily forward, or one might say *as far* forward as understanding the stargates.

Like the fax machine, a "serious blemish on the information landscape" largely derived from "image-oriented" Japanese "culture, language, and business customs," the hyperdrive technology portrayed in the series is a step backward from the ideological principles and simplicity of gate travel.[45] Many seasons of

---

[41] Wood, Martin, dir. "Avatar," *Stargate SG-1*, USA: Sci-Fi Channel, 2004.

[42] Ibid.

[43] Griffiths, Mark, "Online video gaming: what should educational psychologists know?" *Educational Psychology in Practice* 26.1 (2010), pp. 35–40.

[44] Harvey, p. 303.

[45] Negroponte, p. 188.

SG-1 are spent in pursuit of hyperdrive engines, a faster-than-light propulsion technology utilized by a number of the show's interstellar or intergalactic civilizations as an alternative to stargates. The U.S. Air Force eventually acquires such devices through the reverse-engineering of captured Goa'uld vessels and the hybridization of human and Asgard technology.

The result is Earth's first true starship, the *Prometheus*, a vessel which is appropriately named for what Earth seeks to steal from the (false) gods is firepower. Though popular with fans, the F-302 interceptor, the *Prometheus*, and the later *Dedalus*-class battle cruisers are emblematic of how, as the series progresses, humanity's position with regard to the philosophies of the Goa'uld and the Ancients becomes less clear-cut – and, one might conclude, more beholden to pre-existing and conventional notions of space opera, this being made explicit in O'Neill's initial request to name the *Prometheus* the *Enterprise*.[46]

In many respects, hyperdrives are among the least digital aspect of the stargate mythology. The technology is one prized by ruling elites – be they the Goa'uld or the U.S. military – as manifestations of antiquated force projection doctrines. They are valued for reasons of national (or planetary) prestige and military might more than elegance or cooperation, the chief advantage of hyperdrive engines being that one can "take the fight to the enemy."[47] Capital ships and battle cruisers such as *Prometheus* and *Dedalus*, along with Goa'uld motherships, can act as mobile launch platforms for fighter craft, deliver massive numbers of troops, and even subjugate whole worlds from orbit.

Moreover, on *Stargate*, as on much genre television, starships serve as a "symbol of science fiction's colonial expansion," and the existence of hard-power assets such as these runs counter to the apparent intentions of the Ancients that the interstellar community come together in peace and digital cooperation.[48] This attitude is apparent in, for instance, the shipbuilding practices of the Ancients themselves, who – in peacetime, at least – adopt an approach of starfaring *en masse*: "city-ships" with distributed systems and living quarters throughout an internal volume equivalent to that of Manhattan, such as Atlantis, which is capable of transporting an entire community *as* a community.

---

[46] Mikita, Andy, dir. "Unnatural Selection," *Stargate SG-1*, USA: Sci-Fi Channel, 2002.
[47] Mikita, Andy, dir. "New Order" (Part 1), *Stargate SG-1*, USA: Sci-Fi Channel, 2004.
[48] Parrent, Kim Louise, "Travelling Through the Iris: Re-producing Whiteness in *Stargate SG-1*," Unpublished MA thesis, University of Canterbury, 2010, p. 39.

Atlantis itself serves as an expression of the highly networked Ancient civilization, the very definition of Castells's "network society" extensively comprising "informational labor," a class of workers defined as "the creators, designers and disseminators of information flows [...] those who think, plan, and conceive in situations of great uncertainty."[49] A more apt description of the Ancients would be difficult to come by, as would a better example of their digital ideology. A living space as much as an intergalactic technological marvel, Atlantis utilizes transporter booths for instantaneous internal travel (so, again, the conversion of physical matter to information and back again), along with wireless interface designs such as the "control chair," which responds to the occupant's thoughts and is initiated by the so-called Ancient Technology Activation gene, which comes to prominence in *SG-1* and *Atlantis* during the real-world popularization of Wi-Fi availability.

Samantha Carter (Amanda Tapping) and Radek Zelenka (David Nykl) share an awkward moment while utilizing one of Atlantis's transporter booths.

A clear response to developments in the personal computing and communications arenas, the linkage of human minds with technology is a hallmark of the Ancients and cements their position as *Stargate*'s most powerful advocates for digitality, even before their ascension. Throughout *SG-1* and *Atlantis*, much of their technology interfaces directly with the operator and,

---

[49] Webster, p. 6.

while outright cyborgization has never been characteristic of the *Stargate* franchise, the subject of mind-machine connectivity is one which recurs as a means of subverting hierarchical capitalist constraints on information. The downloading of the Ancients' database into O'Neill's brain in both "The Fifth Race" (1998) and "Lost City" is described in terms of a computer analogy: "Your hard-drive has been filled with information [...] in a language your computer doesn't understand."[50]

For the Ancients, a civilization and its information are – quite literally – virtually indistinguishable. It is, after all, no coincidence that the Asgard, allies of the Ancients, demonstrate a similar philosophy in "Unending" (2007), when they decide to give humanity "everything we have [...] and know."[51] What is more, the relationship between the Ancients and the Asgard, two of the most advanced species in *Stargate* mythology, is itself based on the most digital of all concepts: the free sharing of information, much of it of a technical or scientific nature. By contrast, the capitalist-inflected Goa'uld "do not share technology"; they hoard information and clash constantly over the control of physical space.[52]

The Goa'uld practice a kind of capitalism which should be recognizable to anyone in the early twenty-first century, one which has "overcome the limits of time and space" through abuse of the stargate network's communications infrastructure.[53] O'Neill himself implies the capitalist analogy by comparing Earth's adversaries to Mr. Burns, the unscrupulous businessman of his favorite television series, *The Simpsons*.[54] Spurred on by the collapse of spatial barriers, the System Lords are able to transfer labor, raw materials, and military power throughout their interstellar fiefdoms in mere instants. Stargate travel allows for a radically transformed relationship between space and time of a kind which permits the Goa'uld to profit in the former through a reduction in the latter.

Nevertheless, the hegemonic aspirations of Goa'uld pseudo-capitalism are held in check by the open-access philosophy of the gate-builders, the Ancients. Anyone can use a stargate as long as they possess a valid destination address

---

[50] Warry-Smith.

[51] Cooper, Robert C., dir. "Unending," *Stargate SG-1*, USA: Sci-Fi Channel, 2007.

[52] Gereghty, William, dir. "Between Two Fires," *Stargate SG-1*, USA: Showtime, 2001.

[53] Castells, 2000, p. 101.

[54] Wood, "Lost City."

and, although in some cases gates have been relocated to secure military insulations (for example, Earth's gate, along with many of those on worlds controlled by Anubis), the majority remain exactly where the Ancients deposited them: available to all and, especially in the Pegasus Galaxy, enabling exchange of goods and ideas in the truest possible sense; day-to-day economic activities unrestricted by the "hundreds of protocols, declarations and articles that constitute free trade agreements" on Earth.[55]

It is therefore clear that, just as it draws on the language of telecommunications to reflect our increasingly networked society, *Stargate*'s technobabble also echoes the globalized world in which the emergent Information Age is embedded. Not that this should surprise the viewer for, "as capitalism's primary 'value system' becomes 'dematerialized,' so cultural texts seem to reflect 'the dissolution of the material representations of value.'"[56] What could, therefore, be more appropriate than a cultural text such as *Stargate*, wherein the protagonists, along with the physical objects of material value they carry and acquire, are literally dematerialized on a weekly basis?

For their part, the Goa'uld often behave like any large multinational corporation, able to operate with simultaneous decision-making in relation to the processes and conditions of material and labor galaxy-wide – for, via the stargate, a thousand light years is nothing more than a few steps. In the globalized galaxy, the Goa'uld are caricatures of the ultimate capitalists: "posturing egomaniacs driven by an insatiable lust for power. Each one capable of unimaginable evil."[57] "Their society is feudal" and they maintain the enslaved Jaffa as a labor class, chattel of the individual System Lords posing as "false gods."[58] The rule of the System Lords thus combines "immense economic power" with factors officially beyond the reach of Earth's transnational corporations: "factors of territoriality and control of the means of violence."[59] When it comes, however, "capital flight" is quite literally an act of flying away, the Jaffa seizing the Goa'uld fleet for themselves and transmuting labor power into political power.[60]

---

[55] Yúdice, George, *The Expediency of Culture: Uses of Culture in the Global Era*, Durham NC: Duke University Press, 2003, p. 214.
[56] Connell and Marsh, p.2.
[57] Mikita, "New Order" (Part 1).
[58] Wood, Martin, dir. "Politics," *Stargate SG-1*, USA: Showtime, 1998.
[59] Giddens, Anthony, *The Consequences of Modernity*, London: Polity, 1990, p.70.
[60] Harvey, p 294.

Yet, the Free Jaffa State does not come into being on account of military might alone. Instead, a Jaffa rebellion teeters on the brink of failure in the episode "Reckoning" (2005), not because of Goa'uld strategic competence, but due to the unexpected invasion of the mechanical Replicators. Warships, *Stargate*'s allegorical indicator of capitalism, are of little use against digitally fluent robotic creatures able to commandeer space vessels at their ease. Consequently, the series – in what could easily have been one of its final episodes – tendered its grandest gesture in favor of Ancient philosophy. Defeating the Replicators requires teamwork; collaboration between the Tau'ri, the Jaffa and, unexpectedly, System Lord Ba'al; and the activation of all the stargates in the galaxy at once, so as to defang both the Goa'uld and the Replicators in a process whereby the Milky Way is rendered less attractive to the "highly mobile capital" of the insect-like mechanical aliens.[61]

For the stargate network, like the Internet it represents, is at its decentralized heart a "collaborative medium" designed around the sharing of knowledge. As Walter Wriston said only a few months before the *SG-1* premiere, in the Information Age "intellectual capital is at least as important as money capital and probably more so."[62] Digitality is the emergent system incubating within the decaying culture of capitalism, and those who underestimate its power, and do not embrace the modes of thinking it makes possible, are doomed – as the Goa'uld are – to be left behind.

In the *Stargate* universe, humanity realizes the value of cooperation soon after they unlock the gate, with one of the earliest discoveries made being the "meeting place" where the Ancients and the Asgard, along with the Nox and the Furlings, gather "to share knowledge or discuss relations like a United Nations of the stars."[63] Crucially, the model utilized by the Four Races is the exact opposite of the consumerist logic underpinning globalization; theirs is a galactic village which, unlike either our global one or the imperial version of the Goa'uld, is predicated on equality and cooperation (admittedly a straightforward achievement for a post-scarcity culture such as theirs). "Friends share knowledge with one another," Jackson says in "The Nox" (1997) and, more than any military

---

[61] Ibid. p. 295.
[62] Bass, Thomas, "The Future of Money," *Wired* 4.10 (1996), URL: wired.com/wired/archive/4.10/wriston.html (accessed 21 May 2012).
[63] Glassner, Jonathan, dir. "The Torment of Tantalus," *Stargate SG-1*, USA: Showtime, 1997.

mission statement, it is this belief which informs the actions of SG-1. The team utilizes the gate network not just as a means of retrieving alien technology but also to share Earth's story with other civilizations, to make contact with foreign allies, and to coordinate resistance against the established order.

That being said, the dangers of misusing information technologies are obviously manifold. On the one hand, there are the detrimental effects of overreliance on digitality apparent in the final fate of the Asgard in the *SG-1* finale, that of "mass suicide."[64] For centuries, the Asgard transferred their minds from one body to another, yet this led to both an irreversible genetic decline and to a mental state incompatible with following the Ancients to a higher plane. They "made the choice to extend their life through science generations ago. Took any natural physiological evolution necessary for Ascension out of the equation."[65] Equally, the immersive qualities of the digital age (and, one might hazard, science-fiction television) presents social challenges to even the smartest human beings. Carter's ignorance of the Cheyenne Mountain Zoo, for example, acts as a comment on the excessive amount of time she spends going through the stargate at the expense of the real world.[66]

Although the Internet – like the stargate network – has the means of freeing its adherents from global capitalism by connecting and educating individuals and communities, just like Carter, we also have a tendency to spend too much time going through the gate and tinkering with the new toys we discover there. We risk spending too much time in digital space to the detriment of our personal lives and our relationships with those around us. *Stargate SG-1* is a true representation of digitality, not simply because of how it incorporates analogous technologies into its narrative, but also because of how it subtly warns us of the dangers inherent in the digital condition.

Reprinted with the kind permission of <u>Foundation: The International Review of Science Fiction</u>.

---

[64] Cooper.
[65] Cooper.
[66] Waring, William, dir. "Chimera," *Stargate SG-1*, USA: Sci-Fi Channel, 2004.

Same Gate Time, Same Gate Channel: Resurrecting the Brand (Twice) with a Serial Flair

by Robert Jeschonek

The year was 2009. It had been two years since the end of *Stargate SG-1*, the flagship series of the *Stargate* television franchise. The sequel show, *Stargate Atlantis*, had ended in January after five seasons on the Sci-Fi Channel,[1] but one thing was certain: the franchise would return. Its owner, Metro Goldwyn Mayer (MGM), had a new series in production, one that would feature plenty of good old *Stargate* action, while pushing the storytelling in new directions. The question was, would *Stargate Universe* – SGU, for short – get people to watch and clamor for more?

A similar question arose nine years later, when another new chapter in the franchise debuted, this time on the Stargate Command online streaming service. Again, the successor series pushed the storytelling in new directions, bringing a fresh perspective. But would *Stargate Origins* attract swarms of viewers and breathe new life into the mythos? In both cases, the answer was the same. In

---

[1] Rebranded in 2009 as Syfy.

spite of the best-laid plans of producers, writers, cast members, and crew, the new directions did not pan out. Neither *Universe* nor *Origins* generated the kind of interest needed to propel the *Stargate* brand into the future.

Franchise Mania

In the realm of televised entertainment circa 2009, building a successful franchise was the proverbial brass ring. Multiple studios had proven it could be done and had showed how profitable it could be as a long-term strategy, inspiring other developers of intellectual properties to get in on the act. All it took was for a savvy producer and their team to capitalize on a hit series by branching off with additional shows, each a variation on the original theme. With a strong enough core show, a solid approach, and the right cast and crew, the possibilities were vast.

Historically, the practice of spinning off shows from existing hits had been in place since the golden age of old-time radio in the 1930s and '40s. In 1941, for example, the supporting character Throckmorton Gildersleeve was spun off from the successful show *Fibber McGee and Molly* into a new series, *The Great Gildersleeve*, which ran for 16 years.[2] Successful television spinoffs include *The Jeffersons* and *Maude* (both based on 1970s smash *All in the Family*) and *Laverne & Shirley* and *Mork & Mindy* (based on another '70s powerhouse, *Happy Days*).

By the 1990s and the era of televised *Stargate,* the spinoff process had been further refined. Hewing closely to the successful template of a core series, from show titles to episode formats and overall visual and storytelling style, creators were able to develop unified franchises with consistently high ratings. Fans of the original core series found enough familiar elements to draw them in, plus sufficient new aspects to make the spinoffs feel fresh. In this way, *CSI: Crime Scene Investigation* begat *CSI: Miami, CSI: NY*, and others; *Law & Order* begat *Law & Order: Special Victims Unit, Law & Order: Criminal Intent*, etc.; and *JAG* spawned *NCIS*, which spawned *NCIS: Los Angeles* and more.

In the science-fiction genre, *Star Trek* stood as the gold standard, giving birth to *Star Trek: The Next Generation, Star Trek: Deep Space Nine, Star Trek: Voyager,* and *Star Trek: Enterprise.* The producers of *Stargate SG-1* followed suit with *Stargate Atlantis*, which debuted on the Sci-Fi Channel on 16 July 2004. *Atlantis* did well enough that it ran for five seasons and inspired the development of

---

[2] From *Spin-off (media),* accessed 1 Jan. 2022 at wikiwand.com/en/Spin-off_(media).

another series to pick up after it went off the air in 2009. That new show, *Universe,* was meant to capture fans of *SG-1* and *Atlantis* with new tales arising from the same basic *Stargate* concepts and continuity, updated enough to bring in new viewers and strengthen the franchise with fresh dramatic possibilities.

According to executive producer Robert C. Cooper, the new show (airing on what by then was dubbed Syfy) would be a departure from recent stylistic choices, in part looking to the past of *SG-1.* "I think there's going to be a little more *reality* in it," he said in a *GateWorld* interview. "We're trying to get more realistic about the characters. It is more character-driven."[3] It was an ambitious plan, incorporating a new approach while staying true to well-traveled pathways. There was risk involved, as there always is when tinkering with something successful with a devoted fan base... but the potential rewards were enough to encourage the new venture.

Left to right: Ming-Na Wen as Camille Wray, David Blue as Eli Wallace, Lou Diamond Phillips as David Telford, and Robert Carlyle as Nicholas Rush helped to make *Stargate Universe* a show that vastly improved over time.

Producers delivered exactly as promised, stepping through their own personal gate into the great known/unknown, confident that they were going to achieve their objectives. Syfy shared that confidence enough to take the unusual

---

[3] "An Expanding Universe," accessed 2 Jan. 2022 at gateworld.net/news/2009/04/an-expanding-universe/.

step of committing to airing two full seasons right off the bat. As Craig Engler, senior vice president and general manager of Syfy Digital, later wrote:

> Two-season deals are rare in the TV world because they tie up a huge amount of investment (both time and money), but our great track record with MGM and *Stargate* made this seem like as much of a sure thing as you'll get in the TV business. That means before any footage was shot or any actors were hired, we knew there'd be 40 episodes.[4]

Unfortunately, the confidence and two-season deal did not guarantee success and longevity for *Stargate Universe*.

Strange New Gates

When *Universe* first hit the airwaves, it was a departure from past *Stargate* adventures. For one thing, the setting was very different from what had gone before. Instead of the protagonists being based on a planet like Earth or the Atlantean homeworld of Lantea,[5] the central team of *Universe* was in constant motion, traveling the distant cosmos aboard the Ancient starship *Destiny* after gating there to escape an attack by the Lucian Alliance. They couldn't physically return home, so they were very much on their own, though individuals were able to swap places mentally with people on Earth thanks to Ancient communication stone technology.

The new framework for starship-based stories echoed the *Star Trek* franchise,[6] leading the cast on an action-packed journey to "explore strange new worlds" and "seek out new life and new civilizations." This opened up possibilities, so the crew wasn't limited to stargate-based adventures... though the shipboard gate did provide fast access to the surfaces of planets within range, acting as a plot expedient like the transporter device in *Star Trek.*

Motivating Factors

Even as the new ship-based setting expanded the storytelling palette, it helped shape the motivations of key *Universe* characters in new ways. From the start of the series, the protagonists struggled to survive, understand the ship, and find a way home – though these central goals evolved as the show continued.

---

[4] "An Open Letter to *Stargate* Fans From Syfy," 11 May 2011. Accessed 2 Jan. 2022 at gateworld.net/news/2011/05/an-open-letter-to-stargate-fans-from-syfy/.
[5] As in *Stargate SG-1* and *Stargate Atlantis*, respectively.
[6] Especially *Star Trek: Voyager* (1995 to 2001), with its similar "lost in space" motif.

When Dr. Nicholas Rush discovered that *Destiny*'s intended mission was to trace a pattern in the cosmic microwave background that might reveal the secret origins of the universe,[7] the crew's mission became one of exploration and discovery as much as survival.

The starship *Destiny* was built and launched by the Ancients more than fifty million years ago to explore the nature of the cosmos.

The approach was not unprecedented. It had similarities to previous iterations of *Stargate*, in which missions of survival and discovery went hand in hand. On *Atlantis,* for example, a military-scientific team had to survive hostile action on a distant world while mounting exploratory missions through a gate – all the while cut off from Stargate Command (at first, anyway).[8] Despite the shared DNA, *Universe* managed to feel fresh when it came to character motivations. The show's key protagonists acted for reasons other than being ordered to do so, and they came across as complicated, realistic people because of it.

Complicated Individuals

When it came to character traits on *Universe*, absolutes were in short supply. Instead of straight-up heroes and villains painted in black or white, the crew members were mostly portrayed in shades of grey, making their reactions to the new setting and situations realistic and believable.

---

[7] "The Greater Good," *Stargate Universe*, 9 Nov 2010.
[8] Communication with Earth was not established until the end of season one.

Most notably, lead scientist Dr. Rush had a pronounced dark side. At various times, he lied, concealed vital information, spearheaded a mutiny, and even cast doubt on the innocence of the mission commander during a murder investigation. He was egotistical, difficult, obstinate, and borderline pathological... though he could never be described as outright evil. His actions were always in service to the good of the mission, which to him (and the starship *Destiny* itself) was a journey of exploration in search of knowledge.[9]

Colonel Everett Young may have been Rush's nemesis aboard *Destiny*, but he was equally complex. Though Young was driven to provide strong leadership and protect the ship's passengers, he also delved into less-than-noble acts of his own. At one point, he marooned Rush on an alien planet[10] and lied about it to the crew.[11] After a series of failures and personal setbacks, Young became increasingly unhinged and nearly lost command of the ship.[12] When he discovered that Rush had secretly deciphered *Destiny*'s master code and had concealed the information even though it could have saved a life, Young beat him brutally and said he should have killed him.[13]

Other *Universe* characters also had dark secrets or glaring imperfections, from temperamental Master Sergeant Ronald Greer, who'd been up for a court martial before arriving aboard *Destiny*, to medic Tamara Johansen, who'd had an affair with Colonel Young when he was still a married man back on Earth. Together, these complex protagonists added a sense of realism to the show, emphasizing that much human behavior can be mapped in shades of grey rather than simple black and white.

However, the show's inventiveness didn't end with the compelling characters and unique setting (unique to the *Stargate* franchise, anyway). The style of the storytelling also changed from what had gone before, as *Universe* presented highly serialized arcs in place of loosely connected episodic adventures. "Yeah, it's going to be a little more serialized than the other shows,"

---

[9] See this author's other essay, "A Wolf in Sheep's Spacesuit: Nicholas Rush and the Dark Side of *Stargate Universe*," elsewhere in this anthology.

[10] A fate that Rush arguably deserved after embroiling Young as a suspect in a murder investigation because he considered him unfit for command.

[11] "Justice," *Stargate Universe*, 4 Dec 2009.

[12] "Trial and Error," *Stargate Universe*, 2 Nov 2010.

[13] "The Greater Good," *Stargate Universe*, 9 Nov 2010.

Cooper said. "Character-wise, the stories will still hopefully resolve within the hour."[14]

Serial Thriller

Serialization – continuing storylines flowing from one episode to the next – had never gone out of style in daytime television,[15] but it had taken a while to gain a foothold in dramatic programming on the primetime TV schedule. Though *The Fugitive* had featured an overarching storyline with a beginning and an end, and though shows like *Peyton Place* had brought soap opera continuity to nighttime television, the primetime serialization boom didn't really get off the ground until the 1980s. It was then that shows like *Hill Street Blues, St. Elsewhere,* and *L.A. Law* told tightly plotted stories that continued throughout the season, interweaving between episodes and characters to create a lifelike tapestry of incidents, resolutions, and aftereffects.

In the 1990s, series like *The X-Files* and *Buffy the Vampire Slayer* rolled the serialized style back into the science-fiction and fantasy genres,[16] putting it to use in new ways. *The X-Files* focused mostly on standalone episodes but followed a chronological sequence punctuated by "mythology" episodes that developed an overarching plot throughout the course of a season.[17] Similarly, *Buffy* told an overarching story each season, with a "big bad" menace confronted in full by the protagonists in the last episode before summer hiatus. Episodes within the season built steadily toward this climax, while also presenting relatively self-contained adventures along the way.

The series *Babylon 5*, which aired from 1994 to 1998, took science fiction genre serialization to the next level, telling a complete story from beginning to end, complete with elaborate subplots, foreshadowing, and genuine character evolution. By the time *Universe* came along, these shows and others had set the stage for another serialized drama. The smash hit series *24* may have been the ultimate example of how well-executed tight continuity[18] could create tension and bring in huge audiences. Another serialized series, *Lost*, also brought in big

---

[14] "An Expanding Universe," accessed 2 Jan. 2022 at gateworld.net/news/2009/04/an-expanding-universe/.

[15] See pretty much any daytime soap opera ever broadcast.

[16] Where its influence had been felt since the *Flash Gordon* and *Buck Rogers* movie serials of the 1930s.

[17] And the course of the entire series.

[18] Plus a marquee lead actor and cinematic production values.

ratings and buzz. Yet another example, the rebooted *Battlestar Galactica*, had done well enough on *Stargate*'s home network, Syfy, to encourage executives to take a shot at another, similar production.

Thus, when the *Universe* team planned their new effort, making it a serial seemed like a great way to go. The writers generated scripts that linked together to tell one big story, even as smaller individual tales played out in each episode. Season one followed the crew from their arrival aboard *Destiny* through the marooning of Rush and the attempted mutiny, culminating in an assault by the Lucian Alliance. Season two saw the *Destiny* team defeat the Lucian Alliance, gain control of the ship by cracking the master code, and enter cryogenic hibernation (except one volunteer, Eli Wallace) to make the long journey to another galaxy and survive a blockade by murderous drones.

Taken as a whole, the series tells a single story encompassing multiple nested sub-stories, though it does end in a way that leaves open the possibility of further adventures. It's a tighter continuity than that of *SG-1* and *Atlantis*,[19] and it makes *Universe* stand out from those past series. It gives it the feeling of being something new and fresh in the franchise, something very much in tune with the TV landscape of its time. But the producers soon discovered that being new and in tune with the TV landscape isn't always a guarantee of success.

Destiny's End

Despite all the hard work that went into the show's creation, *Universe* did not reach the level of steady ratings success needed to survive beyond two seasons. As Syfy executive Craig Engler explained in a post-cancellation open letter posted at *GateWorld*, the show's numbers were "untenably low" during its first season. It lost a third of its initial audience during the season's second half, leading Syfy to move it from its Friday night slot to Tuesdays for its second season, paired with *Battlestar Galactica* spinoff *Caprica*. Sadly, the first ten episodes of season two continued the downward trend. Syfy then moved the back half of the season to Monday nights, and that was the last straw. (*Caprica* faced a similar abrupt end.)

According to Engler, the decision to cancel the series was made because the ratings weren't "sustainable," though the network had spent a lot of money to make it happen. "We invested tens of millions of dollars and thousands of hours

---

[19] Though those shows' episodes did occur chronologically and led to climactic punctuation points.

of work over many years making and supporting the show," he explained. "We love *Stargate*. There is literally no one other than MGM who supported it more than we did."[20]

Executive producer and co-creator Brad Wright said MGM's financial difficulties in 2010 also hurt *Universe*'s chances for renewal:

> What happened with *Stargate Universe* is MGM went through a major restructuring – basically a structured bankruptcy – that changed everybody. Everyone who I knew at MGM simply was gone within a month of this event. And so even Syfy – who wanted to talk about a third season, or at least have the conversation – really had no one that they could talk to. It was kind of sad. And it was kind of a perfect storm of not great ratings and the studio disappearing.[21]

After months on life support, the plug was officially pulled. *Universe* was cancelled, and Syfy broadcast its final episode, "Gauntlet," on 9 May 2011. It would be nine years until more live-action *Stargate* adventures saw the light of day. Surprisingly, the producers of that revival would go all in on using at least one of the stylistic tools that had been employed so prominently in *Universe*: they would make it even more of a serial.

Species of the *Origins*

By 2018, there had been no new *Stargate* for nearly a decade... and the playing field had changed. Video streaming services like Netflix and Hulu had taken hold, enabling viewers to watch films and TV shows on demand instead of having to view them on broadcast or cable channels at designated times, record them from those sources for later viewing, or purchase DVDs or Blu-rays.

MGM decided it was a great time to launch a streaming service of its own, one tapping into the studio's vast library of *Stargate* content. "We saw a need for a definitive hub for the *Stargate* fanbase to continue to enjoy news and content, both old and new," said Chris Ottinger, MGM's president of worldwide television distribution and acquisitions. "Stargate Command will open a new door for the

---

[20] "An Open Letter to *Stargate* Fans From Syfy," 11 May 2011. Accessed 2 Jan. 2022 at gateworld.net/news/2011/05/an-open-letter-to-stargate-fans-from-syfy/

[21] "New Stargate? Wright Says 'We're Working On It'," 24 Jan. 2019, accessed 2 Jan. 2022 at gateworld.net/news/2019/01/new-stargate-wright-says-were-working-on-it/

community to celebrate and interact with all content in a way that has never been done before."[22]

Stargate Command was launched as a subscription service in early 2018, with the first episode of its flagship show, *Stargate Origins*, made available as a free preview on Feb. 15. The hope was that this content, the first *Stargate* programming in nine years, would bring in droves of fans to pay the $20 subscription fee to access the full series and *Stargate*-related bonus materials.

Ellie Gall as Catherine Langford, *Stargate Atlantis*'s Connor Trinneer as Paul Langford, and Philip Alexander as James Beal did their best with what they were given to make *Stargate Origins* entertaining.

As with *Universe*, producers hoped that providing an action-packed series with classic *Stargate* elements and fresh twists on the formula would ensure success and breathe new life into the franchise. But as had happened with *Universe*, things didn't turn out as expected. The particular mix of elements in *Origins* did not draw throngs of devoted viewers. Perhaps the audience just wasn't there for this particular retro-style serial.

All-You-Can-Eat Serial

Of all the *Stargate* series, none so closely resembled an old-fashioned movie serial as *Origins* did. Unfolding over the course of ten episodes, the prequel followed the first trip through a stargate in 1928 by Catherine Langford, a

---

[22] "MGM Revives 'Stargate' Franchise With 'Stargate Origins' Digital Series & SVOD Platform," 20 July 2017, accessed 2 Jan. 2022 at deadline.com/2017/07/mgm-stargate-franchise-digital-series-stargate-origins-1202131483/.

character who'd appeared multiple times on film and TV as a driving force behind the Stargate Program. Catherine, along with British officer Captain James Beal and Egyptian soldier Lieutenant Wasif, travels through the gate to save her kidnapped archaeologist father, Paul Langford, from Nazis intent on perverting its technology for their own purposes. On the other side of the gate, Catherine and her friends struggle with the Nazis and their godlike alien allies on a desert planet, achieving a pyrrhic victory that leads to freedom for Catherine and her father.

Much like classic film serials, each episode of *Origins* functions as a chapter in the overarching story, advancing the plot and ending on a cliffhanger.[23] Tension builds as the characters move toward a series-ending climax in which all the setup finally pays off. The technique was familiar from *Universe* but had been ratcheted up several notches. *Origins* was much more highly serialized, without the smaller, standalone stories nested within individual episodes of the overall arc. All the storytelling was targeted at moving the narrative forward, and everything that happened onscreen was part of that main story.

The pulpy nature of the overarching story evoked classic serials of the big screen and more recent films like the Indiana Jones series that paid tribute to them. The crusading archaeologist, Nazi villains, and desert backdrop certainly brought to mind *Raiders of the Lost Ark* and its second sequel, *Indiana Jones and the Last Crusade*. The tone was lighter, too, with room for humor and less *Sturm und Drang* than the darker, edgier *Universe*. Everything about *Origins* felt retro,[24] in keeping with its nature as a prequel set in 1928.

But was a brighter, retro serial what *Stargate* fans had waited nine years for? Was it enough to make the Stargate Command streaming service a going concern? There were hints that *Origins* might be the first in an anthology of *Stargate*-related stories featuring different characters and time periods...[25] but would such a format have a chance of success? By now, you know the answers to these questions all too well.

---

[23] Except the last episode, of course, which concludes the tale.

[24] Except, perhaps, for its more contemporary portrayal of homosexuality between Wasif and a male native named Motawk.

[25] "*Stargate Origins* Season 2? Everything We Know So Far," 4 Feb. 2019, accessed 2 Jan. 2022 at gateworld.net/news/2019/02/stargate-origins-season-2-renewed-cancelled/.

Top, Salome Azizi was effectively menacing as *Origins'* Nazi-allying Goa'uld underlord Aset, shown here with her *harcesis* child and servant Renisenb (Ghadir Mounib); right: Michelle Jubilee Gonzalez as Aset's personal guard, Goa'uld warrior Serqet.

The Writing Was on the Gate

Stargate fans did not rally behind *Origins* as hoped. Reviewers were not kind, criticizing the "wooden acting and lack of characterization,"[26] and even claiming the sets and props looked "like cheap knock-offs."[27] Reviewer Moe Akhtar wrote, "Had this not had the word *Stargate* in the title and been funded by MGM, you could be forgiven for thinking this was a polished fan-made project. Had this not aired in ten-minute bite-sized episodes, I doubt many would have had the will to sit through the whole feature."[28]

The exact number of viewers was not publicized, but it wasn't enough to justify ordering a follow-up season or a new series. Not only did the *Stargate* franchise return to hibernation, but the Stargate Command streaming platform died on the vine, closing for good by the end of 2019. All bonus original content produced for the streamer was migrated to YouTube, while MGM's library of *Stargate* programming ended up leased to other paid streaming services.

[26] "*Stargate Origins* Season 1 Review," 15 Feb. 2018, accessed 2 Jan. 2022 at thereviewgeek.com/stargateorigins-s1review/.
[27] "*Stargate Origins* Review," 27 Mar. 2018, accessed 2 Jan. 2022 at thedigitalfix.com/television/review/stargate-origins-review/.
[28] "*Stargate Origins* Review," 27 Mar. 2018, accessed 2 Jan. 2022 at thedigitalfix.com/television/review/stargate-origins-review/.

Left: Tonatiuh Elizarraraz and Shvan Aladdin as Motawk and Wasif, *Stargate*'s first gay male couple; right: Daniel Rashid as a younger version of Kasuf, played by Erick Avari in the 1994 movie.

As for *Origins*, it ended up edited into a feature-length movie titled *Stargate Origins: Catherine*.[29] No one seemed to mourn that young Catherine's adventures went no further than that... though the lack of new filmed *Stargate* certainly left a gaping hole in the *Stargate* fan universe. It's a hole that, to this day, has yet to be filled. Still, as always, hope survives for this resilient and long-lived science-fiction franchise to return.

Stargate: Crystal Ball

The year is 2022. There has been no new *Stargate* for nearly four years. Only one thing is certain: the franchise will return. Having purchased MGM in 2021 for $8.45 billion, Amazon now owns the rights to *Stargate*. According to Mike Hopkins, senior vice president of Amazon Prime Video and Amazon Studios, the chief motivation for the sale was the acquisition of intellectual property (IP) for future development. "The real financial value behind this deal is the treasure trove of IP in the deep catalog that we plan to reimagine and develop together with MGM's talented team," he told *GateWorld*. "It's very exciting and provides

---

[29] Unlike other *Stargate* shows, *Origins* has not been released on DVD or Blu-ray, to the annoyance of completist fans who now have a gap on their shelves they can't fill.

so many opportunities for high-quality storytelling."[30] In his list of MGM IP of interest, Hopkins specifically called out *Stargate*.

When Amazon finally decides to pull the trigger on a new series, co-creator Brad Wright will be ready to take another swing.[31] In late 2020, Wright announced that he was working on a big new project with MGM – and the implications were clear, though *Stargate* wasn't mentioned by name.

> It's very exciting. It's something that we have been talking about for a while now. And I love it – I'm excited to have the possibility of making it someday soon. Or someday, period! I'll say this much: It exists in the universe that you already know. It's not a reboot, it's not a completely new thing. It's a *continuation*. And I'll leave it at that. I'm not allowed to say anything more! I'm sworn to secrecy.[32]

The chevrons, it seems, are aligning. It is only a matter of time before new *Stargate* programming is produced and made available for public consumption. Judging from the example set by streaming service CBS All-Access/Paramount+ and its multiple *Star Trek* series,[33] there could be many thrilling (and lucrative) *Stargate* shows in our not-too-distant future. Will these shows be heavily serialized? Will they dip into the past for prequels to the shows we know and love? Will they bend and twist the *Stargate* concept or revert to the baseline template that made the original series popular? Most importantly, will they get people to watch and clamor for more?

Only time will tell.

---

[30] "Amazon Is Buying MGM. What Does It Mean for the *Stargate* Franchise?" 26 May 2021, accessed 2 Jan. 2022 at gateworld.net/news/2021/05/amazin-buying-mgm-what-does-mean-stargate-franchise-2021/.

[31] If called, of course.

[32] "Brad Wright Confirms New *Stargate* Is (Still) in the Works," 21 Nov. 2020, accessed 3 Jan. 2022 at gateworld.net/news/2020/11/brad-wright-confirms-new-stargate-still-in-the-works/.

[33] Including, at the time of this writing, *Star Trek: Discovery, Short Treks, Picard, Lower Decks, Prodigy,* and *Strange New Worlds*, with other shows currently in development.

Chevron Seven Locked:
An Afterword

by Joseph Dilworth Jr.

> Well, basically, when the gate is dialing, I say 'Chevron one encoded, chevron two encoded' and so on, incrementally up to the seventh chevron – which is a little different, because that's when the wormhole connects. When that happens, I like to change things up a little bit and just say, "Chevron seven locked."
> — Chief Master Sergeant Walter Harriman, "Heroes, Part 1"

Confession time: I wasn't a fan of *Stargate SG-1* when it first started airing. In fact, I didn't watch it at all until just before it moved over to the Sci-Fi Channel for its sixth season. I was a fan of the film, but similarly had not seen it during its initial theatrical run. Thanks to the advent of the home-video market, I was able to see the movie and it quickly became a favorite. But the TV series had aired on Showtime for the first five years, and I didn't have a subscription to that premium service, nor could I reliably find it airing in syndication. Essentially, I simply never had the opportunity to jump on board.

So why am I co-editing a book celebrating twenty-five years of something I wasn't into from the moment it began? Because once I finally did see it, I was hooked – and I realized I had been missing out on something truly special (mirroring co-editor Rich Handley's own personal *Stargate* journey, as recounted in his introduction). Here was a series that excelled at world-building, creating a richly populated universe filled with friends and enemies (and sometimes frenemies) who would show up from time to time. It followed the adventures of three-dimensional characters who were grounded and relatable. And like the best science fiction, *Stargate SG-1* and its spinoffs explored themes, ideas, and messages that were relevant to what was going on in the world. Oh, and it made sure to not always take itself too seriously.

That was probably the biggest hook for me. Sure, it regularly followed tried and true science-fiction and drama tropes, but it always did so on its own terms, either by adding an unexpected narrative twist or by outright acknowledging the cliché. I have often watched movies or TV series on which the characters did something illogical for the sake of the story, and I've wondered why those characters hadn't paid attention to pop culture enough to know why that was a very bad decision. The denizens of *Stargate* seemed to have actually paid attention to their own entertainment, so they frequently avoided the pratfalls or obvious traps and were quick to accept the unbelievable.

From the moment I watched the first episode, I liked what I saw, and that made me a fan. That's the little secret about fandom, by the way: there are no degrees of being a fan. If you hear a piece of music or have a favorite sequence in a film or have watched even a single episode of a series and have thought, "Hey, I like that!"... well, then you're a fan. It's *that* simple. No matter what Internet quizzes or bullying social-media gatekeepers (no, not *that* kind) would have you believe, there is no such thing as True Fans or Real Fans or Uber Fans. There are fans, period, full-stop. I can't tell you what degrees Rodney McKay has earned or quickly remember the name of Nicholas Rush's late wife, but, man, do I love watching, writing, and talking about all things *Stargate*, especially with other fans.

Yes, I quickly became a *Stargate* fan – and not only of *SG-1* but also the subsequent shows, *Stargate Atlantis* and *Stargate Universe*. So much so that when I ran my own pop-culture website, I made sure to cover the series regularly and was fortunate enough to interview several of the cast members and crew, and to review early screeners of the episodes. The highlight of that period was attending the world premiere of *Stargate: Continuum* on the flight deck of the aircraft carrier USS *Midway* during San Diego Comic-Con 2008. It was a surreal experience in a surreal period of my life, and it's something I will fondly remember forever. There was also that time I bore witness to a great practical joke played on my friend Brandon Jerwa during the *Stargate Universe* premiere party the following year, concerning Ming-Na Wen. You can read about that in his essay.[1]

I recall those things not to brag, as I was extremely fortunate to be able to be invited, much less to attend such events. Instead, I recount them as evidence that even behind the scenes, the cast and crew didn't always take themselves seriously and absolutely loved celebrating their respective shows. Anytime I talked to anyone involved in *Stargate*, from actor Richard Dean Anderson to producer Joe Mallozzi to Michelle Rosenblatt in Sci-Fi Channel's publicity department, it was clear that they all took immense joy in making the show and were thrilled that fans loved it as well – you see, they were all fans, too!

I can hear you wondering why I'm going on about the beginnings of my love of *Stargate*. This is an afterword, a glorified epilogue, so shouldn't I be talking about endings and putting a fine point on everything? The last *Stargate* television series ended more than a decade ago, and other than a brief online serial-turned-movie, *Stargate Origins*, there hasn't been anything going on with the franchise in years, right? Well, no, not exactly.

Fan interest in *Stargate* has not diminished in the interim. In fact, it seems to be growing, especially in recent years. There are very active fan groups on the Internet, and conventions continue to celebrate the franchise. Even with COVID-19 having imposed a longer-than-expected break on in-person get-togethers, there have been some wonderful online fan events. Fandemonium Books continues to publish officially licensed *Stargate* novels, while American Mythology produced a few comic book series that officially continued *Atlantis* and *Universe*, and they are in talks to do more.

Just as exciting, in recent years Brad Wright – who, along with Jonathan Glassner, developed *Stargate* for television – has been talking about writing a new script aimed at returning the franchise to our TV screens. This became even more of a possibility recently when *Stargate*'s owner, MGM, was bought by Amazon Studios, which seems keen to exploit many of its IPs, with *Stargate* among those mentioned in press releases.

Many folks in the cast seem willing to return as well. Wright hosts a podcast on which he interviews former *Stargate* cast members, and they all seem excited when he mentions that he's been writing scenes for their respective characters.

---

[1] See Brandon's essay "Fear and Loathing in Cheyenne Mountain," elsewhere in this anthology.

Recently, in fact, Amanda Tapping, Michael Shanks, David Hewlett, and Jewel Staite took part in a livestream table read of a brand-new *Stargate* script... written by an AI, with another being planned to include Richard Dean Anderson.[2] I mean, if *that* doesn't show a special kind of love for your old job, what *does*?

Brad Wright's script for a proposed new live-action *Stargate* TV show will reportedly make the Stargate Program public knowledge, a concept introduced in *Stargate Atlantis*'s finale.

Sure, it's possible Amazon might choose to reinvent the wheel and reboot *Stargate* from the ground up with all-new characters and a new mythos. There have been reboots of lots of other franchises in the past few years, but it seems to be the revivals featuring the returns of the original actors and characters that have been better received. Let's hope that Amazon Studios is smart enough to go for the path with an already established audience clamoring for an update on their old friends.

Time will tell, as Robert Jeschonek notes in his essay preceding this afterword. But giving voice to your love of all things *Stargate* on social media, loudly and often, cannot hurt. Talk proudly about your favorite episode of *SG-1* (it's "Windows of Opportunity" for me) or about how awesome Teyla Emmagan is, or debate why Everett Young never pushed Nicholas Rush out an airlock the first chance he got, or why *Stargate Infinity* was a pile of... well, let's leave that show to its number-one (and only) fan, Rich Handley.[3]

---

[2] You can watch it here: thecompanion.app/2021/11/23/stargate-a-i-full-video/.
[3] See Rich's essay "To *Infinity* and Beyond the Pale," elsewhere in this volume.

Wherever the gate may take fans now that Amazon has acquired the franchise, one can only hope the powers that be remember that at its core, *Stargate* isn't just about action and adventure—it's also hilarious.

So, yes, this afterword is an ending of sorts, a coda to this book of informative, thought-provoking, and irreverent essays (hey, kind of like how the shows are!), but it is not the final note on the *Stargate* franchise. I doubt such a thing will ever be written, as there are too many people who will not let it go away. Let's look back at what was, while being hopefully optimistic for what is yet to come. While we wait, I'm going to go eat some cake.

More *Stargate* is on the (event) horizon. There's talk of cake.

About the Contributors

Leah Battle has worked and lived in California's Coachella Valley for more than twenty years. She has been a professional artist since 1982 but was a creative soul as a child and teen. Leah studied under Tony Askew and Cynthia Martin (not the comics illustrator) and was a student of fine arts and art history at Santa Barbara Community College. She is currently earning her bachelor's degree in art history at Arizona State University. Leah long had a passion for animals and pop culture while growing up, and she started her professional artistic career as a pet illustrator. She was featured on a local news program's series called *Businesses That Work*. After twenty years of pet illustration, human portraiture, and various personal commissions and personal works, she was invited to participate in creating sketch cards for licensed properties (*Star Wars* and *Lord of the Rings*, among many others) and was also chosen to be an artist at *Star Wars* Celebration. This led to a multitude of other opportunities. Leah is currently exploring and working a new personal style in addition to her traditional methods. Her preferred mediums are pen, pencil, colored pencils, and markers on paper, as well as digital painting. This book marks Leah's third digital painting cover for Sequart, following *From Bayou to Abyss: Examining John Constantine, Hellblazer* and *Musings on Monsters: Observations on the World of Classic Horror*.

Alexis Cruz is a veteran actor, writer, director, and producer. He starred in the title role of HBO's Emmy-winning *P.O.W.E.R.: The Eddie Matos Story*; as well as *The Old Man and the Sea*, opposite Anthony Quinn; Larry McMurtry's *The Streets of Laredo*, with Sam Shepard and Sissy Spacek; and the film *Stargate*, starring Kurt Russell and James Spader, later recurring on *Stargate SG1* in his original role of Skaara. A two-time ALMA award nominee, Alexis recurred as the angel Raphael on CBS's *Touched by an Angel*, starring Roma Downey and Della Reese, before playing Martin Allende on CBS's *Shark*, starring James Woods. He has appeared on *Castle*, with Nathan Fillion; in Gregory Nava's *Why Do Fools Fall In Love?*, with Larenz Tate; and in Sam Raimi's *Drag Me to Hell*. In addition to his many film and television credits, Alexis narrated and produced the audio book series *The Catherine Kimbridge Chronicles* for Amazon, and he created *The Unprofessionals: A Sociopathic Bromance*, a graphic novel series. He lives in New York City and is a founding partner of The Mythmaker Group, an IP development cooperative.

Ren Cummins, upon learning that Spider-Man was never going to be a viable career path, promptly shifted past astronaut and detective to glom onto the next, least probable goal: musician. Since that didn't pan out, he finally surrendered to the realization that if he couldn't save the world, then by gum he was going to create new ones. The present tense finds him in the Pacific Northwest with his wife, son, and two dogs, and the unrelenting memory of a cat named Karma. When he's not floating through the aethereal settings of science fiction and fantasy, he enjoys short walks on uncrowded beaches, pretending he can cook, and challenging himself to incorporate genres that have utterly no business coexisting. There is also the lingering theory that he might be a time traveler, but that has yet to be substantiated or repudiated. Ren's ongoing exploits can be reviewed at renwritings.com.

Keith R.A. DeCandido is the author of more than fifty novels, more than eighty short stories, around fifty comic books, and more nonfiction than he's willing to count. He's the author of the *Stargate SG-1* novel *Kali's Wrath*, as well as short stories in the anthologies *Far Horizons* and *Homeworlds*, and he also did a "*Stargate* Rewatch" for the award-winning pop-culture webzine Tor.com in 2015. Find out less at his hilariously primitive website, DeCandido.net.

Joseph Dilworth Jr. is a long-time Internet writer, essaying his opinions about pop culture at places such as *Long Island Pulse Magazine* and his own website, *Pop Culture Zoo*, now called *What Joe Writes* (whatjoewrites.com). Joe is currently the co-host of *The Flickcast* podcast (theflickcast.com), the co-host of *Highlander Heart*, and a writer and editor for several pop-culture books published by Sequart. He also has an unhealthy obsession with obscure 1970s and '80s television. Joe resides in the Pacific Northwest, where he spends time with his family, 3D printing, brewing beer, writing, reading, and still spouting his opinions to whoever will listen to them. Just be warned: never, ever feed him after midnight. Also: be kind, rewind.

Edward Dodds is a freelance writer, editor, and passionate enthusiast of paleontology, meteorology, evolutionary biology, transhumanism, and rationalism. Edward has written short stories exploring acausal blackmail and decision theory within *The Gods Amongst Us*, penned articles on *Star Wars* and other works for entertainment news outlet *The Blast*, published poems for the *South Kilburn Speaks* project, and contributed as an editor to the *Star Wars* novel *Supernatural Encounters* by Joe Bongiorno. Edward is a dedicated fan of science fiction and fantasy, and his favorite works of fiction are the *Stargate* and *Star Wars* franchises.

Jo Duffy is a writer and editor, perhaps best known for her work on superhero comics like *Power Man and Iron Fist*, *Catwoman*, *Wolverine*, *Fallen Angels*, and *Nestrobber*, as well as on *Star Wars*; plus, the English-language edition of Katsuhiro Otomo's *Akira*. Jo has written short stories, critical reviews, essays, forewords, and the odd song or two, along with a couple of movies. She was the managing editor of *Epic Illustrated* magazine, and she also edited a number of comics, including *Elektra: Assassin*, *Dreadstar*, *Groo the Wanderer*, *Doctor Strange*, *She-Hulk*, and *ROM Spaceknight*. Jo is a lifelong fan girl.

Bryanna Elkins is a Canadian-American writer and visual artist who enjoys not only science, but everything science fiction. She is also a published poet. After a decade of acting and modeling internationally, Bryanna is currently pursuing a career in both health sciences and in comic writing and illustration. Visit her online at bryannaelkins.com.

Kelli Fitzpatrick (she/her) is a science-fiction author who writes fiction, screenplays, essays, poetry, and game content. She is a winner of the *Star Trek: Strange New Worlds* contest from Simon and Schuster and has written for the *Star Trek Adventures* tabletop role-playing game line from Modiphius Entertainment. Her short stories have been published by Flash Fiction Online, KYSO Flash, Crazy 8 Press, and others, and her essays on science-fiction media appear online at StarTrek.com and *Women at Warp*, and in print from Sequart and ATB Publishing. Kelli placed fifth in the NYC Midnight Short Screenplay Challenge. A former high school teacher, she is a strong advocate for public education, the arts, and gender rights and representation. She can be found at KelliFitzpatrick.com and on Twitter at @KelliFitzWrites.

Rich Handley edited seventy volumes of Eaglemoss's *Star Trek Graphic Novel Collection* and has worked with DC Comics, IDW, BOOM! Studios, Dark Horse, The

Library of American Comics, Titan Books, ATB Publishing, Sequart, Realm Press, and other publishers. He cofounded Hasslein Books and has written, edited, or contributed to books discussing *Star Trek*, *Star Wars*, *Planet of the Apes*, *Battlestar Galactica*, *Hellblazer*, *Blade Runner*, *Red Dwarf*, *Watchmen*, *Buffy the Vampire Slayer*, *Angel*, *The X-Files*, *Twin Peaks*, *Babylon 5*, *Back to the Future*, *Dark Shadows*, *Batman '66*, *Doctor Who*, classic movie monsters – and now *Stargate*. Rich writes a weekly *Star Trek* comics column for <u>HeroCollector.com</u> and is the managing editor of <u>RFIDJournal.com</u> by day. You can find him online at <u>RichHandley.com</u>. He is not a Goa'uld.

Mark L. Haynes has been working in and around TV, comics, and pop culture for more than twenty-five years, and is the cowriter of the American Mythology comic series *Stargate Atlantis* and *Stargate Universe*. Mark was the cowriter of IDW's *24* comic line based on the hit Fox show. Titles include *24 Stories*, *24: One Shot*, and *24: Midnight Sun*. As the publisher of Realm Press, he guided the artistic development of a comic based on *Battlestar Galactica*, as well as the alien invasion saga *First Wave*. As a screenwriter, Mark has developed stories and concepts for TV, including *Star Trek: Voyager* and *Star Trek: Enterprise*. Mark is the cocreator and cowriter of *Hyperloop*, a new science-fiction TV series in development with Roddenberry Entertainment. In 2019, he established Mark Haynes Productions LLC, based in Los Angeles. Mark and his partners, having established strategic and creative partnerships within the industry, are actively engaged in developing original properties for film, television, and other media. Contact: (323) 482-7655, markhaynes1@gmail.com.

Brandon Jerwa has a long history of writing licensed comics for properties ranging from *Stargate* and *Battlestar Galactica* to *The Bionic Woman* and *G.I. Joe*, and he contributed an essay to Sequart's *Somewhere Beyond the Heavens: Exploring Battlestar Galactica*. He's also a writer and story editor for video games, including *Britney Spears: American Dream* and several *Jurassic World* releases. Brandon currently resides in Seattle.

Robert Jeschonek is an envelope-pushing, *USA Today*-bestselling author whose fiction, comics, and non-fiction have been published around the world. His stories have appeared in *Clarkesworld*, *Pulphouse*, *Galaxy's Edge*, *Escape Pod*, and many other publications. He has written official *Star Trek* and *Doctor Who* fiction and has scripted comics for DC, AHOY, and other publishers. Robert's essays have also appeared in Sequart's *Musings on Monsters: Observations on the World of Classic Horror*, *Somewhere Beyond the Heavens: Exploring Battlestar Galactica*, and *From Bayou to Abyss: Examining John Constantine, Hellblazer*. He has won an International Book Award, a Scribe Award for Best Original Novel, and the grand prize in Pocket Books' *Strange New Worlds* contest. Visit him online at bobscribe.com, find him on Facebook, or follow him on Twitter (@TheFictioneer).

Dr. Anastasia Klimchynskaya fell in love with science fiction by watching *Stargate Atlantis* and is now an academic whose work focuses on the genre. She is a Postdoctoral Fellow at the Institute on the Formation of Knowledge at the University of Chicago, with her current book project exploring the emergence of science fiction in the nineteenth century and its technoscientific and social contexts. Anastasia is a co-organizer of the Philadelphia Science Fiction Conference, as well as an avid Sherlockian.

Val Nolan is the author of *Neil Jordan: Works for the Page* (Cork University Press, 2022). He has published articles in *Science Fiction Studies*, *Journal of Graphic Novels and Comic Books*, *Review of Contemporary Fiction*, and *Irish Studies Review*, as well as book chapters about the *Star Trek* franchise, *Fringe*, *Lost*, and *Battlestar Galactica*. Val's own fiction has appeared in *Year's Best Science Fiction*, *Best of British Science Fiction*, *Unidentified Funny Objects*, and the "Futures" page of *Nature*, while his story "The Irish Astronaut" was shortlisted for the Theodore Sturgeon Award. He is currently a lecturer in genre fiction and creative writing at Aberystwyth University, in Wales.

Frank Schildiner is a martial arts instructor at Amorosi's Mixed Martial Arts in New Jersey. He is the writer of the novels *The Quest of Frankenstein*, *The Triumph of Frankenstein*, *The Spells of Frankenstein*, *Napoleon's Vampire Hunters*, *The Devil Plague of Naples*, *The Land of Everlasting Gloom*, *The Last Days of Atlantis*, and *The Chains of Ares*. Frank is a regular contributor to the fictional series *Tales of the Shadowmen* and has been published in *The Lone Ranger and Tonto: Frontier Justice*, *The Joy of Joe*, *The New Adventures of Thunder Jim Wade*, *Secret Agent X* Volumes 3, 4, 5 and 6, and *The Avenger: The Justice Files*. Frank resides in New Jersey with his wife Gail, who is his top supporter, and their two cats, who are indifferent on the subject.

Darren Sumner founded the leading *Stargate* fan site, GateWorld.net, in 1999, and he continues to serve as its managing editor more than twenty years later. A native of the Pacific Northwest, Darren holds a Ph.D. degree in systematic theology from the University of Aberdeen, Scotland, and teaches in the fields of theology and religion.

ALSO FROM **SEQUART**

SOMEWHERE BEYOND THE HEAVENS: EXPLORING BATTLESTAR GALACTICA
THE CYBERPUNK NEXUS: EXPLORING THE BLADE RUNNER UNIVERSE
BRIGHT LIGHTS, APE CITY: EXAMINING THE PLANET OF THE APES MYTHOS

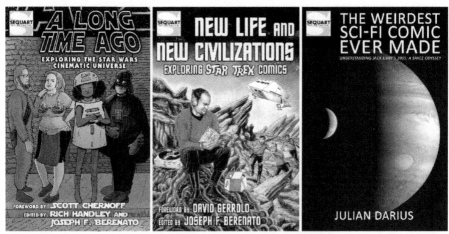

A LONG TIME AGO: EXPLORING THE STAR WARS CINEMATIC UNIVERSE
NEW LIFE AND NEW CIVILIZATIONS: EXPLORING STAR TREK COMICS
THE WEIRDEST SCI-FI COMIC EVER MADE: UNDERSTANDING JACK KIRBY'S *2001: A SPACE ODYSSEY*

For more information and for exclusive content, visit Sequart.org.

BOOKS ON COMICS CHARACTERS:
JUDGING DREDD: EXAMINING THE WORLD OF JUDGE DREDD
FROM BAYOU TO ABYSS: EXAMINING JOHN CONSTANTINE, HELLBLAZER
THE DEVIL IS IN THE DETAILS: EXAMINING MATT MURDOCK AND DAREDEVIL
MOVING TARGET: THE HISTORY AND EVOLUTION OF GREEN ARROW
TEENAGERS FROM THE FUTURE: ESSAYS ON THE LEGION OF SUPER-HEROES

ON TV AND MOVIES:
WHY DO WE FALL?: EXAMINING CHRISTOPHER NOLAN'S *THE DARK KNIGHT TRILOGY*
GOTHAM CITY 14 MILES: 14 ESSAYS ON WHY THE 1960S BATMAN TV SERIES MATTERS
MUSINGS ON MONSTERS: OBSERVATIONS ON THE WORLD OF CLASSIC HORROR
TIME IS A FLAT CIRCLE: EXAMINING *TRUE DETECTIVE*, SEASON ONE
MUTANT CINEMA: THE X-MEN TRILOGY FROM COMICS TO SCREEN
IMPROVING THE FOUNDATIONS: *BATMAN BEGINS* FROM COMICS TO SCREEN
MOVING PANELS: TRANSLATING COMICS TO FILM

BOOKS ON SCI-FI FRANCHISES:
THE SACRED SCROLLS: COMICS ON THE PLANET OF THE APES
A GALAXY FAR, FAR AWAY: EXPLORING STAR WARS COMICS
A MORE CIVILIZED AGE: EXPLORING THE STAR WARS EXPANDED UNIVERSE

BOOKS ON GRANT MORRISON WORKS:
GRANT MORRISON: THE EARLY YEARS
OUR SENTENCE IS UP: SEEING GRANT MORRISON'S *THE INVISIBLES*
CURING THE POSTMODERN BLUES: READING GRANT MORRISON AND CHRIS WESTON'S *THE FILTH* IN THE 21ST CENTURY
THE ANATOMY OF ZUR-EN-ARRH: UNDERSTANDING GRANT MORRISON'S BATMAN

BOOKS ON WARREN ELLIS WORKS:
SHOT IN THE FACE: A SAVAGE JOURNEY TO THE HEART OF *TRANSMETROPOLITAN*
KEEPING THE WORLD STRANGE: A *PLANETARY* GUIDE
VOYAGE IN NOISE: WARREN ELLIS AND THE DEMISE OF WESTERN CIVILIZATION
WARREN ELLIS: THE CAPTURED GHOSTS INTERVIEWS

OTHER BOOKS:
HOW TO ANALYZE & REVIEW COMICS: A HANDBOOK ON COMICS CRITICISM
THE BRITISH INVASION: ALAN MOORE, NEIL GAIMAN, GRANT MORRISON, AND THE INVENTION OF THE MODERN COMIC BOOK WRITER
CLASSICS ON INFINITE EARTHS: THE JUSTICE LEAGUE AND DC CROSSOVER CANON
AND THE UNIVERSE SO BIG: UNDERSTANDING *BATMAN: THE KILLING JOKE*
HUMANS AND PARAGONS: ESSAYS ON SUPER-HERO JUSTICE
THE MIGNOLAVERSE: HELLBOY AND THE COMICS ART OF MIKE MIGNOLA
THE BEST THERE IS AT WHAT HE DOES: EXAMINING CHRIS CLAREMONT'S X-MEN
MINUTES TO MIDNIGHT: TWELVE ESSAYS ON *WATCHMEN*
WHEN MANGA CAME TO AMERICA: SUPER-HERO REVISIONISM IN *MAI, THE PSYCHIC GIRL*
THE FUTURE OF COMICS, THE FUTURE OF MEN: MATT FRACTION'S *CASANOVA*

DOCUMENTARY FILMS:
DIAGRAM FOR DELINQUENTS
SHE MAKES COMICS
THE IMAGE REVOLUTION
NEIL GAIMAN: DREAM DANGEROUSLY
GRANT MORRISON: TALKING WITH GODS
WARREN ELLIS: CAPTURED GHOSTS
COMICS IN FOCUS: CHRIS CLAREMONT'S X-MEN

Printed in Great Britain
by Amazon